ALSO BY JASON WARBURG

FICTION

Believe in Me
Never Break the Chain

My Heart Sings the Harmony

Twenty Years of Writing About Music

∞

Jason Warburg

Wonder Wheel Publications
Seaside, California

ISBN-13: 978-0692539033
ISBN-10: 0692539034
LCCN: 2015956578

Jacket concept, photography and design by Jean-Paul Vest

www.jasonwarburg.com

This is for

Josh and Sarah and Eric

who have been making my heart sing
since the day you arrived

We who love music,
we love the people who make it,
we love the sound of it,
and we love what it does to us,
how it makes us feel,
how it helps *us* love.

– George Harrison

as quoted by Timothy White in *Rock Lives:
Profiles and Interviews* (Omnibus Press, 1991), p.174

Table of Contents

Introduction

"WRITING ABOUT MUSIC," ELVIS COSTELLO once famously said, "is like dancing about architecture."

His point being, don't review my work, because you're wasting your time, and by the way, you look stupid doing it.

Love you too, Declan.

The relationship between artists and those who write about their work (often referred to as "critics"—more on that later) is inherently fraught. Artists—the ones worth paying attention to, at least—pour themselves into their craft, investing not just dollars and hours, but deep personal truths that animate and give dimension to their creations. The critic then "cracks open" the artist's creation and describes what s/he finds inside[1]. Whether Costello likes it or not, there is a symbiosis in this relationship, an ongoing dialogue between creator and audience. The artist may find the audience's observations affirming or enlightening or frustrating or painful; regardless, the critic's job is in this respect identical to the artist's—to tell the truth.

This seemingly simple task is anything but. Legendary *Rolling Stone* music critic Lester Bangs is said to have told younger colleagues something along the lines attributed to him in Cameron Crowe's semi-autobiographical film *Almost Famous*: "Whatever you do, don't make friends with the rock stars." His point being that, as a critic, you should never compromise your objectivity. It still surprises me that Bangs' head didn't explode from the cognitive dissonance of his comment; I can't imagine an act more inescapably subjective than offering your opinion about a work of art. You can muster this and that past example of work that you perceive as similar or related in some way for purposes of comparison, you can dress it all up in elaborate metaphors and brash assertions, but in the end a review can only ever be one person's opinion. One person's truth.

---

[1] Thank you for that evocative image to my friend Mark Doyon. It's the closest I've ever come to feeling like Indiana Jones.

The real question implied by Costello's dig cuts deeper: why write about music at all? What's the point?

Twenty years down this road, I can only report that for me, it comes down to passion. I love music, and I love to write, and the day in early 1996 when I was first given the opportunity to indulge both of these appetites at the same time was a happy one indeed (thank you, Christopher MacDonald). The motto on the home page of *The Daily Vault* (www.dailyvault.com), the website I have written for since 1997 and been editor of since 2003, reads: "Music reviews for music lovers by music lovers," and I aspire to live up to that creed every time I sit down at the keyboard.

Whatever else it accomplishes, I hope this volume suggests something about the role music critics can play as a gateway for the audience to deepen its understanding of a work. That's always my goal, as well as the reason why I still to this day reflexively—and not entirely rationally—resist the label of "critic." While the second dictionary definition of "criticism" is "the analysis and judgment of the merits and faults of a literary or artistic work," the first is much less impartial: "the expression of disapproval of someone or something based on perceived faults or mistakes." To me, that suggests that the first obligation of a "critic" is to criticize, rather than to praise, or simply analyze, the work, and I reject that premise. My job is to narrate my experience as a listener, to explain how the work was received on my end, which buttons it pushed and which it didn't. Any given review might contain both criticism and praise, but my default setting is positive, not negative. I do what I do because I love music, not criticizing those who make it. And on special occasions when I've done my job particularly well, I may also have the privilege of assisting the artist and the audience in achieving the only goal that really matters in art—connection. A shared moment of communication.

Those days are the best days.

Those days have also on occasion led to a total breakdown of Bangs' Axiom, with no regrets. Life's too short for either regret or friendships foregone out of some misguided commitment to "objectivity." When it comes to talking about art, objectivity is a unicorn; you might convince yourself it exists, but good luck ever locating it.

As for our friend Elvis Costello, here's a winking footnote. It turns out that the quote above, long attributed to him, may actually have been coined by comedian Martin Mull; its origins remain murky and the subject of conflicting reports. Either way, the fact that Costello was believed for so many years to have said it speaks volumes about his antipathy for music critics, not to mention the subjectivity of this entire exercise. When it comes to art, people believe what they want to believe.

1

My Musical Life

IF YOU ASK ME, "BECAUSE I'VE ALWAYS done it" is a terrible reason to do anything.

I've been writing about music for 20 years now, scrapping away in small venues like an aging club band with more stubbornness than sense, never making a dime at it, consuming thousands of hours of an already full life listening to music and writing about my reactions to it. It's a fairly ludicrous thing to do.

And so I make sure to stop every so often—usually about once a year—and ask myself *Do you really want to keep doing this?* I've taken breaks here and there, going quiet for weeks or months at a time to focus on fiction writing or my day job or just life away from the computer screen. But I always come back, and on *The Daily Vault*'s 15th birthday in 2012, I took a moment to consider why:

> *I thought about doing a list of 15 of these—those musical moments that make the hairs on the back of my neck stand at attention, that live on in memory long after the song has faded out—and the only hard part would have been keeping it to 15. Moments like when the drums come thundering in at 3:40 of Phil Collins' "In the Air Tonight." Or when the Edge's force-of-nature circular guitar riff infiltrates, then obliterates the synth wash during the opening sequence of "Where the Streets Have No Name." Or when Moon's hair-on-fire drum fills, Daltrey's banshee scream and Townsend's Armageddon guitar crash headlong into the closing verse of "Won't Get Fooled Again." The immortal opening chords of "Limelight" and the brilliant closing solo of "Oye Como Va." The slinky electric piano and bee-sting guitar that fuel Tom Petty's "Breakdown"; the majestic church organ Rick Wakeman uses to blast "Awaken" into the stratosphere; Peter Buck's mandolin residing at the very heart of "Losing My Religion"; the little waver of emotion that*

sneaks into Mary Chapin Carpenter's voice on the verses of "Come On Come On." The furious precision of Mick Fleetwood's drumming driving "Go Your Own Way," or the sublime bridge of Fountains of Wayne's "All Kinds of Time," the best song about football in the history of the game. The headlong thrash of "American Idiot"; the uplifting drive of "Stars"; the understated anguish of "Fire and Rain."

I could go on and on (obviously). These moments are the tapestry of my musical life, and in this place I am reminded of them again and again.

The other thing that writing about music keeps reminding me of is that the process of acquiring new musical memories—those moments that make the hairs on the back of your neck stand at attention—never ends. Every year I come across a new artist, a new album, a new song that stops me in my tracks and commands my heart to sing the harmony. It's a perpetual voyage of discovery, and the beauty of doing it on my own terms, captaining a small ship of hardy, like-minded souls, is that we get to chart our own course.

*

The roots of my passion for music run deep. Deeper than skin, deeper than bone; truth be told, it's actually in my DNA.

My grandfather Gerald Warburg was the third child, and second son, of a successful banker. The world of finance was likely his expected destination, but he had other ideas. Like his youngest brother Eddie, he left the banking to others more suited to it and gravitated instead toward the arts, becoming, before his 30th birthday, a well-regarded cellist and member of New York's Stradivarius Quartet.

I never knew my grandfather—we lived on opposite coasts and he died when I was eight years old and had met him just once—and I have serious doubts about his potential to appreciate the finer points of bands like AC/DC and Green Day. But that visceral, inescapable attraction to an art form that you recognized from early on was destined to become a central part of your life—that, I have come to understand profoundly, and to this day it fuels the indefinable bond I share with a man I never knew.

My musical education started early and benefitted hugely from my status as the trailing, by-far-the-youngest of four brothers in our household. The treasured moments when I was invited to hang out with my older brothers often revolved around listening to music in their rooms—because let's face it, they didn't want little brother around for most of the rest of what went on in there during their teenaged years in the second half of the 1960s. My early childhood memories are set to a never-ending loop of the Beatles, Byrds and Stones, Buffalo Springfield and Crosby, Stills & Nash, spiked with Motown classics and intriguing glimpses of soul-jazz artists like Les McCann and Stanley Turrentine. My mother's influence was strong, too, given her habit of cranking up the volume on bolder, more dynamic classical artists like Mozart and Beethoven (the original rock and rollers). The point is, in my memories, the irregular rhythms of our at-times tumultuous household were punctuated by moments of pure musical bliss, and I bathed in those beams of light like a sun-drunk kitten.

During my teenaged years, music moved closer still to the center of my existence. In time-honored adolescent tradition, I asserted my independence at first mostly by making myself scarce, barricading myself in my room with my record collection, or going off on long adventures with cars full of friends. Our playground was the San Francisco Bay Area circa 1978-79, a teeming nexus of musical invention whose citizens included Santana, Jefferson Starship, Journey, Sammy Hagar, Steve Miller, Boz Scaggs, the Grateful Dead, the Tubes, the Doobie Brothers and more. We often spent these nights blasting the custom mixtapes we had spent hours designing and assembling at home, carefully hitting pause on the cassette recorder before lifting the needle off the LP and exchanging one record for the next.

Only in the dimmest recesses of our hormonal, adrenaline-craving young brains did we—the revolving band of four to eight guys ages 16-17-18 that I spent most weekends with—understand that we might be experiencing the most carefree moments of our lives. Love and loss and work and responsibility barely made a dent in our collective consciousness during the first two of the three years we spent together, as sophomores and juniors in high school, just old enough to drive and just young enough not to be focused on the road ahead. We lived like a band of lost boys during those years, relying mostly on each other and the music that formed the soundtrack of our lives. I only ever met Sammy Hagar once, after following his cherry-red Trans Am into a Mill Valley hardware store parking lot in 1979, but his presence, and that of fellow travelers like Ronnie Montrose and Pete Townshend and Bob Seger and Tom Petty and a hundred others informed our days and nights like a script informs an actor. These musicians helped shape our world, and we loved them unashamedly for it.

*

At this point in our story, we flash forward 16 years. Your protagonist is fully grown—physically, at least—married to his college sweetheart and helping to raise three active children. He's been through good times and bad in his first career, working for a series of public officials, and though he doesn't know it yet, he's in the process of transitioning into a second career in the non-profit world. Through all of these changes, music has remained a constant presence in his life, though he's still never learned to play a note of it himself. (Granted, he could probably suss out the chords to "Smoke on the Water" again if you give him ten minutes, but that's about it.)

Instead, the nucleus around which his creative life has come to orbit has turned out to be writing—mostly non-fiction, and mostly in service of his employers, though by now he's also authored a number of op-eds under his own name and powered through an awkward first attempt at a novel. And then one day in 1996, the magic of the Internet—more precisely, America Online, back in that dimly remembered moment when it was somewhat useful—brought him to the attention of the editor of a local startup arts and entertainment paper. Said editor, having concluded the young man was not without talent, and was more importantly both sane and eager, asked him what he wanted to write about.

Music, answered the young man, with wide eyes and absolute commitment. *I want to write about music.*

And his world changed once again.

*

The first stage of my career as a music writer lasted 14 eventful months. From my first review column for *On the Town* magazine (March 1996 - May 1997, may she rest in peace) to my last, the drama behind the scenes of our scrappy little zine was as compelling as anything we ever published in its pages. BUT. In the midst of all that chaos, sturm and drang, the moments when I was able—no, privileged—to sit down at the computer and write about music were pure small-n nirvana. Finding the right words to express my reaction to and thoughts about music became a reservoir of joy that helped to fuel me through the darkest alleyways of that adventure.

When it was over—the "over" part landing largely on my shoulders, since by the end I was not just the music columnist, but also the publisher, editor, and layout artist—I took some time away from music writing. I needed that space to recover my equilibrium, not to mention get my career back on the rails, but within a few months I began to feel that space filling up again, the space from which all of those words and ideas and glorious moments of connection with the music had come spilling out.

I needed an outlet for it. And that's when I found the *Vault*.

The Daily Vault (www.dailyvault.com) was launched in January 1997 by Chicago-area music writer Christopher Thelen, who remains to this day among the best friends I've never met. In the beginning it was Chris, his cousin Bill Ziemer and a couple of other frustrated music writers bashing out 500 words on whatever album demanded their attention that day, with just enough knowledge of HTML between them to found what would become (and it seems like a reasonable enough claim, even if no one *really* knows) the longest-running independent music review site on the web.

In the fall of 1997 I stumbled across the *Vault* and wrote to Chris, and he soon invited me to join his merry band. Six years and a couple of thousand reviews later, Chris announced he was stepping down as editor and asked if anyone on the writing staff might want to take the reins and keep the site going. With no knowledge of HTML or the technical side of website management, and zero experience dealing with artists or labels or publicists, I did what any sensible person in my position would do: I wrapped this opportunity in a bear hug and ran with it just as fast as my legs would carry.

From that point forward, both the site and I have enjoyed essential support from numerous partners who have freely offered their help. I've tried to thank them all in the acknowledgments later on, but three can't wait: my initial partner in crime and fellow writer Duke Egbert, who held the title of site publisher in 2003-04; my good friend Benjamin Ray, who served as the site's first assistant editor from 2005 to 2008; and the extraordinarily talented Melanie Love, who took over as assistant editor in 2008 at age 17, and continues in that role today.

Over the years, the *Vault* has expanded its scope to include artist interviews, concert reviews, the occasional book or film review (where there's a strong music connection), and essays about the music business itself. Today it features a staff of ten regular writers whose ages range from mid-20s to mid-60s. While the current crew is mostly American, over the years we've published the work of writers hailing from Australia, Canada, Great Britain, India, Ireland, the Netherlands, Norway, the Philippines and South Korea, as well as half the states in the USA.

Writers come and go and, with surprising frequency, come back. And while I can't speak for anyone but myself, I like to think that we all experience the same thing at times: the gravitational pull of music drawing us back into its orbit, and that primal need to express what it feels like when the rest of the world drops away and all that exists in the entire universe is you, and the music.

It's a moment worth remembering, and celebrating, and sharing with anyone who will listen.

~Segue~

Liner Notes

With lemming-like predictability, the mainstream cultural pundit herd has been quick to declare the death of the album as an art form. No one has the time or attention span required to sit through 40 or 50 or 60 minutes of music any more, they say. Singles and EPs are a more efficient mode of delivery of new music for both listeners and artists. And if people are reluctant to pay $1.29 for a single, who's going to pay $9.99 for an album they'll never find the time to finish?

Anyone remember the whole "e-books are going to make physical books extinct within a decade" prediction? How's that playing out for you?

It seems these sorts of cultural prognosticators are obsessed with the idea of consumption as a zero-sum game. Consumers either want x or y; they couldn't possibly want both. Which is silly on the face of it, since consumerism is ultimately all about choice. As a consumer, I want the product I want, in the form that I want it, at the time that I want it, at the price that I want it.

One result of which is, physical books continue to be a major segment of the market, along with e-books, just like albums continue to be a major segment of the market, alongside singles and EPs. I'm old enough to remember the tail end of the era of the 45 RPM vinyl single. They were 99 cents by my teenaged years, rather than the 25 cents they were when my older brothers were little, but they were around, and still selling, even at the height of the album's predominance, the 1970s.

While I appreciate the art of the single, trying to capture an essential idea or moment or mood in one three-minute song, and have enjoyed a few EPs in my time (three of which are reviewed in Chapter 7), my focus as a listener and writer has always been on albums. Albums allow the artist room to tell a story—not just a scene, but a full-blown three-act play. They present a much fuller experience of what an artist has to offer. And they require you to invest. That investment—of time, and attention, and emotional engagement—is the essence of the connection between artist and audience, and that connection is what art is all about. You can communicate a lot in three minutes, but the experience is inherently

11

limited, and limiting; to really get to know an artist and understand what they're all about—to really connect—you need more time.

And that's why 95 percent of this book, and 95 percent of the material published on *The Daily Vault*, consists of album reviews. We take our time, we go deep, we explore. You could call it "slow music" if you wanted to slap a trendy label on it, but the bottom line is, it's the only way I know how to listen and react to music. Exploring that connection between artist and audience requires complete attention and engagement, and takes time. If you don't have that kind of time, or don't think popular music is an important enough topic to be worthy of that kind of (mostly) serious consideration, then you should probably leave this book where you found it and move on.

*

The other thing about albums is: they have liner notes.

If you think of the music on an album as a play, the liner notes are the playbill: the cast of characters and production staff who brought the work to life. This provides both backstory and context to the work. Who helped to make it, and how? A bedroom album performed and recorded entirely by the singer-songwriter who created the songs not only *sounds* different from a studio album recorded at a professional venue with a full band, it *feels* different. The personality and emotional character of the work is fundamentally influenced by the context in which it is created and performed, and by the performers and tradespeople who contributed to its creation.

There is also, for anyone with even a tinge of interest in things like history and genealogy and cartography, something genuinely fascinating about mapping the family trees of various bands[2]. When did the bass player leave, and where did he go, and (if such is known and/or relevant) why? What act did the producer make an album with previous to this one, or even farther in the past, and how might those experiences have shaped his/her approach to making the current one? All of this information contributes to the context—the scenery and costuming, to extend the metaphor—of the play being performed before your ears. It fills out a landscape that is otherwise incomplete.

---

[2] If the above sentence strikes a chord with you, your next move should be to go out and purchase every volume of Pete Frame's remarkable *Rock Family Trees* series (there are four as of this writing).

Once upon a time, thanks to a year spent in England as a child, I could recite the names and years of reign of every English king and queen from 1066 to the present. Now I can do the same with any number of bands, most notably the Windsor Castle-worthy family tree of Yes. You could have a lively argument about the intrinsic value of either set of facts, but only one will contribute to your understanding of how five ambitious young Brits came to create a piece of music as monumental as "Close to the Edge."

*

Ticking down the checklist of Things We Should Talk About First: a word about the interviews that you'll find interspersed between chapters beginning after chapter 2.

When I began writing about music in 1996, it honestly didn't occur to me that I would ever have the opportunity to interview actual musicians. The idea of having a conversation with one of my musical heroes—or even a working musician anyone had ever heard of—was completely foreign and somewhat terrifying to me. I wouldn't know where to start.

Except, I soon realized, I would. By 1996 I had probably read a thousand artist interviews and profiles in *Rolling Stone* and *Creem* and other bastions of the '70s music press, consuming them like candy, year after year. Here could be found insights into the artist's experiences, approach and creative process that weren't available anywhere else. Interviews—the good ones, anyway—weren't just a conversation, they were a joint exploration of the artists' mind and methods. Maybe this exploration would lead only to familiar lands with familiar customs—after all, in the media age it seems every celebrity and athlete has learned the art of giving an interview without actually saying anything; you just mouth clichés until the person holding the microphone gets bored. But the interviewers who did their homework on their subjects and engaged them on their terms and somehow managed to charm their way past their subject's outer defenses—these explorers sometimes brought home what could only be described as gold: insights and nuances and unguarded moments that would otherwise never have found their way into the larger world.

I don't have any particular aptitude for interviewing—my inner music geek has an annoying habit of asserting his awkward, fumbling self in these situations—but at least I take it seriously. Over the years, I've turned down twice as many interview opportunities as I've accepted,

13

simply because I didn't know enough about, or care enough about, the subject's work to make an interview worth their time or mine. And our time is too valuable for that.

That being true, every interview represented here was with an artist whose work reached me in some powerful way, whose music had weight and substance and meaning in my world. I never expected to have the opportunity to speak with any of them, and in every case, from my very first interview with Danny Federici of Bruce Springsteen's E Street Band, I did my best to treat that opportunity as a rare and priceless fluke. At least two of the interview subjects found here—Ronnie Montrose and Jon Anderson—are genuine musical heroes of mine. The opportunity to speak with them and explore their creative process was both a gift and a privilege.

*

Finally, about the ratings included in these reviews: let's just agree up front that they're problematic. I've never been a big fan of rating systems for works of art, whether presented in the form of stars or grades or ten-point scales. They are highly subjective and somewhat capricious measures of relative worth, and have little broader relevance since every reviewer takes their own individual approach to them. Ratings should always be taken with a large grain of salt. That said, *The Daily Vault* has now published around 9,000 reviews under its letter-grade rating system, so I think it's safe to say we're committed.

And ratings are not without value. As a reviewer, I know how tempting it can be to hide behind vague or neutral descriptions that might allow me to insist to the artist that I liked their work when in fact I had to force myself to listen all the way to the end. A rating draws a line in the sand and offers, all clever turns of phrase aside, a bottom-line estimation of how the work in question measures up. It seems to me that, however arbitrary ratings may feel at times, they do add some value for the reader, as well as holding the reviewer accountable. Whether you loved an album, hated it, or didn't care much either way, as a reviewer, you owe the reader (and the artist) an honest answer, and ratings can function as a sort of fail-safe mechanism to ensure that you deliver one.

As for the internal logic of my own ratings: well. Let me try to explain.

I once described an album as "flawlessly imagined and executed" — and proceeded to give it an A-. Several days later, a puzzled comment about this on the group's Facebook page made me realize that I couldn't really blame them for feeling like "Huh? We made a perfect album, but still only got an A-?"

For me it's about balancing intrinsic value with relative value. The album in question was indeed flawlessly imagined and executed. It also happened to occupy the melodic rock / power-pop genre, the acknowledged progenitors of which are the Beatles.

In terms of intrinsic value—in other words, compared only to itself—the album is so good it's hard to imagine the artist improving on it. That said, I gave the Beatles' *Revolver*—arguably the point of origin for the entire power-pop genre—an A- also. Was the album I'm referring to here better than *Revolver*? No. Was *Revolver* better than its follow-up, *Sgt. Pepper's Lonely Hearts Club Band*, which I gave a straight A? In my opinion, no.

So, there's a certain hierarchy at work in my ratings that combines the intrinsic value of an album with its relative value. It's an inexact science, obviously, but my hope is that this at least helps to clarify the method behind the seeming madness.

And now, on to the reviews.

2

Classics 1959-1975

ONE OF THE MANY MISLEADING THINGS about using the term "classic" to describe any artistic work is that there are really two kinds of classics: consensus classics and personal classics. Consensus classics are works that most observers tend to agree have unique, often groundbreaking qualities that set them apart from others of similar genre and proficiency (see *Macbeth*, the *Mona Lisa*, *Sgt. Pepper's Lonely Hearts Club Band*). Personal classics are in the eye of the beholder. You may think Alanis Morissette's *Jagged Little Pill* is a classic album. Well, then, it is—for you personally (for me, it's a classic in the "overrated" category).

I originally wrote much of the above paragraph in 1997 as the opening for my review of the self-titled 1973 debut album by Montrose, an album that was on endless repeat through the teenaged years catalogued in Chapter 1. Sixteen years after graduating from high school, I was feeling a tad defensive about calling what was at one time my favorite album of the 1970s a "classic," choosing to frame it as a personal rather than a consensus classic.

Still, I think the distinction has validity. There will always be the albums everyone loves, and the albums *you* love; the songs everyone remembers hearing on the radio in high school, and the songs *you* remember as the soundtrack for those pivotal moments in your life that made you who you are today. The albums that are universally praised, and the ones you have a special connection with that few others share.

Yes, that first self-titled Montrose album, for all its undeniable energy and charisma, is full of goofy, melodramatic, adolescent lyrics; that's exactly why it spoke so profoundly to our band of goofy, melodramatic adolescents. Was it as musically significant to the world as *Sgt. Pepper's Lonely Hearts Club Band*? Not exactly. But it was that significant to *us*. And that makes it, for our purposes here, a classic.

*

The reviews of classics found here are split into two chapters based on year of release. The 1959-1975 period represents the heart and soul of classic rock and Motown and the tail end of the classic era of jazz, as well as the roots of power-pop and new wave and punk and progressive rock. You'll find hints or exemplars of each in the pages ahead, reviewed from the singular perspective of a guy who was born in 1962 and grew up with this music all around me, even if I wasn't able to fully appreciate the experience until long after the fact.

Was the music of this era better than anything you might hear today? That's a value judgment that every individual has to make for his or herself. What I would say is that, in context, the music of the 1960s and early '70s was fresher, and braver, and far less calculated than almost anything you'll hear on your radio today. The music industry didn't truly become an industry until around 1972. For most of the era covered in this first chapter, musical acts were free to explore and experiment and expand their musical visions beyond the boundaries imagined by label executives and image consultants. They just dreamed, and played, and grew. And we grew with them.

*

A final note, before we begin. The review of *Who's Next* that kicks off this section is in fact the first album review I ever wrote, for *On the Town* in 1996. I revised it slightly before publishing it on *The Daily Vault*—as I've done over the years for my entire original run of *On the Town* reviews— and again for publication here, though not substantially. Like the album it describes—one of my absolute favorites—it holds up. Let the windmilling begin.

*

The Who
Who's Next
MCA Records, 1971
[Published on *The Daily Vault* on 4/6/2005]
[Adapted from a review originally published in *On the Town* on 3/19/1996]

From the hypnotic opening riff of "Baba O'Riley" (a.k.a. "Teenage Wasteland") to the crashing closing bars of "Won't Get Fooled Again," this album is, quite simply, a rock and roll masterpiece.

You can argue for *Tommy* or *Quadrophenia* as ground-breaking art forms, but *Who's Next* was truly the Who's seminal album, with Roger Daltrey, John Entwhistle, Keith Moon and Pete Townshend all in peak form, playing and singing some of the most powerful songs Townshend has ever composed, from the above two classics to nuggets like "Bargain," "Gettin' in Tune" and "Behind Blue Eyes." (Ironically, the songs that comprise *Who's Next* were originally intended to be part of a larger rock opera project to be called *Lifehouse*. When the concept didn't quite pan out, the best elements were distilled down to this album.)

Decades after it was recorded, three elements in particular have cemented this album's landmark status. First is Townshend's introduction of the synthesizer as a rock instrument—we take it for granted today, but in 1971, synthesizers were a brand-new technology, and planting one in the middle of a pounding rock song was unheard of. Some musical historians believe "Baba O'Riley" was in fact the first use ever of a sequenced synthesizer in a popular recording.

Second is the drumming. If you think it takes no talent to be a rock drummer, take a long, hard listen to Keith Moon's jaw-dropping performance on this album, in particular on "Won't Get Fooled Again." There is no other word for it but awesome. The beauty is, Townshend and Entwistle's work on guitar and bass is so rhythmic that it gives Moon the freedom to go wild on the kit, pounding out massive rolls and fills where others would keep to a simpler pattern—and it all still fits together like magic.

The third landmark element is the album-ending opus that is "Won't Get Fooled Again." A thundering eight-and-a-half-minute indictment of both establishment oppression and starry-eyed idealism, it is both Townshend's most overtly political statement and one of the most powerful rock anthems ever recorded. The closing minute, all windmilling Townshend power chords and crashing Moon drum fills, punctuated by a nerve-shattering Daltrey scream, is one of the great goosebump moments in rock history.

As if all that isn't enough, in 2003 MCA re-released *Who's Next* in a deluxe edition, complete with rare alternate takes and live versions of these songs, several unreleased tracks from the *Lifehouse* sessions, and liner notes about the project from Townshend himself. It's a fitting tribute to an album that remains, decades later, among the best rock and roll records ever released.

Rating: A

*

Miles Davis
Kind of Blue
Columbia/Legacy, 1959
[Published on *The Daily Vault* on 3/08/2007]

It's been called—repeatedly—the greatest jazz album ever made. Miles Davis' 1959, five-track, 46-minute album *Kind of Blue* has over the decades grown so legendary as to become almost unreviewable. But if we must...

Much has been said by Davis' fellow musicians and jazz aficionados over the years about the technical aspects of these five compositions and performances. If you're looking for that sort of analysis here, you're in the wrong place. I can't come close to explaining the musical significance of measures and scales or modal jazz or tonal organization. Whatever science or magic was worked on these charts is beyond my ken.

What I can tell you is that when Bill Evans' piano and Davis' trumpet play their little counter-pointing duet over Paul Chambers' gentle, insistent bass line and Jimmy Cobb's swishing hi-hat towards the end of "So What," it crystallizes into a kind of transcendent beauty and truth. It literally sounds, as Cobb famously said, like music that must have been made in heaven.

What I can tell you is when Evans takes over the early minutes of "Freddie Freeloader" with his fluid lines and phrases before handing the melody off to Davis, it is sweetness personified, a musical hot fudge sundae with John Coltrane's zingy, zesty tenor sax solo the finger-snapping cherry on top.

What I can tell you is that the middle section of the sublime "Blue in Green," where Miles' trumpet solo melts into Evans' piano solo melts into Cannonball Adderly's tip-toeing alto sax, makes my heart sing and my eyes well.

What I can tell you is that when Coltrane's tenor and Adderly's alto and Davis's trumpet wind their way through the sinuous opening bars of "All Blues," weaving lines over and under one another in a kind of jazz ballroom dance, it is the sound of Michaelangelo sculpting, of Da Vinci painting. What I can tell you is that when Davis himself busts in with a solo of his own over Cobb's jittery snare and steady hi-hat, it is not just the epitome, but the very definition of cool.

What I can tell you is that, in addition to foreshadowing the multicultural bent of Davis' future career arc, "Flamenco Sketches" is among his definitive moments as both a player and arranger, giving all three of these legendary horn players the platform to blow some of the most instinctively sensitive and sensual solos of their careers.

And finally, what I can tell you is that I have never heard an album in any genre more deserving of being called the greatest of its genre. There are very few albums that any person wishing to describe themselves as a fan of American popular music simply must own. This is one of them.

Rating: A

*

The Doors
The Doors
Elektra Records, 1967
[Published on *The Daily Vault* on 12/8/2005]

More than 40 years down the road, it's tough to parse the legend from the reality when it comes to those icons of the avant-garde, The Doors.

There are those who maintain the band is vastly overrated, and those who devour every morsel produced by its still-churning publicity machine, fed most notably over the years by the "I-was-there" writing of former manager Danny Sugerman and the fictionalized film fantasia of Oliver Stone. All of which tends to argue for the simple act performed here: listening to, and reacting to, the music.

From the first whispery tingles drummer John Densmore coaxes out of his cymbals, to keyboardist Ray Manzarek's throbbing, otherworldly organ work, to guitarist Robby Krieger's wild, stabbing figures, to lead singer Jim Morrison's recklessly urgent vocals, leadoff track "Break on Through" simply shouts menace at the listener. It might come off as rather tame, put up against Marilyn Manson, but just remember (a) this was 1967, and (b) Marilyn Manson and a thousand other envelope-pushing acts owe their very existence to the Doors. Juxtaposed against the sunny melodies of the Beach Boys and the earnest creativity of the Beatles, this stuff was pure nitroglycerin.

One of the secrets to the Doors' raw, eerie sound is the absence of a bass player. On their songs you'll often find the organ or guitar matching rhythm with Densmore's stuttering, jazzy drums, amplifying the sense of chaos. Not just Morrison but the entire band sounds vaguely unhinged much of the time.

They further that impression with their multiple-personality approach to song choices. From gritty r&b ("Soul Kitchen") to darkly atmospheric ballads ("The Crystal Ship"), from psychedelic blues ("Alabama Song (Whisky Bar)") to pounding, exuberant pop ("Twentieth Century Fox"), the Doors recognize no boundaries. Even when they do compose the perfect single—the timeless, rippling, urgent "Light My Fire"—they insist on including a lengthy instrumental bridge that's by turns brilliant and bizarre.

But then, this debut was designed to shock. How else do you explain the intense imagery of Morrison's imaginative lyrics, the discordant music of cuts like "End of the Night," the melodramatic flourishes of the Oedipal epic "The End"? It's the original shock-rock, no makeup, costumes or props needed.

Yes, a big part of the appeal is atmosphere—after all, Morrison was never much of a singer, and his "poetry" is wildly inconsistent in quality— but the atmosphere these four created was absolutely riveting in the context of the times. The Doors grabbed the '60s by the lapels and shook the entire decade until it was dizzy. Rock music—real rock music, not the watered-down mainstream swill—would be a lot of things after *The Doors*, but it would never again be safe.

Rating: B+

*

The Beatles
Sgt. Pepper's Lonely Hearts Club Band
Apple / Capitol Records, 1967
[Published on *The Daily Vault* on 10/18/2006]

Of all the reviews that have ever run on *The Daily Vault*, few have caused more coffee to be spit in the general direction of computer screens than our esteemed founder Christopher Thelen's C+ review of *Sgt. Pepper's*

Lonely Hearts Club Band. (And yes, the "F" he gave Yes' *Tales From Topographic Oceans* was right up there, spit-take-wise, but let's try to stay focused here.)

For five years since Chris's review of *Sgt. Pepper's* ran, we have received a steady trickle of complaints and demands for some sort of counterpoint. I suppose the amusing part is that the counterpoint finally comes from me, the guy who inherited the site from Chris and who for years got by with only the Red (*1962-1966*) and Blue (*1967-1970*) albums to my name.

But Chris... dude. *Sgt. Pepper's* is an A. Not just any old "A," but pretty much the "A" standard by which every album that's been issued since must be judged, given that a huge proportion of them never would have existed if not for this album. Without *Sgt. Pepper's*, there could be no Pink Floyd, no New York Dolls, no *Ziggy Stardust*, no *Close to the Edge*, no Ramones, no Sex Pistols.

Would there have been a Jimi Hendrix, a Cream, a Jefferson Airplane? Yes, but their impact—and likely, their imagination—would have been blunted considerably if the Beatles had not paved the way ahead of them. They might well have languished in obscurity, freaks who had somehow, somewhere gotten the misguided idea that free-form creativity infused with socio-political awareness—dare we say it, art—had a place in popular music. Just as it could only have been Nixon who went to China, it could only have been the Beatles—those poppy, foppy, lovable, globally popular icons—who dragged the mainstream kicking and screaming toward the idea that popular music and art were not an either-or proposition. You could solve that equation in a way that included both a wide audience and innovative, challenging artistic product.

The Beatles had been driving towards an achievement like *Sgt. Pepper's* through their previous two albums, taking a few tentative exploratory steps on *Rubber Soul* before racing forward with the highly experimental *Revolver*. *Sgt. Pepper's*—the first album recorded after the band formally ceased touring to concentrate on studio work—was where they first attempted to use their new-found freedom to make an artistic statement.

The conceit around which the album was built is telling. Paul McCartney's vision of the Beatles as a psychedelic-uniformed bar band was both parody and rejection of their clean-cut, identical-suit-and-tied formative years. The self-mocking title tune complements the visuals perfectly, a brilliantly disorienting sound collage of cocktail-party crowd noise, thumping guitar riffs, stately horns, fat gang vocals and one of Paul's best blues shouter lead vocals.

The rest of the disc fills out the vision of a reinvented band playing reinvented music. The smartly-arranged harmonies on "With a Little Help From My Friends" might be old Beatles, but John's emotionally rich counter-culture lyric and Ringo's brilliantly understated lead vocal are miles ahead. From there things range farther and farther afield, from the starry-eyed psychedelia of Lennon's "Lucy in the Sky With Diamonds" to the earthbound sentimentalism of McCartney's "When I'm Sixty-Four'; from the poignant story-telling of Paul's "She's Leaving Home" to the otherwordly spiritualism of Harrison's strictly subcontinental "Within You Without You." Before it's over you get a barnyard symphony ("Good Morning Good Morning"), a harpsichord-and-electric-guitar duet ("Fixing a Hole"), and enough big, echoey background vocals to make Brian Wilson blush ("Lovely Rita"). Not to mention quite possibly the most daring Lennon-McCartney collaboration ever in the haunting, surreal, multi-part closer "A Day in the Life."

Almost as remarkable as the range of music to be found on *Sgt. Pepper's* is the fluidity of the structure, tracks flowing into one another without so much as a cleansing breath in between. This soundtrack-to-an-uninterrupted-dream technique has been imitated many times since — notably on Pink Floyd's *Dark Side of the Moon* — but has rarely stitched together this diverse a group of songs this effectively.

With *Sgt. Pepper's*, as perhaps with no other album in history, context is everything. No song illustrates this better than the oft-maligned Lennon number "Being for the Benefit of Mr. Kite." Taken on its own, "Kite" is a weird little circus-freak of a tune, full of odd instrumentation and even odder lyrics, all of which ends up feeling like an inside joke gone horribly wrong. At least, taken in isolation. Taken in the context of *Sgt. Pepper's* — not to mention the broader artistic revolution that it helped to fuel — "Kite" serves the album's virtual topic sentence, i.e. "There are no boundaries to popular music anymore; we have erased them. See?"

Viewed in context, the whole of *Sgt. Pepper's Lonely Hearts Club Band* is in fact considerably greater than the sum of its parts. "Mr. Kite" might not make the Top 25 on your iPod, but that doesn't change the fact that the album whose creative spirit it personifies is arguably the single most influential musical work of the 20th century.

Rating: A

*

Les McCann & Eddie Harris
Swiss Movement
Atlantic Records, 1969
[Published on *The Daily Vault* 2/20/2003]

Over the years I've noticed that *Daily Vault* Founder Christopher
Thelen and I invariably open our jazz reviews with the same "I have no
idea what the hell I'm talking about here" mea culpa. And the truth is, we
don't—it's one of the handicaps of growing up suburban white bread in
the years spanning 1975 to 1990. Jazz simply wasn't part of our teenaged
musical vocabulary.

Thankfully, that has not prevented me in my adult years from
enjoying fabulous jazz albums like *Swiss Movement*.

Les McCann arrived at the 1969 Montreux Jazz festival in Switzerland
as a pianist and bandleader with a reputation for soulful, funk-infused
jazz. For his part, Eddie Harris was already well-known for his rippling,
eloquent sax phrasings. Their impromptu teaming at the festival, joined by
noted trumpeter Benny Bailey, generated one of the great live jazz albums
of its day, an all-too-brief set of five tracks that simply bubbles and froths
with the pure joy of playing.

It's amusing now to have "Compared to What" plastered across the
airwaves as part of a Coca-Cola advertising campaign, but if you want the
real real thing, you have to come here for it. McCann's take on it, besides
featuring the only vocals on this album, is simply smoking hot. Never
mind the dated '60s lyrics; in McCann and Harris' hands, this thing has a
groove you could drive a truck through, and Harris and Bailey's horns
wail triumphantly between its choruses.

Harris and especially Bailey shine even brighter on "Cold Duck
Time," a Harris composition the band literally learned the day of the show.
The smooth swing of the basic melody doesn't take long to devolve into
dueling solos, Harris' sax alternately juking and soaring before Bailey
comes in and simply blows the crowd away with a trumpet solo that starts
out suave and stylish and builds to a controlled frenzy before falling back
again.

McCann's piano work is consistently rich and effervescent, nowhere
moreso than on the aptly-named "You Got to Get It in Your Soulness,"
where his alternately playful and lyrical solo carries the first half of the
song. Harris' smooth, masterful solo is again the perfect complement,

segueing into a blistering trumpet run from Bailey and a closing full-out jam. The remaining two tracks ("Kathleen's Theme" and "The Generation Gap") are equally entertaining.

Swiss Movement truly caught lightning in a bottle, turning out to be the singular highlight of not one, or even two, but three distinguished jazz players' careers. I'll be the first to concede that every well-versed jazz fan out there already has this album. But for those of you who, like me, are relative beginners, I can't say it loud or often enough—if you are the least bit curious about what great live jazz sounds like, go get this disc, NOW.

Rating: A

*

Led Zeppelin
Led Zeppelin II
Atlantic Records, 1969
[Published on *The Daily Vault* 8/16/2005]

Not many sequels outdo the original—but those that do, usually do so by treating the first in the series as a stepping-off point rather than a template.

On their sophomore release, Led Zeppelin pays respect to the industrial-strength electrified blues that was the foundation of their sound, but makes a quantum leap in terms of creativity, audacity and pure musical charisma. It might not be the first true heavy metal album, but it's surely one of the most influential of all time. More than another disc in their catalog, *Led Zeppelin II* is a mother lode of monstrously crunchy and delicious guitar riffs that slam into you like a sonic wave pool, one after another after another.

The opening salvo, "Whole Lotta Love," is a hard rock immortal built around Jimmy Page's dirty-sweet chugging riff, one of those timeless musical avatars that immediately burrows deep into some primal head-thumping corner of your subconscious. The psychedelic mid-song breakdown, Robert Plant's orgasmic cries and the boom-boom-solo guitar explosion that kicks the song back into gear... it's hard to capture in mere words the impact music this bold must have had in 1969, but the historical record shows it was huge.

The rest of side one (for those of you born before 1980) is a rich suite of amped-up blues numbers that each start slow but keep revving the engine until they explode into a chorus or a solo or some other form of pyrotechnics, as Plant and Page work voice and guitar into a sexually-charged frenzy. A line like "The way you squeeze my lemon / I'm gonna fall right out of bed" from "The Lemon Song" might sound ridiculous when read on the screen or page, but under the spell of a band this focused and charismatic, it sounds nothing short of revelatory. (And don't miss John Paul Jones' shining moment holding the entire song together with his intricate bass line.)

Side two is where the hooks take over completely. It's hard to imagine the beginning electric guitar player who hasn't tried to learn the riff that kicks off "Heartbreaker" by the end of his/her first few months on the instrument. (As for the solo/jam that fill the song's rangy middle section, good luck with that...!) Like a train with no brakes, "Heartbreaker" barrels right into the propulsive "Living Loving Maid," not one of the group's most complicated tunes—it's basically the same fat hook repeated about 50 times—but definitely one of their most hummable.

"Ramble On" starts in with a palate-cleansing acoustic opening, a lilting verse that promises a wistful sweetness until drummer John Bonham kicks in the bottom end and another thundering hook is upon you. This track also cemented the band's reputation for fantasy-tinged lyrics with its multiple Tolkien references.

And then there's "Moby Dick," which is a decent riff-rocking instrumental wrapped around—deity help us all—a three-minute drum solo. In several decades as a rock fan, the only times I have ever found a drum solo remotely interesting have been when I was standing within a few feet of the person playing it. Otherwise, it's a built-in bathroom break—a reasonable idea for a concert, maybe, but for a studio album, not so much...

The boys close out *II* with a more direct nod to their roots in "Bring It on Home," as Plant mumbles and wails over an opening acoustic-and-harmonica traditional blues verse, before Page kicks in with another thunderously fat electric riff that carries the middle section to a brief acoustic reprise/wrap-up.

The discs that followed *II* would find Zeppelin exploring the outer limits of the ideas heard here—grinding blues, pastoral acoustic numbers, and abstract fantasy-tinged lyrics. There were many high points to come, but only one or two albums as consistently memorable as this one, and surely none with a greater impact on their musical peers.

Rating: A

*

Yes
Close to the Edge
Atlantic Records, 1972
[Published on *The Daily Vault* 12/10/2001]

Some albums are simply collections of songs; others grow over time to personify entire genres of music. Think '60s rock and the Beatles' *Sgt. Pepper's Lonely Hearts Club Band*, '70s soul and Marvin Gaye's *What's Going On*, hard rock and Led Zeppelin's untitled fourth album, or jazz and Miles Davis' *Kind of Blue*.

And when you get around to progressive rock, think Yes, and *Close to the Edge*.

Typically, Yes arrived at this milestone album—the consensus high-water mark of the band's decades-spanning career, even among its own fractious fan base—in other than the advised manner. By the time it went into the studio to record this, its fifth album, the four-year-old band had already been through two guitarists and two keyboard players. But the additions of classically-trained prodigies Steve Howe on guitar and Rick Wakeman on keyboards took the entire group to the next level musically, precisely the goal of co-founders Jon Anderson (vocals) and Chris Squire (bass and harmony vocals) and jazz-influenced drummer Bill Bruford.

The band's early experiments with extended pieces of music ranged as long as ten minutes, but resulted in only one significant commercial success, an edited version of the bounding, exuberant "Roundabout," off the first album to include both Howe and Wakeman, 1972's *Fragile*. Buoyed by this breakthrough, the quintet took on a more ambitious goal: to burst the very boundaries of their chosen form, to catapult the music not mere minutes but miles out of the four-minute verse-chorus-verse box by crafting virtual rock and roll symphonies, complete with shifting, flowing movements and extended, virtuosic instrumental passages. It was a form of composition familiar in jazz and classical music, but groundbreaking for a five-piece rock band. The mere idea of a 15-to-20-minute rock song was regarded as preposterous, so if the music wasn't exceptional, the entire experiment could have fallen flat to the point of drawing ridicule.

And there's your punchline: the music WAS exceptional.

Diving straight into the deep end, Yes kicks off with the nearly 19-minute "Close to the Edge," the first and arguably still the best of the band's many long-form pieces to come. Opening with ambient nature sounds, the song abruptly crashes into the hard-edged first movement, Howe's urgent, jazzy, almost atonal electric guitar runs in the forefront while Squire and Bruford play a dizzying rhythmic duet underneath, and Wakeman fills in the flanks with a heady mix of keyboard tones. Three minutes in, the first shift carries the music to a gentler tempo, taking a key theme from the opening and transforming it from a harsh exclamation to a soft, beautiful melody line as Anderson's vocals enter.

These opening few minutes alone are complex, startling and brilliant—and only the beginning. Anderson's "sound painting" approach to lyrics was at its pinnacle here, choosing words that surrender meaning to sound, creating a strangely hypnotic form of sung poetry. Nowhere is its effectiveness clearer than in the quiet middle sections here ("I Get Up, I Get Down") where Anderson's vocals play off Squire and Howe's harmonies before flying high alone over Wakeman's rich, evocative church-organ synths. It's a shimmering, gorgeous moment, a virtual cathedral of sound. As the music picks up again, Wakeman gets his chance to shine as the keys take over the melody explored by Howe in the opening and carry it off in a fresh new direction.

The amazing part is that the entire piece holds together exceptionally well, the movements complementing and amplifying one another's themes while flowing seamlessly from one to the next. The ultimate effect is exhilarating in a way that's difficult to capture in words. At the risk of sounding as air-headed as some of Anderson's latter-day lyrics, it's like watching an incredible sunset; every individual aspect of it simply reinforces the uniqueness and beauty of the whole.

Next up is "And You and I," a four-section, ten-minute symphony of shimmering beauty. The cornerstone of this delicate piece is Howe's keening slide guitar, whose notes during the opening and closing sections angle up into the sky like fireworks. The star of the middle sections is the three-part harmonies between Anderson, Squire and Howe, soaring alongside the slide. Wakeman's synths also decorate the melody throughout the middle sections, especially the harder-rocking third segment, while Squire and Bruford add low-end accents that function more as flourishes than rhythmic markers.

The closing, relatively concise nine-minute "Siberian Khatru" starts out as close to a straight-ahead rock song as this edition of Yes ever came, with Howe picking out a swift, looping melody as the rhythm section kicks in with a complex time signature that Howe both apes and embellishes, urging them on. The chorus breaks the music down to provide some room for the terrific harmonies provided by Anderson and Squire. The closing minutes feature Howe again, blazing through an intricate series of solos as Bruford and Squire keep the rhythm racing along to the track's abrupt, dramatic finish. Maybe the ultimate compliment to the rippling energy given off by this song is that it's probably held down the opening slot on more set lists than any other track in the band's history.

If there was any down side to *Close to the Edge*, it was simply this: it was a huge accomplishment for a band still so early in its career. In the decades gone by since, they have yet to match its combination of power, subtlety and pure musicality—though thankfully, there have been a few near-misses. No matter when the band ultimately calls it a day, though, the five who were there will always have this accomplishment to look back on: the ultimate progressive rock album, the singular masterwork of its genre.

Rating: A

*

Carly Simon
No Secrets
Elektra, 1972
[Published on *The Daily Vault* 12/12/2006]

I was nine years old when *No Secrets* came out, making me an unlikely candidate to have been a fan the first time around. My older brothers were a different story, though, and on those occasions when little brother was allowed into their teenaged sanctum back in '72-'73, this LP was often on the turntable. I might not have understood what half the songs were about at that point in my life, but the sound and feel of this album—warm, honest, intimate—left a lasting impression.

Of course, the cover photo also made a lasting impression on my brothers... but that's to be expected.

Carly Simon had gotten her feet wet in the New York music scene in the mid-'60s, but it wasn't until decade's end that an Elektra exec heard a batch of her demos and, over the objections of his own A&R staff, signed her as a solo artist. Her self-titled debut spawned the surprise hit "That's the Way I've Always Heard It Should Be" and was followed just eight months later by *Anticipation*, whose title track she wrote while waiting for Cat Stevens to pick her up for a date.

Her third album, *No Secrets*, was the one that fully crystallized Simon's emerging sound—revealing, deeply personal songs brought to vivid life by her powerful vocals—and thrust her to the forefront of the female singer-songwriter scene that had been rapidly coalescing around pioneering talents like Carole King and Joni Mitchell.

The rocket engine that propelled this album into the stratosphere was the international number one hit "You're So Vain," a brilliantly rendered portrait of an ex-lover whose charisma is matched only by his ego. "You had me several years ago / When I was still quite naïve" sings Carly, pushing towards the instantly memorable chorus, which features Mick Jagger—along with Warren Beatty, often hypothesized as the song's subject—singing harmony on the classic line "You're so vain / You probably think this song is about you."

"The Right Thing to Do," the album opener and another top ten hit, is among Simon's more optimistic numbers, a song about overcoming doubt and affirming the healing powers of love. Here and in tracks like "The Carter Family" and "Waited So Long," Simon personalizes her lyrics to the point where every word she sings feels autobiographical, whether it actually is or not. And isn't that the definition of good storytelling?

The title tune is another of Simon's very best, capturing both the perils of intimacy and the consequences of getting what you want and not liking the results. "You always answer my questions / But they don't always answer my prayers" goes the key line here. In its own way, the cover image subtly portrays and reinforces this theme—there is a raw sensuality in the shot, yes, but also a disarming openness and vulnerability to the world's pains and joys.

This distinctly female meshing of vulnerable innocence and earthy maturity has a way of making the oddest juxtapositions feel natural, as when the gently lilting childhood nostalgia ditty "It Was So Easy" segues right into the steamy r&b romp "Night Owl," where Carly's growling, playful lead vocals match wits with boogie-woogie piano, sassy sax and a chorus of girl-group background vocals.

To put a fine point on it, there are some aspects of the tones and arrangements on this disc that feel a bit dated today, and anyone with an aversion to assertive string sections backing pop vocals is going have a problem, but such quibbles can't obscure the timeless essence of this album. It's a knowing, artful look at life and love through the eyes of a young woman at the vanguard of a new era, making art that asked and answered questions that were simultaneously intimate and universal. As a result, *No Secrets* deservedly became one of the milestone discs of the singer-songwriter movement.

Rating: A-

*

Stevie Wonder
Innervisions
Tamla, 1973
[Published on *The Daily Vault* 4/18/2008]
[Adapted from a review originally published in *On the Town* 4/2/1996]

The crime of Stevie Wonder's remarkable career is that a generation exists today who think of him principally as the guy who sang that cheesy ad jingle ("I Just Called to Say I Love You," from the otherwise-forgotten 1984 soundtrack album *The Woman In Red*). Let the truth be known: this man was and always will be one of the great ones, even if the years since his 1972-76 heyday haven't matched what went before.

Coming fully into his own after a decade of youthful Motown-formula hit-making, Wonder produced in *Innervisions* perhaps the best of a string of spiritually-tinged, socially-conscious funk-and-ballad albums he issued in an astounding five-year burst of creativity in the early '70s. (*Music of My Mind, Talking Book* and *Fulfillingness' First Finale,* and the double album-plus *Songs in the Key of Life* are the others.) The remarkable footnote here is that during this period Wonder was, as a twenty-one-to-twenty-six-year-old former child star, almost singlehandedly writing, arranging, producing and playing the extremely mature and complex music on these albums. (Not to mention, he's blind.)

Innervisions was the peak of Wonder's skillful melding of spirituality and sensuality, layering his social consciousness, philosophical explorations and simmering romanticism over a series of driving dance rhythms and knockout melodies. "Too High" opens things up with characteristic inventiveness, a smoldering, funked-up rhythm chart establishing the groove before Wonder layers high counterpointing background vocals on top. It's just a brief vignette before the song proper starts, yet it encapsulates Wonder's brilliance beautifully. He's got the groove nailed, but doesn't settle; instead he adds orchestral touches that take the song to a whole new level.

That groove—and everything Wonder adds to it—is what *Innervisions* is all about.

Even the contemplative "Visions"—a daring choice for track number two, as it's the slowest and most serious song on the album—shows great imagination in the way the rather classical acoustic guitar melody is complemented by gentle, jazzy electric licks that give the song its texture and resonance.

"Living for the City" is where Wonder's vision really takes off, though, as he faces weighty social issues head on while grounding his message in driving rhythms. The song's topical subject matter and structure—especially its "theater of the mind" spoken bridge—mark this one as a creative milestone, an exceptionally potent illustration of the urban black experience circa 1973. Late in the song Wonder forgoes lyrics entirely for a powerful crescendo of r&b groove counterpointed with a gospel vocal chorus.

The album's other high point is the pulsating funk groove of "Higher Ground"—so joyfully exploited by the Red Hot Chili Peppers in their brilliant, thrashing 1989 cover—which lifts you right off the floor even as Wonder essays one of his most intensely spiritual lyrics. But truthfully, there's not a weak moment to be found on *Innervisions*. The lush romantic drama of "All in Love is Fair," the burning Latin-inflected funk of "Don't You Worry 'Bout a Thing," and the sweet keyboard melodies of "Misstra Know-It-All" and "Golden Lady" each have their part to play in the album's overall impact.

Innervisions is one of those right-voice-at-the-right-time albums that's a milestone not just for the artist or even the genre, but for the entire era. It's got more groove than a 78 RPM LP and more soul than a gospel choir, and it's the single best album of Wonder's storied career.

Rating: A

*

Pink Floyd
The Dark Side of the Moon
Capitol Records, 1973
[Published on *The Daily Vault* 8/27/2004]

By 1973, Pink Floyd's early days as a psychedelic jam band were waning, and the band was in search of a new focus. Founding lead singer and songwriter Syd Barrett had by then taken his own chemically-induced trip to the dark side, never to return, and while the remaining band of David Gilmour (guitar & vocals), Roger Waters (bass & vocals), Richard Wright (keyboards) and Nick Mason (drums) had talent aplenty, they lacked direction.

Not for long. *The Dark Side of the Moon*—with lyrics by Waters and music by the whole band—would launch Pink Floyd from a quirky footnote to end-of-the-'60s English psychedelia to global icons, guaranteed stadium sellouts any time they chose to hit the road for the rest of their careers.

It's been said that 1975's *Wish You Were Here* is the band's tribute to Syd Barrett. *The Wall* (1979) was of course the band's magnum opus, a massive concept album about—again—a rock star who grows up alienated from society and gradually goes mad. Thematically, *Dark Side* is a dry run for both, the original template from which their later ideas seemed to spring. The key themes are all here—dislocation and alienation, societal greed crushing individual identity, and eventual retreat into madness.

This album contains classic lines—"Hanging on in quiet desperation is the English way"; "Money, it's a gas, grab that cash with both hands and make a stash"; "And if the band you're in starts playing different tunes / I'll see you on the dark side of the moon." And classic moments—the layered, pulsating synthesizers of "On the Run"; Clare Torry's orgasmic vocals on "The Great Gig in the Sky" (now that's what I call an explosion of soul...); the fantastically atmospheric special effects sprinkled throughout the album—clocks, cash registers, snatches of conversation; not to mention the endlessly sampled "Money," simply the most spot-on examination of greed ever recorded.

The production is truly incredible—crystal-clear without losing the band's sometimes-raunchy edge, and full of creative flourishes. In collaboration with engineer Alan Parsons—who would go on to have quite a career of his own as a producer and bandleader—the band created a full-spectrum aural experience that was ground-breaking in its unpredictability and inventiveness.

The most remarkable thing about this album today, though, is the way it flows seamlessly from moment to moment, track to track. It was, if not the very first concept album, the very first concept album to not just stick to a set of ideas and themes all the way through, but explore them fully, evocatively, and without intermission. *DSOTM* is, in essence, a single 44-minute piece of music broken up only by the need on the original version to flip the LP over on your turntable. And not only does it work, it's bloody brilliant every step of the way.

If you only own ten rock albums, this has to be one of them; without this disc, the storyline is incomplete. Absent the smashing success achieved by *DSOTM*, there would be no space-rock, no symphonic rock, no electronica, no elaborate production effects, no stadium-sized laser shows, no (and he would be the first to admit it) Alan Parsons Project. All of those ideas and concepts and dreams can be traced directly back to the success of this landmark album. No respectable rock collection is complete without it.

Rating: A

*

Montrose
Montrose
Warner Brothers Records, 1973
[Published on *The Daily Vault* 11/11/2002]
[Adapted from a review originally published in *On the Town* 2/18/1997]

In 1997 I described the debut album from hard-rock pioneers Montrose as a "personal classic," as distinguished from a consensus classic. The implication was clear: *I love this album, but your mileage may vary.* Fair enough, but isn't that a given?

So, no qualifiers this time around. *Montrose* is a hard rock classic, period.

The massively thundering herds of overdubbed guitar from maestro Ronnie Montrose are one reason (though I also enjoy the subtler purposes to which he put his superb musicianship on later solo albums like *Open Fire*). The clumsy but sincere explications of adolescent fervor and angst from singer "Sam" Hagar (soon to be Sammy, as in the shaggy fellow with a raft of moderately successful solo albums and a platinum-selling stint with Van Halen) are another. Pounding rockers like "Rock the Nation," "Bad Motor Scooter" and especially Hagar's chord-crunching anthem "Make It Last" provide a raw, clear vision of life easily embraced by hormonal, melodramatic seventeen-year-olds (and still fondly recalled by some of us now traversing middle age).

I admit, today some of the lyrics on this album sound slightly goofy to me ("One Thing on My Mind"? Gee, what do you think *that* could be?).

34

But its simple message of enjoying life and reaching for your dreams while ripping out a few choice air-guitar riffs remains even now a powerful antidote against adult-style angst. I mean, just listen to their Chuck-Berry-with-the-volume-on-ten take on the Elvis nugget "Good Rockin' Tonight." This band—Montrose, Hagar, Bill Church on bass and Denny Carmassi in a career-making performance on the drums—is having so much fun it'd be criminal not to join in.

Plus, standing tall in the midst of this eight-song blitzkrieg (no greasy power ballads here, no sir, leave that shit for the hair bands) are a couple of absolute pillars of American hard rock. First comes "Space Station #5," its spacy, effects-laden intro exemplifying the sonic experimentation that was to become an enduring theme of Montrose's work. At least, that's your focus until the intro explodes into one of the most memorable, propulsive riffs in guitar hero history. You've got to love the finish, too. Some bands fade out; this band fades *up*. As in, the closing jam accelerates faster and faster until another bit of sonic trickery launches the melody off its moorings and phase-shifts it from speaker to speaker until it breaches the upper atmosphere.

The patient yang to "#5"'s hyperactive yin is the immortal skin-pounder "Rock Candy." Sure, they might've come up with something a little subtler for a refrain than "You're rock candy, baby / You're hard, sweet and sticky," but the music is five minutes and seventeen seconds of thumping, grinding greatness, one of the transcendent hard rock performances of all time. It's one of those rare songs where an audience hearing it played live will sing along not just to the entire lyric, but to *every note of the guitar solo*. I mean, DUDE.

This band and this album, heavily influenced by Led Zeppelin and Deep Purple, in turn influenced bands from Van Halen (that virtual Montrose tribute band) to AC/DC. It might not be brain surgery, but it is beyond any doubt some of the fist-pumpingest, lighter-snappingest, party-heartiest guitar rock ever, and for me personally, it's a link of memory to places and friends and moments I'll carry with me forever. Rock and roll doesn't get much better than that.

Rating: A

*

Queen
A Night at the Opera
Hollywood Records, 1975
[Published on *The Daily Vault* 10/13/2004]
[Adapted from a review originally published in *On the Town* on 1/7/1997]

This is one of those albums that, at the time, absolutely blew me away.

I mean, who WERE these guys? On one song they would chord-crunch like Led Zeppelin, on the next they'd do a letter-perfect straight-ahead pop song, and on the next they'd come off like a baroque chamber orchestra flying on acid. Topping off all the bizarre musical identity changes, production trickery and dramatic flourishes was this little coda: "No synthesizers." Now how in the hell did they pull that off??

The key lay in understanding that this was always a band made up of four distinct individuals, all of them talented musicians and songwriters in their own right. There was earthy, hard-rocking drummer Roger Taylor; soft-spoken, romantic bassist John Deacon; adventurous, sweet-voiced guitarist Brian May; and on lead vocals and piano, the one and only Freddie Mercury, who shared elements of each of the other three's musical identities, in addition to being the performer for whom the word "flamboyant" would undoubtedly have been invented, if it didn't already exist.

On this career-making album, the band kicks off with the blistering bile of "Death on Two Legs," a miles-over-the-top kiss-off message to their former manager which, whether they would ever admit it or not, likely inspired legions of nascent punks with its thoroughly unleashed anger (try "You suck my blood like a leech" — for an opening line). From there it's wild ride through bizarre British-class-system-deconstructing numbers like "Lazing on a Sunday Afternoon" and "Good Company," dramatic rock numbers like "Sweet Lady" and "The Prophet's Song," the pristine pop sentiment of Deacon's classic "You're My Best Friend" and the folk-tinged historical romance of May's "'39."

And then there was that completely off-the-wall psychedelic/operatic six-minute number near the end that no one thought radio would ever play. Now what was that one called? Oh yeah — "Bohemian Rhapsody." I'm guessing maybe you've heard of it.

A Night at the Opera was the disc that would catapult Queen from British hit-makers to global superstars. As with many landmark albums, it became part milestone and part millstone, with every album that followed compared in some way or another to the musical and commercial success they achieved here. Be that as it may, the music is what counts—and it is simply amazing.

Rating: A

*

Bruce Springsteen
Born To Run
Columbia Records, 1975
[Published on *The Daily Vault* 4/12/2005]
[Adapted from a review originally published in *On the Town* on 4/29/97]

In the liner notes to his 1995 *Greatest Hits* album, Bruce Springsteen describes the song "Born to Run" as "my shot at the title. A 24-year-old kid aiming at 'the greatest rock'n'roll record ever.'"

The kid did okay.

Born to Run—the album and the song—is a rock and roll fever dream, the most evangelical sermon ever preached in the Holy Church of Rock as Redemption. On this album, a brash young singer-songwriter fresh out of the New Jersey club scene set some of the most evocative American street poetry of the 20th century to an electrifying set of recklessly expansive rock and roll.

The musical and thematic rhythms of the iconic opener "Thunder Road" mirror the album's as a whole: the young narrator wages a determined battle against the despair around him until both he and the music finally erupt in life-affirming passion. The key instruments—guitar, piano and sax—play off one another in a flurry of mood-shifts that dazzle with both their audacity (after all, it's only rock and roll) and their precise emulation of the lyrics' emotional tenor. The reconstituted E Street Band— now featuring Roy Bittan on piano and Max Weinberg behind the drum kit—tears into the song's climax as if the players' lives depend on it. The lyric's themes—the desperate fight to keep hope alive in a dark and dangerous world, the redemptive powers of love and faith—are timeless and expressed in a one-of-a-kind, street-wise yet highly literate and sensitive voice.

From that remarkable beginning, the momentum only builds.

"Tenth Avenue Freeze-Out" shows off Springsteen's love of rhythm and blues with a dynamite groove and swinging horn section. A quarter-century later it had become a standard, one of the staples of the 1999-2000 E Street Band reunion tour. Turning the energy up even higher, "Night" and companion piece "She's the One" play the irrational cockiness of youth against the unquestionable certainty of a driving rock beat.

"Backstreets" and "Jungleland" are where I start to run out of superlatives. They are impossibly grand, ambitious and intense goodbyes to the Jersey shore street life romanticized so effectively by Springsteen on his first two albums, beautiful cries of agony and frustration at the loss of his friends, his youth, his world. Together, this pair of extended suites constitutes one of the most musically and emotionally complex mini-rock operas on record. Both feature remarkably patient, evocative arrangements that allow the songs to build and support the lyrics until they take on a mesmerizing, epic quality that has rarely, if ever, been matched.

And the title track? A simply amazing lyric (this is great American poetry here, folks) set to a four-minute full-out multiple-crescendoing rock and roll symphony. For one person at least, the ambitious young kid hit his target. "Born to Run" is pure musical ecstasy and, for my money, the greatest rock'n'roll record ever.

The corner Bruce Springsteen turned artistically on *Born to Run* would shape the rest of his career. His songs were expansive but no longer cluttered, and every note played by the E Street Band was fueled with an unstoppable energy and determination. That in itself makes for great music. The capper was that Springsteen dared to make it all sound like it mattered, like rock could and should aim higher than it ever had before. He dared us all to believe in rock and roll as art, maybe even salvation. Some of us still do.

Rating: A

~Segue~

Interview: Ronnie Montrose

[Published on *The Daily Vault* 4/27/1998]

One of the occupational hazards of being tagged as a guitar legend after your first album is that your reputation tends to precede you forever after.

"Mercurial" is an adjective that's been attached to guitarist Ronnie Montrose's name so many times it's almost a part of it. Add to that "innovative," "enigmatic," "technically brilliant" and most of all, "uncompromising," and you're closer to the complete picture. In a career spanning three decades, Montrose has confounded critics, managers, record companies and perhaps even at times his audience with albums that have over the years ranged far from the mainstream rock sound that marked the launch of his career.

Montrose's early session gigs with Herbie Hancock and Van Morrison paved the way for a stint in the Edgar Winter Band that saw him play on the hits "Frankenstein" and "Free Ride" from 1971's They Only Come Out at Night. *From there he went on at the age of 25 to found the seminal hard rock band bearing his name with Sammy Hagar, Bill Church and Denny Carmassi. Their first album, titled simply* Montrose, *remains a fresh and familiar air-guitar player's icon 25 years after its release, which spawned such FM rock staples as "Rock Candy," "Bad Motor Scooter" and the blistering "Space Station #5."*

The band line-up shifts began almost immediately, though, as first Church and then, after a second album, Hagar left. Throughout his career, Montrose has pushed the envelope with his exploration of sonic tones and textures using both guitars and synthesizers, and the depth of his determination to avoid the beaten path hasn't always made it easy for those around him to stay with the program.

From Montrose through the experimental guitar-and-synth band Gamma and a string of indie-label instrumental guitar albums, the one thing it's become apparent Montrose has never been willing to do is compromise his musical vision. Right or wrong (to which a chorus of admiring fellow players would likely add, "Right!"), his relentless pursuit of new frontiers to travel with his instrument has never been less than interesting, however distant from the commercial mainstream it has taken him.

At least as intriguing as his stories about musical adventures with the likes of Hagar, Morrison and Winter, though, is the man's keen sense of self. Back on the nightclub circuit, clearly in the second half of a career that once saw him fronting one of the biggest acts on the West Coast, Montrose shows every evidence of having achieved a somewhat remarkable state of mind for a quote-unquote guitar hero. Call it self-awareness, or perspective, or simply maturity; Ronnie Montrose has no illusions whatsoever about what his dogged commitment to do it his way has cost him professionally and financially—but neither does he have any regrets. He is at peace with the totality of his musical career to a degree that few artists who strain to grasp the brass ring ever achieve.

The Daily Vault: When did you first pick up a guitar? And when you did, did you know right away? Was it a "this is how I want to spend my life" kind of feeling?

Ronnie Montrose: It was. My friend had a guitar when I was 17. And the first time I held it, the first time my fingers touched the strings and I made a chord, I knew it was something that was resonant with me. I mean, I had friends who had saxophones and pianos, and while those were great, with the guitar there was something about the tactile connectedness, the left hand / right hand and wood and strings that just... worked. It was the pure joy of playing music with it and just strumming it that got me started. It certainly wasn't "Wow, now I have something that I'm really going to be able to make a living with!" It had nothing to do with any idea like that. When I was 17 I just fell in love with it. And I'm 50 now, so it's been 33 years. [Mel Brooks *High Anxiety* voice] "And they said it wouldn't last..." (Laughter)

On the first few records you played on, you played with Herbie Hancock, Van Morrison and Edgar Winter. What was it like starting out as the "new kid" and working side by side with big talents like that?

With Herbie Hancock I just went in and played sort of a wah-wah, *Shaft* rhythm guitar part. And as I recall, David Rubinson, the producer, even at a certain point worked the wah-wah pedal. I had the rhythmic right hand that I've been very fortunate to have, but I was completely out of my league and over my head and I was very aware of it, as was everyone else, though everyone else was cordial. And I had a great time. David Rubinson at that time was basically my mentor; he got me on some sessions and helped me a lot.

Van Morrison was the same kind of story. I had listened to Van, listened to "Gloria" and "Mystic Eyes" and all those songs I love. But I wasn't aware of his absolute prowess over composition, how gifted he actually was as a songwriter. By no means was I on a level where I felt like I could interact with a talent like his.

It seemed like that same thing happened with Edgar Winter. For some reason—and I'm sort of beginning to understand it as I grow and become somewhat "sage" myself—you do seek out wise men. One of the reasons that Van and Edgar gravitated towards me was that I was fresh and talented and had lots of energy and a willingness to work within the parameters that were there and yet still add my own fire.

Let me ask about a song I heard on the radio the other day driving home: "Frankenstein." How much fun was that to play on?

It was a lot of fun, because it was a thing that wasn't supposed to be a single, it was just Edgar messing around on an ARP synthesizer. The reason we called it "Frankenstein" was that it was an assemblage of parts of different songs Edgar had been working on. There were a couple of parts that were actually from Edgar's *Entrance* album. The whole thing was just a gothic rock showcase for Edgar's newfound fascination with the synthesizer. It was amazing to hear that thing on the radio in its day. Of course, in hindsight everyone knows exactly why that was a smash single, because sounds like those synths and effects were just unheard of in a power rock format.

Did you have any inkling at all when you wrote and recorded that first Montrose album what a lasting impact and long shelf life it would have?

Absolutely none. We had a couple of managers come up and listen to me, Sam, Denny and Bill play "Rock Candy," "Rock the Nation," "Space Station #5" and "Bad Motor Scooter" at rip-roaring levels. And one management agency went out and had a meeting and then came back in and said, "Guys, if this were 1968, we probably could do something here, but this isn't going to work. You might want to think about changing your music and getting up with the times." At which point we just kind of closed ranks and adopted the attitude that *was* that band, which is, "If you like it, fine. If you don't, take a hike. We're playing this music, and we love this music." Oh, the folly of youth and testosterone. (Laughter)

What would you consider the highlights of the whole Montrose experience—both incarnations, with Sammy Hagar and with Bob James—

(Laughter) Sammy is funny—he calls the first two Montrose albums THE Montrose albums, and the third Montrose album the FIRST Bob James album. And in a way, bless his heart, he's right, because there is no "Montrose" without me and Sam and Denny and Bill, in my mind. And only later have I come to realize that. *Everyone* knows that. It's like any seminal band—without the original members, it just isn't the same. I don't care what incarnation it is—and this is just me editorializing here—but there is no Deep Purple without Ritchie Blackmore and Ian Gillian. Original members make up a band, and when bands have that big of an impact on the general consciousness, any other incarnation is pale and historically irrelevant.

You guys did a little mini-reunion for one song on Sammy's last album. Would you ever consider trying it again, for an album or a tour?

There's been talk about it. We're not quite sure if it could work or not for all of us. If it happens, it seems like this year may be better suited for everyone than anytime. Getting together with all four of us in the studio was like a high school reunion. It was great because we had a chance to catch up and talk about everything, not just the record business or even music. We talked about our families and the other things going on in our lives. Ten years ago I would have told you [a reunion] would not be a possibility. Now I can't say that. Now I would say that it could be a possibility.

After four albums of fairly heavy rock with Montrose, you first solo instrumental album *Open Fire* caught a lot of people by surprise with its string section and mandolins and Edgar Winter's jazzy keyboard textures. Was that your intent? Were you consciously trying to go a different direction and challenge your audience with the music on that record?

Most assuredly not. I was consciously trying to make the music that I *felt like making* at that time. That particular musical foray was completely comfortable and natural to me, much to the dismay of those in the music "business." *Open Fire* did, however, afford me wonderful recognition from

42

the one and only Tony Williams [a highly respected jazz drummer/bandleader], who recently passed away. So while many of my rock fans were not too pleased with that record, I was pleased and honored to be invited to travel to Japan with Tony, who wanted me to play on his *The Joy of Flying* album. That's the thing—any situation is potentially double-edged, where music is concerned.

In 1979, when the *Open Fire* phase was done and Gamma was coming together, were you still thinking maybe you'd get back to instrumental music down the road?

Yeah, never a doubt, because playing melody and chord structure sans lyrics has always been so deeply a part of me.

Gamma put out three albums of amazing music in a pretty short period. What were the highlights for you of that band and that experience?

The first Gamma record was great for me because I was writing and playing at a very fast pace. Working with Ken Scott [producer of *Gamma 1*] was great because we were experimenting, and I was afforded the chance to go off on all kinds of little sonic forays. Like, for example, the intro to "I'm Alive" was a microphone tapped against my knee and processed through a vocoder. Also a lot of different guitar tones and chord changes and fun sonic experiments. And it was great, the energy of that lineup. It was the original Gamma lineup, and once again, I guess there was an essential quality to it.

There were good and bad parts working on all three Gamma albums, but another highlight was doing the third Gamma album [*Gamma 3*], because I was working with Mitchell Froom and we were experimenting quite a bit. And also, we were bucking the system—management and the record company were trying to get us to play the "Let's make a single" game, and it was fun engaging in combat with that mindset and saying instead "Let's make interesting music, and hope it comes out well."

At a certain point after Gamma ended, you went in the direction of all-instrumental albums. You had to know that was not the recommended career path if your only priority was to have a big commercial success.

I can't state it any clearer than to say that I was following my muse. Everyone tried to steer me into making popular music, from any manager I was with to any record company I was with, and in fairness, understandably so. Because without an artist who makes popular music, management and record companies and booking agents don't survive. So as a result, you're faced with the dilemma of saying, "I know I should be doing this kind of music, but I don't *feel like* it."

So in the end, I just followed the music, for better or for worse. I'm not saying I've made brilliant instrumental solo albums, but I certainly have taken the path that seemed appropriate to me at the time. In hindsight, are there things I would change on my records? Sure. Are there approaches I would take differently? Yes. But that's what any artist would do.

One of the rewards for making instrumental music has been that, at one point, I was in a period of making records where I reached a serious existential moment of self-doubt. I was making records that I knew were not going to get played on the air a lot, just working off the knowledge that there were enough people that enjoyed this music that I could survive. But it almost got to the point that I'd make records and I'd get them out and get no response.

And you need some kind of response. If you write a review, you like to have somebody go, "Hey, nice review." If you repair a car, you like to have somebody go, "You know, you did a damn fine job on that car." Or you paint a house—you know what I'm saying? When you do something, it's important to get feedback. And I reached a point where I specifically remember sending out *Mutatis Mutandis*, or maybe *The Diva Station* to magazines and newspapers and industry people, and signing a little note saying, "Call me back and let me know what you think," just to get their feedback. And, as God is my witness, I got not one single response to my mailings. Not even to say "I don't like it." *Zero* response. And that was a pretty low point for me.

But now, the reason I'm so up and so joyful in spirit is that, because of this wonderful world of e-mail, I've gotten e-mails from across the country and around the world from people who specifically write to tell me about *The Speed of Sound* or *Mutatis Mutandis* or *The Diva Station* or other records that I've done, and say, "You know, that record really touched me. That got me through some tough times." And that, right there, period, end of story, is all I need; I am a happy man because of that. Because I know somewhere, the music that I've made has touched and reached—I don't care how *many* people—as long as I've gotten through to *someone*. That's all we all hope for, really, is that sort of validation.

The *Mr. Bones* album is really unique and fun in that it works as a video game soundtrack—I can almost see what's going on on the screen in my head—and it also works as an instrumental guitar album. Tell me how you got involved in that project and what it was like working on it.

It was a long project. The producer of the project told me that it would take six months, and it literally took two years. I never thought I'd work on a project for two years. Going into it, they wanted this game to be guitar-based. It was different from other games because of that, because Mr. Bones is a guitar player, and the whole thing is based around guitar playing. [Video game producer] Ed Annunziata's original concept for the game was nothing but guitar and a lot more of the sort of Southern old blues guitar, but that's not my nature. We sort of found our levels after he invited me into the project. He never imagined the music could go that far out in different areas, and different forms, but it all made sense. And I guess that's sort of what I do with instrumental music and synthesizers and the things I'd done with Gamma, is take the music to those different levels.

Mr. Bones was also great for me to flex my underscoring ability, which I've always known I had. I just sort of dove into it. All the music on the segue parts between the game levels, those were me, and I knew that I could do them. Ultimately, I'm sure I will end up composing music for films.

The making of the *Mr. Bones* CD was one of the most fun times I've had in the studio for a while, because it came at a point where I'd worked long and hard though an arduous journey from beginning to end of the video game project. And after all that work was done, the fun was getting to put great musicians together and not specifically play music for the game, but rather to take these sketches of music from the video game and make a bona fide full-length CD. It was fast, it was loose, and it was a lot of fun.

Tell us about the concept and process behind your new live album. What made you decide it was time for a live album?

We actually recorded it right before I did *Mr. Bones*. I was playing live with my then-studio band, Michele [Graybeal, on drums] and Craig [McFarland, on bass]. We were just sort of having fun playing live trio music, and a really long-time old friend of mine named Jim Mathews suggested, because he had some recording equipment, that we go out and record a few gigs. And we tried it, just for the fun of it, and one night just happened to be spectacular. It was totally loose, raw. It was a packed house—a small crowd, but it was packed—and it was a magical night.

And the reason I haven't finished it before now is, of course, that I was working so hard on *Mr. Bones* that I didn't have time. The [live] tape's been around for a couple of years, but we just got to the point now where we could go back and finish it.

At first, because of the temptation of multi-track, I was going to say, like a lot of guitar players do, "Well, a live album is a live album, but I'll just go back and fix this little guitar note." It dawned on me later that that was the absolute wrong thing to do. Now it's against my philosophy, which is, let the mistakes stay where they are. That way the listener will get the same exact experience as the people who were there having a great time at the concert got, as opposed to the listener getting sort of an "edited for TV" experience. And it's called *Roll Over and Play Live*.

What tracks are on the album?

Different pieces of music from my instrumental albums. A lot from *Music From Here*, which was my current album at the time, plus a couple of older songs and about a half dozen new songs we wrote in rehearsal specifically for the shows.

You've explored a lot of territory as an instrumental artist; do you think you'll ever try the rock-band-with-vocals setting again?

I may not do the rock band with vocals, but I will absolutely do the vocal thing again. I've been working with a great artist recently, a singer-songwriter named C.J. Hutchins. I'm producing his record for him out at my home studio, and we're basically finishing the mixes right now. His project is called *Out of These Hands*, which is the name of a song that he and I co-wrote. He brought me 40 songs and let me pick the cream of the crop, and I gave him song chorus ideas, and he was absolutely brilliant at coming up with the appropriate verse and the right feel and nuance.

It made me realize that I really do love working with lyrics and working with singers. My problem is—one of these stigmas for me is—when a singer who's looking for a guitar player hears the name Ronnie Montrose, they immediately think, "Well, I better start screamin'." You know? "I better start to cinch it up, and try to scream and I better cop a pose." But that's not where I'm at at all right now with lyrics and vocals and songs in general. So I'm very much looking forward to doing a vocal album, but it won't be a vocal album that is a rehash of *Montrose*, it'll be a vocal album that is where I'm at now, currently. It'll be a collaboration with someone who's at the same place I am right now, which is hopefully at a deeper lyrical level and less rock-oriented.

What's the difference for you between playing electric and acoustic? What do you usually use to compose on?

Basically, composing, there's hardly any difference between electric and acoustic when I compose a melody or a chord structure. But there is an attitude that seeps in when I compose at 100 decibels. There's a certain thing that comes out, maybe a powerful passage of chords that you wouldn't find at home with an acoustic guitar. But really, for me they're pretty interchangeable.

Tell us about your plans for your website, and what kinds of things people are going to be able to find on it when it's up.

I'm so stoked! The website is going to be www.ronnieland.com. It's going to have an editorial page, obviously, because I'm a long-winded kind of fellow. (Laughter) And lots of great photos, and some features about things that have happened in my life. I'm also really enjoying exploring the possibility of getting my music out to people on the website. One of the great things about the website and Internet is that I'm able to network with people who are looking for my music or for other music and sort of be the catalyst that connects people to find my music or any other music. There'll be a bunch of my CDs, and some downloadable audio... and that's about as specific as I can get right now. We're just now roughing out all the features.

Do you have any sort of target date yet?

How about yesterday? (Laughter) My son Jesse, who is a programmer, is helping me set it up, as is my wife Michele, who is not only a talented drummer, but a gifted illustrator and artist and is creating a real look and feel on the site. One of the prerequisites for site was we all agreed we did not want it to look like it came from a "Website Building 101 kit." Instead of using standard graphics, we're using a lot of hand-rendered art.

I'm also looking forward on the site to connecting people and getting feedback from people about both specific and not-specific things. It might be "What chords did you play on this song?" but it also might just be being a catalyst for dialogue.

Another interesting thing that has happened to me with this world of e-mail and the Internet is that I'm finding it very easy to discern who has legitimate questions about things. The way I figure it, if you're backstage at a concert, you sometimes meet people where you can carry on a wonderful conversation and dialogue with them... and then sometimes you're meeting a person who's had quite a bit too much to drink, and who's shaking his fist and going "You rock, dude!" I just figure that, when I get a letter from someone who is pretty proficient on a keyboard and can articulate themselves, I'm probably going to be able to communicate with them. So e-mail has been a wonderful filter.

Not there's anything *wrong*, mind you, with "You rock, dude!" (Laughter) I don't mind that. It's just that, that's the level that conversation is going to stay at.

What other guitar players do you admire the most? And what do you think of instrumental guitar artists like Joe Satriani and Eric Johnson?

It's an interesting thing that happens with guitar music; it sort of waxes and wanes. I'm at the point now where, anytime anyone succeeds in any way playing any type of instrumental guitar music, I'm gonna stand up and cheer. I'm long past that point—I think it's kind of a youthful thing—looking at guitar music as a competition, or guitar playing as calisthenics or gymnastics. I've sort of left that mentality and mindset by the wayside. It's not that I'm being diplomatic, it's just that I think that mindset is sort of horrid.

That having been said, I do, like anyone else, have certain tastes. So I can tell you that the players that I listen to and enjoy are players like Adrian Legg, Chris Rea and Billy Gibbons. My complete hero is Daniel Lanois. My dream come true would be for Daniel to be able to produce a record for me, because he takes an approach that I really, really enjoy, which is just such a non-slick approach.

There's an album he produced for Emmylou Harris that had a completely different sound that I thought was wonderful for her.

Uh-huh. Absolutely. And his album *For the Beauty of Wynona* is just a devastating record. Some of the finest guitar tones I've heard. If you don't have it, you should get it, as well as the *Sling Blade* soundtrack.

Sounds like I've got some shopping to do. Okay, last question. You've put some really interesting, thought-provoking little quotes and phrases on most of your albums since *Gamma 2* in 1979. The last one, on *Music From Here*, says: "The only path to the here and now is the one that we have traveled." Are you where you want to be? Is there anything you'd change if you could?

That's really the point of the quote. Once you realize you can't change things, that you're going to be here and you're going to be now, it's pretty difficult to stray off that path into worrying about what might have been.

How that quote came about is that I was sitting there at one point thinking "You know, there are a lot of things I would change." But pretty soon I realized, had I gone to an "investor" a few years ago, or done the "economically sound thing," buy a house and build up equity and do all of those things, I wouldn't be talking to you right now. I wouldn't be married to the woman of my dreams right now. I would have never met people and friends that I have now. And I wouldn't be playing the music that I'm playing right now.

All of us can look back and say, "I should have done this..." —and this is what irritated me at the time—it's all based on this idea of success. People say, "Well, if only Ronnie would have done this..." and it's not just me they're saying that about, it's any artist who hasn't succeeded to that level of making a string of gold or platinum records. The music business is based on that, and of course everyone wants to rationalize their value system and say "Well, at least it's a quality record." But to that mindset, a quality record means nothing in and of itself.

So when people were saying "Where did Ronnie go wrong? Why didn't he go the gold and platinum record route?" I started thinking about it, and I looked around at all the wonderful things in my life right now. And I thought, had I gone down that road, I never would have met the people that I know now, and have the family and friends around that I have now. The other side is that, if you're not now where you want to be, then the awareness that you're the one who's taken the path to where you are can remind you that you have the ability to go where you want to be.

The bottom line is this: I am very—no, extremely—happy. I'm healthy, I have a wonderful wife, my children are doing great, I have wonderful friends, and I'm playing music. Everything is good in my life. The *only* thing I could use... is a little more money! Like everybody else! (Laughter) And since that's my only problem, I don't really have any problems right now.

3

Classics 1976-1996

SEPTEMBER 1976 WAS THE MONTH I started high school, and also the month the band Boston's self-titled debut was released. I came of age, in other words, just as the nearly simultaneous rise of disco and punk was threatening to drown out rock and roll completely, despite the best efforts of neo-traditionalists like Springsteen. And then *Boston* arrived, a record that ascended the charts like the rocket-ship guitar on its cover and didn't come down for years, one of those albums that everyone I knew had, or wanted, or had at least heard and been impressed by. The sound was fresh and clean and *huge* and the album took over radio for not just weeks or months, but years, and is still heard frequently today on any classic rock station worth its salt.

It also arrived as a symbol of the changes that had been busy taking hold across the entire breadth of popular music itself over the previous decade. Boston was a band driven more by technology than human connection, the original bedroom album, recorded in guitarist / songwriter / producer Tom Scholz's basement with occasional assists from a few friends (notably, lead singer Brad Delp). When the label signed Scholz and got hold of the music, they determined the final lineup of the band he would later take out on the road in support of the album, and encouraged Scholz to present the scrappy-bar-band backstory heard on the self-mythologizing track "Rock & Roll Band" as Boston's own, rather than a pastiche of stories he'd heard from musician acquaintances.

Rock was back, in other words, but it was a different kind of rock. It was the beginning of corporate rock, with the puppet strings of label executives and mercenary bean-counters more and more visible to an increasingly skeptical and cynical public. The Vietnam War and Watergate scandal had purged the nation of whatever innocence it had left, and the music business was no exception, having morphed in a handful of years into the music *industry*, an increasingly monolithic and uber-capitalist force bent on manufacturing widgets of pre-fabricated entertainment for the mass consumer market.

In many ways, it's been so ever since. Waves of fashion will always rise and fall, and the rise of the Internet has opened up the playing field somewhat for independent artists, but big media and big corporations still have a chokehold on the mass market. It takes a special kind of artist to break through the lowest-common-denominator clutter and make music that's memorable, both then and now.

That's the focus of this chapter, for the most part—artists in the second and subsequent, splintering waves of rock, and albums old enough now (20 years-plus being my personal cut-off point) to be considered classics. This is also where you as a reader become even more a prisoner of my tastes as a listener and writer, moving steadily forward into favored genres like singer-songwriter, power-pop, mainstream hard rock and British art-rock.

A final note on this chapter: if this second wave of classics feels heavy on the '70s, it is. As a musical decade, I *hated* the '80s—the tinny drums, the strangled guitars, the processed vocals, the lifeless synthesizers looming like clouds of inhuman metallic dust—and the '90s still feel recent to me, though I managed to zero in on a trio of albums worthy of the term "classic" from each of the latter two decades. From the beginning of my high school years in 1976, through the beginning of my music writing career in 1996, these are the albums I've reviewed that, for one reason or another, strike me as genuine classics.

*

Boston
Boston
Epic Records, 1976
[Published on *The Daily Vault* 3/28/2005]

First opener: You think steroids are a problem in baseball? Consider the steroidal growth of the electric guitar sound between 1966 and 1976... from the tinny strums of early Yardbirds to the cavernous, electrifying, interstellar-rocket-engine-buffed-to-a-crystalline-shine tone of Boston.

Second opener: I blew my daughter's mind with this one just the other day in the car. "Peace of Mind" was blasting away and she, a 15-year-old acolyte of Green Day, Maroon 5, et al, was bopping along. "Nice guitar sound, huh?" said I. "Yeah!" exclaimed she. "This album came out 29 years ago," said I. ".....!....." said she. (So young, yet so eloquent.)

Third and final opener: Most people think of Boston in terms of huge riffs and pristine production. What's always made them special to me, though, is the weird juxtaposition in much of their material between larger-than-life music and introspective, sensitive-guy lyrics.

I mean, sure, lead vocalist Brad Delp could have been the guy standing on the back of the couch belting it out at the top of his lungs at your high school party. But Boston's composer / guitarist / producer / mastermind Tom Scholz would have been the guy sitting by himself in the corner staring at the lava lamp. Except instead of spacing out, he would have been drawing a perfect schematic of the thing in his head while trying to get up the nerve to talk to the equally shy girl sitting in the opposite corner of the room.

The backstory of this band is the stuff of rock and roll legend... at least, among the pocket-protector crowd. Scholz was working on his master's in mechanical engineering at M.I.T. when he started tinkering with demos for some of these songs, working in his basement with a 12-track recording unit. Upon graduating, he was immediately snatched up by Polaroid and installed in their product research and development shop.

Meanwhile, he kept writing and playing and was eventually drafted into guitarist Barry Goudreau's band to play keyboards. Within a matter of months, Scholz was playing guitar and leading the band, which by then included Delp on vocals, Fran Sheehan on bass and John "Sib" Hashian on drums. A four-track demo recorded in Scholz's basement studio landed the band an instant contract with Epic.

It's not hard to see why. This disc starts strong, opening with the single that broke the band, and never looks back. "More Than a Feeling" is classic Scholz, a number that starts out gentle, then steadily gains momentum until the soaring solos achieve escape velocity—all in support of a somber, contemplative lyric. "When I'm tired and thinking cold / I hide in my music, forget the day / And dream of a girl I used to know / I close my eyes and she slips away," goes the key verse. Yes, Virginia, Boston is the shy guy's air-guitar band.

The next two cuts are equally classic. "Peace of Mind" features the propulsive pairing of acoustic rhythm and electric lead guitars, a dynamite melody line, and an upbeat, philosophical lyric you can sing along to. As for "Foreplay / Long Time," if you've never listened to this one at high volume while blasting down an empty road with the top down, you really need to make it happen sometime. The opening section, a throbbing two-minute instrumental, segues gently into a sunburst of a guitar solo that leads to a powerful verse, a doubly powerful chorus, and eventually to two more solos, each packing more punch than its predecessor. I could — and did — listen to this one over and over.

Later on, Scholz gets playful with "Smokin'," featuring some of his best organ work and a finger-snapping lead vocal from Delp, and bangs out a decent piece of guitar pop in "Something About You." To be fair, there is some lyrical cheese here, notably in the self-laudatory and mostly fictional "Rock & Roll Band" and the lounge-quality seduction piece "Let Me Take You Home Tonight."

But even with a fall-off in songwriting quality in the third act, you can't mark this disc down much. It is simply a milestone in rock, and side one (those first three cuts for you young 'uns) constitutes one of the great slabs of '70s guitar rock ever recorded. If you've ever played air guitar in your life — especially if you were alone in your room and wearing dorky-looking headphones at the time — this album is a must.

Rating: A-

*

Peter Frampton
Frampton Comes Alive!
A & M Records, 1976
[Published on *The Daily Vault* 5/28/1998]

Once upon a time in the land of music, just before the Sonic Plague that was disco and just after the birth of the Metal Dragon, came upon the land a young prince (no, not that Prince — it's a metaphor, dammit!).

This young prince was lithe and blonde and long of hair, and spoke in the soft, lilting tones of an Englishman, setting the hearts of all the young maidens in the land to pittering and pattering... and yet he could also pound out a tasty, jamming eight-minute cover of "Jumpin' Jack Flash" if the mood struck him. Truly, for his one brief shining moment, this prince had it all.

Leading into *Frampton Comes Alive*, nothing particularly suggested Peter Frampton was about to issue the biggest selling live album of all time (15 million units and counting... paying attention, Garth?). Sure, he'd produced several well-regarded singles with Brit-pop bands The Herd and

Humble Pie, and shown off some very solid guitar work and melodic tunesmithing on three solo studio outings.

But despite the strength of his musical chops, he'd been passed off as something of a lightweight thanks to his forays into sentimental, acoustic love songs. What *Frampton Comes Alive* let him do was show both sides of his musical personality, the crooner and the rocker, and do it in the charged setting of a high-energy live show. As Cameron Crowe says in the liner notes, this album is "a testimony to Peter Frampton in his natural habitat." His lack of sustained success in any other context makes these words ring truer today than ever.

Recorded largely in the cozy confines of San Francisco's legendary Winterland, *Frampton Comes Alive* captures the energetic, yet unmistakably clean and terribly British pop-rock sound Frampton featured on songs like "Something's Happening" and "I Wanna Go to the Sun." Many songs dabble in blue-eyed funk, with the aptly-named "Doobie Wah" in particular sounding like it could have been borrowed from an early Doobie Brothers album. "(I'll Give You) Money" ventures even farther into the land of Cream, featuring a fat guitar sound over a simple blues beat and a couple of shimmering, authoritative solos from Frampton.

The keys to Frampton's kingdom clearly came, though, in the songs where his generally gentle approach to lyrics melded with a choice radio-friendly riff or two, as in the monster hits "Show Me the Way" and "Baby, I Love Your Way." Songs for the ages? That's debatable, but a great pop song is still a great pop song. You think those girls in the audience screaming out the chorus of "All I Want To Be (Is By Your Side)" cared whether it was the most original approach they'd ever heard?

"Show Me the Way" also featured a relatively obscure rock instrument, the talkbox (the other main practitioner being Joe Walsh). Frampton's inventive use of it as a melody instrument to supplement his own voice provided a funky edge to an otherwise straightforward pop song. It was, in hindsight, a brilliant addition.

The talkbox gets a real workout on the other big song here, the fourteen-minute (and surprisingly coherent at that) musical tour de force "Do You Feel Like We Do." Frampton's made-for-concert refrains segue perfectly into Bob Mayo's entertaining keyboard jam, some sharp soloing from Frampton, and then a minutes-long ride through the outer reaches of talkbox territory, ending in a breakout full-guitar finish. It's a piece of work that manages to be elegant, funky and hard-rocking all at once, and it's quite possibly the best thing he's ever recorded.

There can be no question, however, that the album as a whole represents Frampton's musical high-water mark. It was, in fact, an achievement from which he never seemed to recover. Decades later, Peter Frampton has become the answer to an obscure musical trivia question. But for a year or two in the mid-'70s, this prince was the guy every girl wanted and every guy wanted to be... and this album is all the evidence you'll ever need that he didn't do it on looks alone.

Rating: A-

*

James Taylor
Greatest Hits
Warner Brothers, 1976
[Published on *The Daily Vault* 6/28/2014]
[Adapted from a review originally published in *On the Town* April 16, 1996]

One of the unique joys of popular music as an art form is the way certain songs etch themselves into your life's memories. A decade (or several) down the road, three familiar chords can snap you back to the moment you first stepped into your college dorm room, or bared your soul to a new-found friend, or kissed that intriguing someone who was destined to become a fixture in your life. Songs become temporal bookmarks that way—put your finger on the marker, flip the book open, and boom, you're back where you left off all those years before. One album that performs this minor miracle for me, again and again, is James Taylor's *Greatest Hits*.

The first time I was really exposed to JT, in my first month of college, his brand of gentle, introspective folk-pop did nothing for me. I had headed off to UC Davis in full head-banger AC/DC rebellion mode, certain if the music didn't make your eyeballs bulge on the downbeats, there wasn't any point. It was around the fourth late night I was forced to spend hanging out in the student lounge, thanks to my freshman year dormitory roommate's resounding success with the ladies, that his secret finally dawned on me—it was that damned acoustic folkie sensitive-romantic crap he put on every time he "entertained" in our room. "Don't Let Me Be Lonely Tonight," indeed.

As I learned over time, though, there's a lot more to "Sweet Baby James" than romantic noodlings and pleasant acoustic guitar melodies. The man frequently writes from the depths of his soul, from deep blue and white hot interior landscapes few artists are brave enough to explore with his degree of honesty and sincerity. When he sings "I've seen fire and I've seen rain, but I always thought that I'd see you again," it doesn't matter whether you know he wrote the song after the suicide of a young woman he had gotten to know during his own stay in a psychiatric ward—just the emotion in his voice tells you he is doing a lot more by singing it than simply entertaining. This performance is an exorcism of grief.

JT unflinchingly shows you both sides of the coin of life, always carrying on, rhyming the bad with the good, the sad with the sweet, the absurd with the devastating. The wonder is that as he lopes through middle age, once-shaggy hair now mostly a memory, new albums an increasing rarity, his audience stands intact, waiting impatiently for the annual summer tour. After all, what could be more comforting and uplifting to a person feeling beaten down by the brutally alienating modern world than to know that they aren't alone, that someone has visited the same dark corners of the soul that they have, and come back singing about it?

Taylor's *Greatest Hits* album covers every major single from his extremely fertile early period (1968-1976), including songs that capture in three minutes' time the essence of solitude ("Country Road"), solace ("Something in the Way She Moves") and the redeeming power of love ("Shower the People"). The melancholy "Carolina in My Mind," written during a homesick stretch spent in London, is sprinkled with references to friends who "hit me from behind" and other tangled relationships, culminating in the narrator's flight back inside his own imagination. Both a gifted songwriter and an expert interpreter of others' compositions, Taylor delivered an early soft-rock anthem in his comrade Carole King's "You've Got a Friend."

The sometimes solitary Taylor ("Walking Man") has always had a playful side, too, though, as heard in the rollicking singalong "Mexico," the exuberant Motown cover "How Sweet It Is (To Be Loved by You)," and especially the rascally blues stomper "Steamroller." A musical Renaissance man of sorts, Taylor has always been defined most by his humanity and accessibility as an artist; whether or not you really do, his songs make you feel like you know him.

And that's the key to this album's time-traveling powers, at least for me: it pulls you in, it engages you in a conversation. It takes you back to times and places when you felt or did momentous things—like sitting in your freshman year dorm's student lounge late in the evening, passing the time getting to know the woman who would turn out to be the love of your life.

Rating: A

*

Fleetwood Mac
Rumours
Reprise Records, 1977
[Published on *The Daily Vault* 12/31/2012]
[Adapted from a review originally published in *On the Town* 4/30/1996]

Some bands are simply groups of musicians who enjoy playing together. Others either begin as, or grow to be more like, a family. The problem with the latter situation is, of course, that families have been known to behave somewhat dysfunctionally from time to time. (*"No,"* says the reader, pausing between throwing darts at a photo of her hyper-critical mother-in-law. "Really? Where'd you get *that* idea?")

The trick, one supposes, is in turning dysfunction into worthwhile art. And the hands-down winner in this category (at least in the subcategory of late 1970s popular music) has got to be Fleetwood Mac. Here we have a band that, at ten years old, had already had more personnel walk in and back out than Madonna's doorman. Add to that two disintegrating long-term relationships (between vocalist/keyboardist Christine McVie and her bassist husband John on the one hand, and vocalist/guitarist Lindsey Buckingham and vocalist Stevie Nicks on the other) and just to make sure everyone's involved, let's see what happens if the fifth member's (drummer Mick Fleetwood) marriage falls apart and he has a fling with one of the others on the rebound (Nicks).

Recipe for disaster, right? Fire in the hole; instant musical roadkill. Except that it produced *Rumours,* an enduring classic and one of the biggest-selling albums of all time.

This album, shot through from the bittersweet hit "Dreams" to the just plain bitterly autobiographical "The Chain" with equal doses of heartbreak and recrimination, sets hard truths to brilliant pop melodies and knockout three-part harmonies. Buckingham, Nicks and McVie's voices meld so gorgeously on songs like "Second Hand News," "Don't

Stop," and "You Make Loving Fun" that you are tempted, momentarily, to overlook the fierceness of the clenched-jaw "Never Going Back Again" and the brutally hard-driving kiss-off anthem "Go Your Own Way" (the latter featuring one of the greatest drumming performances in the history of the pop single).

Throw five headstrong, badly wounded people into a situation (the studio) with powder keg written all over it, and they collectively produce the best music of their lives. Maybe there's something to that old chaos theory after all.

Rating: A

*

Bob Seger & the Silver Bullet Band
Stranger in Town
Capitol Records, 1978
[Published on *The Daily Vault* 2/18/1999]

Listening to *Stranger in Town* today, twenty years after adding it to the party-time soundtrack of my sophomore year in high school, the thing I'm struck by is—amazingly, considering the personal context it has for me—what a mature album this is.

The guy a few unkind critics labeled a Midwestern Springsteen lite actually nailed down some of the difficult truths of adult relationships here a full ten years before Springsteen was ready to tackle the subject himself on his 1987 *Tunnel of Love* album. The fact that Seger had five years of gigging around the Midwest under his belt before Springsteen was out of high school may have played a part in this. But the key is really the way Seger seamlessly melded hard-driving rhythm and soul music with his searching, often brutally frank lyrics.

The album kicks off in high gear with what is arguably Seger's greatest song, "Hollywood Nights." That's probably sacrilege right there for any number of Seger fans, but give me a minute.

His 1976 breakthrough hit "Night Moves" may be the obvious pick from Seger's large catalog, but for me, "Hollywood Nights" has all the emotional nuance and resonance of the former coupled with even greater musical drive. The thundering double-time backbeat at its core is absolutely relentless, as is the unflinching lyric. In "Night Moves," Seger narrates from the point of view of a grown man looking back nostalgically on himself as a teenager trying to sort lust from love, and sex from hope. The central idea is a struggle through a whirlpool of overwhelming emotions that are impossible to tame.

In "Hollywood Nights," Seger explores similar ground from the point of view of a young adult experiencing with great immediacy what it's like to fall so hard in love that you lose all control of your emotions. "And those Hollywood nights / In those Hollywood hills / It was looking so right / It was giving him chills," he sings urgently, and it gives them to me, too. The song is a portrait of the familiar devastation that results when feelings of that magnitude aren't reciprocated. Love is portrayed here as an almost terrifying loss of control, something that can simultaneously uplift and consume you... scary, and true.

Thoughtful observations about what love is and isn't, and what it can and can't do for you, reverberate through most of the eight other songs on this album. Two of them — "Still the Same" and "We've Got Tonite" — were substantial hits (#4 and #13, respectively), and have their charms. The latter's whole attitude — jaded and world-weary but still capable of giving in to romantic impulse — feels remarkably true-to-life.

Still, I prefer some of the lesser-known tunes here. "Till It Shines" is one of my favorite Seger songs. There's something in the imagery and the tone that seems to sum up Seger's entire persona of the road-hardened romantic, bringing to bear a lifetime's worth of hard lessons that make him wish he could start all over. Next is a track that's more topical than ever in the '90s — "Feel Like a Number," Seger's driving barroom rocker about feelings of disconnection and alienation in a society that treats people like statistics rather than individuals. "Brave Strangers" is impressive as well. While the lyric isn't much more than a clever rewrite of "Night Moves" (he even tosses in a reference to "hiding in the backwoods"), the song is arranged and sung with such fire and conviction you can't help getting caught up in the story yet again.

"The Famous Final Scene" is the perfect closer to this cycle of songs about how love revs you up and knocks you down (and still leaves you wanting more), a resigned parting ballad about two lovers whose time has passed. They both know what's coming, and play out their final scene just the way they knew it had to go, without recriminations. It's a measured, mature take on a topic that many artists would reduce to a single juicy kiss-off line, repeated twenty times. Seger plays it dead serious and nails it.

Oh, yeah, and then there's that one other song. But y'know, as much fun as "Old Time Rock and Roll" is, I just couldn't quite reconcile a discussion of the thoughtful lyricism of *Stranger in Town* with the inevitable image of 17-year-old Tom Cruise dancing around the living room in his jockeys. (And if you've never seen *Risky Business*... well, I'm betting you will now.)

Rating: A-

*

Van Halen
Van Halen
Warner Brothers Records, 1978
[Published on *The Daily Vault* 6/11/2004]
[Adapted from a review originally published in *On the Town* 11/12/1996]

Kick back for a second and let the music hit you... the pulsating bass, the pounding drums, the playful tinkle on the ivories, the wild-animal cries from the leather-pantsed, sweaty-maned singer, and... and... what the hell is that thing that sounds like a cross between an electric guitar and a howitzer?

Welcome to Circus Van Halen, where never-before-heard feats of electric guitar derring-do are summoned up with deliberate, repeated, stunning ease. Feast on the chiming chord shifts and monstrously fat chorus riffs of "Ain't Talkin' 'Bout Love"; let your eardrums savor the band's driving, thrashing, ecstatic take on the Kinks' classic "You Really Got Me"; step back in awe at the sheer savagery with which the band attacks the opener "Runnin' with the Devil"; cackle with glee at the sassy lyric and effortless virtuosity of "I'm the One," or the lounge-y Vegas start and blistering hard rock finish of "Ice Cream Man."

Trace the impossibly cool flying VH symbol into a homemade poster (for this part it helps a lot to be 15 years old and male). Marvel at the pioneering, fretboard-hammering, string-bending, tone-melding style that would make Eddie Van Halen one of the most-imitated guitar heroes in rock history. Finally, stand back in wonder and absorb the awesomeness that is Eddie's "Eruption"—a concise two-minute solo statement on the guitar, straight out of the gate: here's my best, I dare you to top it. In the decades since, no one has—not even Eddie.

Of course, time has taken a toll on the band. Heavy metal is, after all, typically a young man's sport, even allowing for the mainstream pop-metal leanings Van Halen has opted for ever since the band's second album (a shift in tone previewed here on "Jamie's Cryin'"). And the ghost of old Leatherpants David Lee Roth—one of the biggest buffoons in rock history—haunted the group for decades even as the remaining trio forged on with VH mark II singer Sammy Hagar. More recently, with Hagar and founding bassist Michael Anthony both on the outs with the famously mercurial Van Halen brothers, Eddie and drummer Alex reunited with Roth and installed Eddie's son Wolfgang on bass. Whatever, dudes.

As this once-great band continues its slow fade into history, though, let's stop and appreciate for just a moment this smashingly original, powerhouse debut and the way it forever reshaped the landscape of hard rock—not to mention the repertoire of an entire nation of air-guitar players.

Rating: A

*

Tom Petty & the Heartbreakers
Damn the Torpedoes
MCA Records, 1979
[Published on *The Daily Vault* 9/8/2008]
[Adapted from a review originally published in *On the Town* 6/11/1996]

The whole band vs. singer-songwriter thing kind of goes out the window when you get to these guys. Here is one of the great American rock and roll singer-songwriters of the last half-century, whose killer band's outside session credits read like a *Who's Who* of rock and roll (try: U2, Don Henley, X, Stevie Nicks, Indigo Girls, Jackson Browne, Tracy Chapman, Jeff Healey Band, the Jayhawks, Crosby, Stills & Nash, Brian Wilson and Eurythmics, to name but a few). Either is a force alone; together, they are one of the major rock and roll bands of their era.

Coming out of Florida in the mid-'70s, Petty and the Heartbreakers had a string of terrific singles off their first two albums—"Breakdown," "American Girl," "I Need to Know" and "Listen to Her Heart" —but their third LP, *Damn the Torpedoes*, is the one that made them. Taking Petty and lead guitarist Mike Campbell's heavily Byrds-influenced chiming guitar sound and fattening up the roles of both keyboard player Benmont Tench and the group's harmony vocals, co-producer Jimmy Iovine gave the band a fuller, cleaner sound than they'd ever had before. Add to that the most consistently high-quality set of songs in Petty's very respectable writing career, and you've got a double-platinum knockout.

"Refugee" launches the album strongly with tight playing from Campbell, Tench and drummer Stan Lynch in support of one of Petty's strongest pleading/snarling vocals. It's barely over when "Here Comes My Girl" kicks in, with Petty using an emotionally raw spoken-verse style that preceded rap by a decade to cut right to the heart of what the best relationships are all about:

> *Every now and then I get down to the end of a day and have to stop and ask myself why I've done it*
> *It just seems so useless to have to work so hard and nothin' ever really seems to come from it*
> *And then she looks me in the eye, and says 'We're gonna last forever' and man, you know, I can't begin to doubt it*
> *No, because it just feels so good and so free and so right, I know we ain't never gonna change our minds about it!*

Then, delivering a superb one-two-three punch of album sequencing, the band launches directly into "Even the Losers," a blistering piece of self-affirmation that has grown into an anthem for the romantically crashed-and-burned ("You could kiss like fire and you made me feel / Like every word you said was meant to be / No, it couldn't have been that easy to forget about me"), not to mention one of the few album tracks important enough to make it onto Petty's 1993 *Greatest Hits* package.

Here Petty is in his more usual element, writing about the baffling, sometimes self-destructive ways humans behave when they're attracted to one another. The rest of the album examines these questions entertainingly with the huge radio hit "Don't Do Me Like That," the funny/edgy rockers "What Are You Doin' in My Life?" and "Century City," the brooding "You Tell Me" and the wistful "Louisiana Rain."

Damn the Torpedoes and full speed ahead 'til it hurts; that's Petty's message, and he makes it a pleasure to hear on this milestone album, a high-water mark for both the band and the decade.

Rating: A

*

AC/DC
Highway to Hell
Atlantic Records, 1979
[Published on *The Daily Vault* 12/14/2005]

I love this album.

This qualifies as semi-news since I am a middle-aged father of three who, if a *Highway to Hell*-era Bon Scott were to ring the bell to pick up my 16-year-old daughter, would answer the door with bared teeth and a Louisville Slugger gripped tight in my hands.

But, see, I love this album.

Part of the reason is, it's lived two lives with me. One happened when the album first came out in 1979. I was, well, 16 at the time, bowing down before guitar-brandishing greats like Van Halen and Montrose, and the Young brothers struck me as among the high priests of the great rock riff. (Clearly, Jack *"School of Rock"* Black agrees…) The second time around, repurchasing a bunch of old favorites on CD in my late 30s, was no less joyful an experience.

Can you tell I love this album?

One way albums make the leap from good to great is by simply never letting up. In a career that's seen plenty of greatness, but also plenty of filler, AC/DC has never issued a more consistent album than this relentless 10-song slab of ringing, stinging rock and roll (and yes, I'm including the also-great *Back in Black* in that statement). There isn't a clunker in the bunch; not even close. And it contains not one, not two, but three of their greatest cuts ever, the timeless, iconic title track, the hilarious, propulsive "Shot Down in Flames," and the thundering, electric "If You Want Blood (You've Got It)."

The music and lyrics, of course, have all the subtlety of a three-megaton warhead. That's the point. Yes, the lyrics are full of giddy double entendres, but it's cleaner than the average network sitcom, and twice as funny. Anyone who thinks vocalist Bon Scott was a loud-mouthed simpleton hasn't been listening; the guy put a lot more craft into his lyrics than you might expect from a brawling, alcoholic ex-chauffeur. He's arguably the wittiest cad in the long and storied history of rock and roll hooligans.

Kudos also go to producer Robert John "Mutt" Lange, who gave the band's already big sound even greater punch and clarity. Angus and Malcom Young's guitars have never sounded more muscular and vibrant, and the Cliff Williams-Phil Rudd rhythm section plays like their hair is on fire. Surprisingly, though, it's the subtler touches I've come to appreciate the most over the years—the little "Woo!" Bon lets out as "Shot Down in Flames" gets going; the huge background vocals the boys put up on "Walk All Over You"; the way Rudd crashes the cymbal every single time Scott sings "blood" in "If You Want Blood (You've Got It)."

Finally, a word about Angus and Malcolm's playing on this album. Gargantuan. That's it. *Highway to Hell* is 50 minutes of one of the great riff machines in rock history at the very top of their game. Any wannabe guitar player who doesn't own this album doesn't really wanna be.

It's true, you see—I love this album. (Maybe I should have just stopped there.)

Rating: A

*

The Pretenders
The Pretenders
Sire, 1980
[Published on *The Daily Vault* 9/7/2007]

Male singers swagger.

Female singers might preen or wail or enchant or provoke, but throughout the brief history of rock and roll up to 1980 that essentially Stones-ian swagger, that sneering, occasionally brutal self-confidence had always been the province of men—until Chrissie Hynde claimed it for her own.

The Pretenders' self-titled debut is a monumental rock and roll album, one that both changed the way the rock world viewed women and changed the way the few female rockers active at the time viewed themselves. The message of this album—full of aggressive, balls-out rockers and equally gentle, heartfelt ballads—was that a woman could in fact be both tough and tender, could spit and swagger and bully and still be a dewy-eyed romantic underneath.

The album kicks off memorably with the visceral post-punk snarl of "Precious," a showcase for both guitarist James Honeyman-Scott's furiously inventive riffing and Hynde's kiss-me-now-before-I-kick-your-ass stage persona. By the time Hynde's rant reaches its natural climax— "But not me baby, I'm too precious / Fuck off!"—the average 1980 listener had been bludgeoned into giddy submission.

The two in this disc's one-two opening punch is "The Phone Call," another furiously churning rocker in which Honeyman-Scott's lead guitar is again both muscular and creative while Hynde simply assaults the microphone with confidence and attitude. On these first two the vocals seem to be purposely fast and slurry; it's hard to make out some of Hynde's words, but the boiling-over emotions behind them are indelible.

"Up the Neck" and "Tattooed Love Boys" hint at the smoother Pretenders sound Hynde and drummer Martin Chambers would steer the band into on later albums, after Honeyman-Scott and bassist Pete Farndon's untimely deaths. They're both loose yet highly melodic pop-rock tunes with the occasional rough edges polished by sultry vocals and sublime hooks.

On an album of this quality, even dated throwaways like the instrumental "Space Invader" have a role to play, showing the group's range and sense of humor, while also setting up the intro to the frenzied, deliriously catchy "The Wait," another album highlight.

The second half of the disc (side two for us old-timers) is generally softer than what came before, but no less remarkable. The band's luminous, role-reversing, spot-on cover of the Kinks' "Stop Your Sobbing" led composer Ray Davies right into Hynde's arms, and why wouldn't it? "Brass in Pocket" is similarly brilliant ear candy. And the closing "Mystery Achievement" gets the crowd back on its feet with a loose, rather Who-like arrangement spotlighting the rhythm section under some of Hynde's most ebullient vocals.

The Pretenders is without a doubt one of the great debut albums in rock history. The fact that it is also one of the most influential albums of all time by a female-fronted group is simply one more reason it deserves your attention. Chrissie Hynde swaggers; Chrissie Hynde rocks.

Rating: A

*

Peter Gabriel
So
Geffen Records, 1986
[Published on *The Daily Vault* 4/12/2014]
[Adapted from a review originally published in *On the Town* 2/4/1997]

This, by far the most successful album of former Genesis frontman Peter Gabriel's solo career, offers two unique elements at its core that press every song firmly into memory—space and intensity. Gabriel, an art-house scion with an eye for the avant-garde (see the multiple award-winning video for this album's big hit "Sledgehammer") and an ear for international rhythms, combined these passions most successfully on this album of remarkably well-produced and personal songs.

The element of space is evident on every song—the airiness of the production on both quieter tunes like "Mercy Street" and workouts like the gleefully sarcastic "Big Time" is at times almost overwhelming (or am I listening too loud again?). The brooding atmospherics of songs like the pulsing, cascading "Red Rain" would sound merely odd without the hugeness the production grants them. With it, they are completely absorbing.

Space and intensity may be combined the most effectively on the three songs filling the core of the album: "Don't Give Up," "That Voice Again" and "In Your Eyes," offering intense looks at (respectively) despair, internal conflict and overwhelming attraction. "Don't Give Up," with guest vocals by Kate Bush, is a particularly tight little two-character play about spiraling depression and inspirational reinforcement. "In Your Eyes," at the opposite end of the emotional spectrum, is one of the truly great songs about falling not merely head over heels but mind over body, soul over the horizon in love with someone: "In your eyes, the light the heat / In your eyes, I am complete... In your eyes, the resolution of all the fruitless searches."

The CD version adds a bonus track to the original album's contents, an arty chanted duet with Laurie Anderson which, while interesting, lacks precisely the elements which made the original so strong—space and intensity. It makes for an odd finish to a fantastic journey, but then that jibes with Gabriel's general aesthetic, and in no way subtracts from this album's status as the high point of the former Genesis frontman's solo career.

Rating: A

*

U2
The Joshua Tree
Island Records, 1987
[Published on *The Daily Vault* 11/15/2004]
[Adapted from a review originally published in *On the Town* 4/30/1996]

One of the things that separates much of the best rock music from its peers in this or any other genre is social consciousness. Rock and roll started out as much more than just a rougher, faster dancing beat—it was music that dared to stir strong emotions, that wasn't afraid to confront the listener musically and, over time, lyrically as well. This is why U2 is a great rock and roll band, and *The Joshua Tree* is a great rock and roll album.

The album is actually summed up effectively in its first two minutes. The opening song, "Where the Streets Have No Name," begins as a low, resonant hum, building into an ominous wall of sound before shifting to a brief, contemplative gospel organ melody that's swiftly overtaken by the slow, steady eruption of one of guitarist the Edge's best pulsating, shimmering riffs. Then the riff explodes forward, momentum building as Adam Clayton's bass and Larry Mullen Jr.'s drums kick the lower end into gear and the entire song blasts off like a screaming sonic rocket, climaxing as Bono cries out in a voice equal parts desperation and determination: "I want to run / I want to hide / I want to tear down the walls that hold me inside / I want to reach out and touch the flame / Where the streets have no name."

This is quintessential U2—anthemic guitar melodies powering a blistering cry for release, for a hope to sustain you through hard times. The band's spiritual roots in Christianity are constantly apparent; the cultural touchstones of their songs are crosses and angels, thorns and heaven, Jacob and Cain. In songs like "I Still Haven't Found What I'm Looking For," though, they essay their belief that the right spiritual answers are never simple ones, and that what works for one person doesn't necessarily work for another.

The poetry of some of Bono's best lyrics adds another majestic element to this, the band's most consistent album. "Bullet the Blue Sky" dazzles not just with the Edge's buzz-saw lead and the coiled intensity of the vocal, but with vivid images like "Suit and tie come up to me / His face red / Like a rose on a thorn bush / Like all the colours of a royal flush." The underappreciated acoustic gem "Running to Stand Still" follows with an even more surrealistic lyric, a preview of sorts to the band's '90s material, which took the music off into a similarly experimental, somewhat psychedelic direction.

Looking back at this album from the vantage point of the 21st century, it's easy to appreciate the size of the challenge U2 faces every time it enters a recording studio, trying to both recapture the old magic and move the music forward. The raw, unself-consciously spiritual rock and roll they pioneered here has never been matched since by them or anyone else; *The Joshua Tree* still stands as a milestone for one of rock's premier bands and, indeed, rock and roll itself.

Rating: A

*

Eric Clapton
Unplugged
Reprise, 1992
[Published on *The Daily Vault* 11/28/2008]

The unplugged concept was just gathering steam when Eric Clapton sat down for his turn to be featured on MTV's *Unplugged* series. The custom of artists who normally work in electric format scaling back to acoustic instruments in front of a live audience is generally traced back to a pair of primary sources—Elvis Presley's famous 1968 comeback concert, and Pete Townshend's June 1979 acoustic performances of "Pinball Wizard" and "Won't Get Fooled Again" as part of the Amnesty International fundraiser *The Secret Policeman's Ball*.

As the '80s wore on, acoustic music came back into vogue with artists like R.E.M. and Indigo Girls exploring the folk roots of their own music, and by 1987 MTV was catching on, televising an acoustic performance by Jethro Tull. By 1989-90 MTV formalized the concept into a series of specials featuring a variety of different electric artists playing *Unplugged* before a small studio audience in an intimate venue.

In the meantime, guitar hero Eric Clapton was going through a particularly difficult stretch in his life, as he sought to recover emotionally from the accidental death of his four-year-old son Conor, as well as the loss of his friend Stevie Ray Vaughan. At the time of his January 1992 appearance on *MTV Unplugged*, the only new music he had issued since 1989's *Journeyman* album had been a single deeply poignant tribute to

Conor, "Tears in Heaven," released on the 1991 soundtrack to the movie *Rush*.

The emotional context of these performances is key to their power. For while *Unplugged* is far afield from just about every other album Clapton has ever recorded, for some of us, it's among the high-water marks of his long and storied career.

One reason is that, as good an electric guitar player as Clapton is (don't forget the old London graffiti "Clapton is God"), he may be even better on the acoustic. Some of his riffing here, on both instrumentals like "Signe" and old blues standards like "Hey Hey" and "Walkin' Blues," is absolutely stunning. It's hard to imagine any other player matching the combination of precision, fluidity, rhythmic intuition and soulfulness that Clapton manifests on his instrument here. He also benefits from the backing of a spectacularly tight all-star band including Andy Fairweather Low (Dave Edmunds, The Who, Roger Waters) on guitar, Chuck Leavell (Rolling Stones, Allman Brothers Band, Aretha Franklin) on keys, Nathan East (George Benson, Bob Dylan, Phil Collins) on bass and Steve Ferrone (Tom Petty, Steve Winwood, Average White Band) behind the drum kit.

A second reason arises from the reality that Clapton, for all his wonderful songs and performances, has never been a great singer, only a pretty good one. On this album, though, he never has to push his voice beyond its natural capabilities, and as a result he sounds relaxed and in the groove at all times and delivers arguably the best vocal performance of his career. He pays more attention to vocal arrangements here, too, flavoring tracks like "Nobody Knows You When You're Down & Out" with effective background vocal support from Katie Kissoon and Tessa Niles.

A third is the way he transforms two of his most famous songs in ways large and small. When he launches into "Tears in Heaven" with no introduction, the crowd immediately hushes. While he doesn't vary the arrangement much—it was a gentle, quiet ballad already—he delivers the vocal of a lifetime, a weary man gathering strength enough to wring every last bit of emotion out of a song that is already supercharged with it. When he sings "Time can bring you down, time can bend your knees / Time can break your heart, have you beggin' please / Beggin' *pleeee-ease*," it's one of the most devastating moments in the history of recorded music. When he finishes, rushing ahead into the opening chords of the next song as if willing himself forward, lest he bog down in the emotion of the moment, the audience goes from stunned, church-like silence to firm, damp-eyed applause that forces him to hold up until they finish.

The greater musical transformation is achieved with his signature tune, the unrequited love epic "Layla," which is made over completely into a gentle, deliberate soliloquy against a skittering, jazzy backdrop. Considering the song itself is an imagined conversation occurring entirely inside Clapton's head, putting it in this context makes perfect sense and breathes magnificent new life into a song that was already a classic.

There will always be those purists who cry foul when you mess with a song as iconic as "Layla," or an approach as cherished as Clapton's earthy electric blues-rock. But *Unplugged*, in addition to marking Clapton's return to the music-making arena, remains one of his most accessible and interesting albums. As for the non-purists, they bought over ten million copies of this disc, so it's safe to say Mr. Clapton did something right.

Rating: A

*

Counting Crows
August and Everything After
DGC Records, 1993
[Published on *The Daily Vault* 9/18/1998]

I've fantasized once or twice that if I ever wrote a song it might sound something like "Mr. Jones." That is, a stripped-down, rootsy rock sound (Van Morrison yada yada yada) backing lyrics that are both personal and universal, filled with irony, insight, clever pop culture references and killer alliteration.

It's probably a good thing I stuck to reviewing.

Adam Duritz, lead singer and chief songwriter for the Crows, is a poet, and a damned fine one. To appreciate the Crows (and not everyone does) you have to accept that statement—that, and everything that goes with it. Yes, the band's sound is underdeveloped and somewhat derivative on *August and Everything After*—crawling along in its infancy here, as evidenced by their subsequent, musically much fuller sophomore album, *Recovering the Satellites*. And yes, a cheery album this isn't; more like eleven shades of misery, from sardonic detachment all the way down the spiral to writhing emotional agony.

What you have to do is get past all that, and get to the meat of the album—all those lovely, dazzling, precocious, attention-craving (and deserving) WORDS Duritz packs into these songs.

71

From the first lines of the haunting opener, "Round Here," Duritz proves he isn't just another chicken-scratch lyricist: "Step out the front door like a ghost / into the fog where no one notices / the contrast of white on white." The song itself is a travelogue of the madness that's an inherent element of love, chronicling a relationship that's going around the bend at the same time as the narrator's lover apparently is.

In the midst of "Mr. Jones," Duritz's witty deconstruction of his own rock-star fantasies, and the closest thing to an upbeat tune here, he calls out to his audience "Believe in me / Help me believe in anything / I want to be someone who believes" — capturing, in the space of three desperately sung little lines, the very heart of the relationship between performer and audience. Then later, he sings "When everybody loves me, I will never be lonely," his voice cracking with self-loathing at the bullshit promise of stardom that he realizes some part of him has actually bought into.

The other occasional criticism of the Crows has focused on Duritz's unique approach to singing. And truly, his swerving, note-skipping vocal contortions can at times be distracting to the point of annoyance. But, as perhaps only Dylan and Springsteen have managed before him, Duritz overcomes the limits of his vocal instrument by injecting his delivery with an emotional fire and intensity that overpowers everything else.

Still, there are a few things on *August* I really don't care for that much. Even clever, literate navel-gazing gets old deep in the slower sections of this album. But then, just as they're winding things up and you're starting to feel maybe just a little bit let down, you get to THE song. The sure-thing personal Top Ten of All Time tune "A Murder of One."

The song, a devastating plea to a friend trapped in an abusive relationship, is as finely crafted and emotionally explosive as any of the truly great rock anthems. Over a steady, propulsive beat: "Are you happy where you're sleeping? / Does he keep you safe and warm? / Does he tell when you're sorry? / Does he tell you when you're wrong?" Chills. The music builds. "All your life is such a shame, shame shame / All your love is just a dream, dream, dream....You don't want to waste your life / You don't want to waste your life.... Change, change change..." More chills. Duritz speaks his peace, to no avail. The music peaks, fades, settles, and then slowly builds up steam once again until it positively erupts as he wails "CHANGE CHANGE CHANGE / CHANGE CHANGE CHANGE / etc." It's a goosebump moment.

Mark McGwire would be the first to tell you that you can't hit a home run every time you come to bat—but that's part of the reason it's so sweet watching the ball sail out of the park. As far as I'm concerned, Duritz can write as many sad-and-lonely busted-relationship songs as he wants, as long as every so often he throws in a piece of sheer rock and roll poetry like "A Murder of One."

Rating: A-

*

Dave Matthews Band
Under The Table and Dreaming
RCA Records, 1994
[Published on *The Daily Vault* 6/16/2003]

In music, as in life, making a good first impression can count for a lot. Here are 10 reasons to love this, the 1994 major-label debut of a little group you may have heard of—the Dave Matthews Band.

1. The biting lyrics and irresistible-yet-exotic hooks of early singles "Ants Marching" and "What Would You Say."

2. The manic-depressive juxtaposition of "Best of What's Around" (a classic dose of "cup is half full" optimism) with "Rhyme & Reason" (dark, dangerous, obsessive).

3. The ecstatic musical friction between singer/guitarist Matthews' crooning voice and horn player Leroi Moore's swooning sax on the gorgeous, sublimely seductive "Lover Lay Down."

4. The diverse arrangements, spotlighting a seemingly endless variety of different instrumental "looks" song to song among the virtuoso ensemble of Matthews, Moore, Boyd Tinsley (violin), Stefan Lessard (bass) and Carter Beauford (drums).

5. The amazing dynamics—almost prog-rock in the way they shift gears and mix styles—of songs like "Jimi Thing," which moves rapidly from soaring melodies to driving funk to a shimmering sax solo.

6. The interpolating melody lines and superb sax fills of "Warehouse."

7. The sheer musical density of this album, featuring layer upon layer of melody and counter-melody.

8. The exquisite tension in the music, lyric and delivery of "Pay for What You Get."

9. Tension and release, tension and release... when this band is on, it's as sensual as any in rock.

10. Last but not least, *Under the Table and Dreaming* is simply the best job this band has ever done of merging its various musical personalities—

earthy jam band, eclectic virtuosos, hooky popmeisters, exorcists of the dark corners of Matthews' soul. In the hands of producer Steve Lillywhite, the music is intricate but focused. Unlike *Before These Crowded Streets*, there's no aimless wandering here; it's about the songs, not the players. But unlike *Everyday*, this is a band album, with the spotlight on the entire group's ability to play together with and off of one another in order to generate amazing soundscapes. This debut launched the DMB off toward the stratosphere, and it's no wonder; it's still the best thing they've ever done.

Rating: A

~Segue~

Interview: Jon Anderson

[Published on *The Daily Vault* 5/13/13]

Jon Anderson will always and inevitably be best known as the co-founder, lead voice and lyricist for iconic progressive rock band Yes. The group's flights of musical fancy, tenacity, and rough-and-tumble internal politics have all become legend over the past very eventful 45 years. Those at-time bruising politics resulted in Anderson's replacement in 2008 by a tribute band singer, since replaced himself by current Yes vocalist and Anderson soundalike Jon Davison. Anderson himself seems to have taken this tumult in stride; there were a few understandably bitter words in the immediate aftermath of his ouster, which took place while he was too ill to perform, but since then he has expressed nothing but openness to whatever the future may hold, while pursuing a terrifically productive solo career. First came Survival and Other Stories, *a solo album cataloguing his recovery to good health and musical rebirth, then the 2010 duo album* The Living Tree *with fellow Yes expatriate Rick Wakeman, extensive touring both with Wakeman and on his own, and more recently the release of "Open," an Internet-only 20-minute single carrying echoes of the classic Yes long-form symphonic prog approach.*

One thing it's apparent the 68-year-old Anderson will never do is stop creating new music; it's simply in the man's blood. Taking a break from crafting the follow-up to "Open," Anderson describes by phone the sunny patio overlooking the ocean he is occupying not far from his San Luis Obispo home, announcing that "I've been in the studio for the last six hours, but I had to get out of there!" Much like his free-form lyrics, his sentences don't always flow in predictable ways. What shines through is that his intention, his spirit, is as strong as ever, his vivid imagination rich with ideas and insights and visions that emerge in one intense burst after another. A half hour spent on the line with Jon Anderson is a travelogue of musical adventures led by a man who was born to create, and has had a hand in producing some of the most memorable musical moments of the rock and roll era. From watching the Beatles play in Liverpool, to conceptualizing an app containing his entire musical catalog, in his lifetime, Jon Anderson has truly seen—or imagined—it all.

The Daily Vault: **Looking back on your career, you've been making music for 50 years now. How does that feel?**

Jon Anderson: It's amazing! You know, I was talking to a young friend today called Alvin, who comes up every month to work on his guitar playing—he plays and writes some beautiful guitar concertos. He's only 18, and I reminded him that I started when I was 18 years old with my brother's band The Warriors. It was like, the beginning of the beginning of opening the doors of modern times. After the Beatles came out with a single called "Love Me Do," my brother and I went to see them play up near Liverpool, and there they were, four guys on stage playing amazingly well. I think they'd only got two microphones and that was the sound system, but it was amazing. And everybody sang, and everybody screamed, and everybody enjoyed the show, and from that moment, I just wanted to be a Beatle, I think. Like a million other people! (Laughter)

A member of our writing staff suggested a question that I'd like to ask about your lyrics. He said that your lyrics tend to suggest rather than describe scenes, and emotions, and drama, and create moods and textures with sound, rather than using more standard narrative approaches. And he was wondering, what were the seeds of somewhat abstract but very emotional songs like "Yours Is No Disgrace" or "Awaken"?

I think that, more than anything, I realized when I started writing songs that I would write lyrics that were sort of free-form. I knew what I was trying to say, but I didn't really want to say it, I wanted to free-form it. I'd sing a song the first time around and then listen to the cassette and try to figure out what I was trying to say. I'd write things down and look at them later and say, "Well, these are metaphors for something"—how I was feeling about Vietnam, or how I was feeling about music and peace and love, feeling still like a hippie from the '60s.

"Yours Is No Disgrace" [from 1971's *The Yes Album*] really had a lot to do with Vietnam, and the world changing, and how things like wars are really out of our control. A lot of the time people feel incredibly guilty for the things they've gone through and really, we should not feel disgraced, because it's part of the life experience. "On a sailing ship to nowhere, leaving any place" is the earth—we're on a sailing ship that flies around the sun, and it's not going anywhere, it's going round and round.

"Awaken" [from 1977's *Going For the One*] is from another important time. By the end of the '70s I'd come to terms with feeling that I was learning about spirituality more and more, and I felt that I had to wake up, and that I wanted to sing about waking up. So I wanted to call a song "Awaken," because I was going through an awakening feeling, that feeling of connection, which wasn't really anything I could put my finger on. It wasn't really anything to do with any one religion; it seemed to have a lot to do with all religions, sort of all interconnected somehow.

I was reading some of your recent interviews this week, and one quote in particular jumped out at me [from an interview by *Vintage Rock*]. You told a wonderful story about the School of Rock kids who wanted to play "Awaken" with you, and the story finished with this comment: *And someone said to me: "Why did you do* Tales From Topographic Oceans?" *I said, "Well, if we hadn't done that, we wouldn't have done 'Awaken'."* **And I have to confess that personally, I've never been a huge fan of *Topographic Oceans*, but if that's what it took to produce "Awaken," it was worth every minute.**

It's interesting, because people ask me why we did *Topographic*, period. And it's because we were left to our own devices, and music was a very open book to the band, and I was wanting to experience an adventure in music rather than writing music for the radio. We'd had some experience writing songs and hoping they would get played on the radio, but radio was—"Oh, we're not going to play that, it's eight minutes long, we don't play 'And You and I,' and 'Close to the Edge,' we're not going to play *that*."

And it was like, "Well, screw you, then." Because music is not just making money, music is all about the experience and the adventure. And when we did *Topographic*, I really jumped into that incredibly big well of the musical experience, and I can only say that 25 years later, we performed the first movement ["The Revealing Science of God: Dance of The Dawn"] and the last movement ["Ritual: Nous Sommes du Soleil"] of *Topographic* with a full orchestra, and it went down incredibly well, audiences around the world loved it. This was about 2001 or 2002, and it just reinforced that music is really a lot more about creation rather than how much money you make out of it. It's funny you mention you weren't particularly keen on it, but I understand. But if you listen to "Revealing," it's 20 minutes long and it's my wife's favorite piece of music—and she wasn't a Yes fan!

It was painful to admit that to you, because I love so much of the work that you and the band have done. *Topographic* **was tougher for some of us, more of a challenge for the audience.**

Oh, yeah! Sure. And it was a challenge for us to create, and I would say in interviews that, whatever we learned, the audience will learn along with us, and it might be good, it might not be great, but at least it's ours.

I'd like to ask a little about "Open." Over the course of your career you've seen the music industry go through wave after wave of change. And here you are presenting this big, 20-minute suite of music as an Internet-only release, and I'm wondering how you see the future of the music industry unfolding, both in terms of your own career, and in terms of all the artists who are just starting out today who are trying to figure out how to break through and have an impact.

Well, like everything, I think necessity is the mother of invention. When I came to realize that record companies were not interested in my work anymore, I tried to use the Internet as a vehicle, and then I realized there are thousands of people doing it, it's not just me. My website doesn't have that much music on it, just about 12 tracks, but then I started thinking about creating an app that I could use to put all this music up I've been creating in the last ten years. And then I want to evolve that app, and create a situation where people can get new music every month, and then every six months they'll get albums that they've never heard from me before, with Vangelis or by myself. The idea is that within the next five years, the app itself will have probably all the work I've ever done, and be up to 12 or 14 hours long.

That's an amazing concept.

And the idea would be to "visualize" everything, so that not only are you listening to music, you're actually seeing a visualization of it at the same time. In the '60s you had those lights at gigs in San Francisco with bands like The Doors, they were just projections at first and then it evolved over the years from projection to these large scale giant TV monitors you have all over the stage now, and you're getting incredible visuals using computer animation. I think that's part of the experience of the 21st century, music as a visual experience as well.

"Open" seems to echo the scope and structure of some of the longer Yes works that we were just talking about. Could you talk about how it came together, and what the process of creating it was like? I know you worked with other musicians over the Internet.

Right. I'd recorded an album called *Survival* and I had about 30 or 40 songs that I'd written with different people around the world. So I picked out a dozen for an album, and then realized that one album really wasn't enough to express how I felt. I released it and it did pretty well, and a lot of people liked it.

And then I thought, "I think I should try a long-form piece," because it's part of my DNA to do long-form pieces. I was the one who pushed the band into doing long-form pieces. It's an interesting story, because when *Close to the Edge* was released in '72, there was a lot of FM radio in America, and they would play the whole album. Within six months of it being released, FM radio was no more, because it wasn't making much money, it was really a lot of collegiate radio. It wasn't good business for regular stations, so they stopped playing long-form music.

And in a way, that made me want to do even more long-form pieces, I just wanted to rebel against the idea, that they wanted to restrict us, just because our music isn't making them enough money, because they wanted to sell advertising space. During the period it was a really difficult experience. But over the years I've contended that music can be a journey, and that's why I decided to do "Open," because I really wanted to say to myself, "I can create another journey." And that's what I did.

"Open" is essentially an orchestral piece. I was curious what led you in that direction, rather than using more traditional rock instruments as you did in the long-form pieces with Yes. Was that in any way a carryover from the experience of making *Magnification* [the 2002 album featuring Yes with an orchestra]?

Probably. *Magnification* was a good experience, I enjoyed it, and I enjoyed touring that music. I just knew that I had a friend who lived 20 minutes away named Stefan Podell, who's a beautiful orchestrator, and we'd been talking about doing some work together for about three years. I just did a sketch of the whole piece on guitar, and then gave it to him, and he came back about two weeks later with a beautiful sketch of the orchestration.

79

And the more he did, the more I wanted, so it became more about the orchestra, and I just loved the idea. I'm actually working on a second one now. This next one is called "Ever" and I might have said there would be no orchestra this time, but I just put an orchestra on it this morning! It's kind of betwixt one and the other right now.

Do you think you'll eventually release these two long pieces on a CD, or do you see yourself moving more in the direction of Internet-only releases?

I think I'm just going to work toward Internet releases and using the app right now. But there's a record company that's releasing all the classic Yes stuff, Audio Fidelity, and they're a very, very nice company and if they wanted to release some of my work I'd be very happy to work with them. I've even thought about vinyl as well, for fun.

On a different subject, we lost [founding Yes guitarist] Peter Banks recently. I read somewhere that you had been in touch with him not too long ago. And I just wondered if there were any particular memories of Peter that you'd like to share.

Peter was a really nice guy, and he was in the band with Chris when I first joined that band, called Mabel Greer's Toy Shop. And Peter came up with the name Yes. I kept saying "We've got to have a short name, Mabel Greer's Toy Shop is so long." And so one day I said "Why don't we call ourselves Life?" And Chris said, "Well, let's call ourselves World." And Peter said "Why don't we call ourselves Yes?" And we looked at him and said "The Yes?" And he said, "No, just Yes." And so that was it, and it was like, "cool."

And for a couple of years Peter was with the band, and everything was going really well, and then we got to a time when I wanted to rehearse 24 hours a day and not everybody was into that. I felt, we're lucky to do what we do, and we should rehearse every hour, minute, second God has given us. And that didn't go over too well with Peter, and it came to a point after that where we had to start thinking about bringing someone in, and we found Steve Howe. It was hard to let go of Peter. He didn't really like working out the structures much, while I was more into structure every day, though I don't really know why.

Over the years I kept bumping into Peter and we'd always say "Hi, how're you doing," and then a couple of years ago we got in touch because a friend of mine got in touch with him and he wasn't very well. So I sent him an e-mail and we talked two or three times last year, and talked about doing some songwriting, and he said "When I get better, I will." His health wasn't good. And then I spoke to him early this year, I think it was in February. And things happen, you know, life moves along and people go off to the next world. I'm sure he's happy.

When you did *The Living Tree* album with Rick Wakeman a couple of years ago, the setlist on your tours included a number of Yes songs. Was it a special challenge to take those songs out of the band context and reinterpret them in a duo setting? Did that freshen up the songs for you as a performer?

I think it made it an interesting way of presenting a song, just with a piano and guitar. It was great with Rick, because he's such a talented piano player, and the songs always seemed to sound great, and the audience loved hearing them. Of course, when you're not in the band, you have to decide, do I perform songs I wrote for the group, or not? But I love singing them, and I wrote them for the group, and the audiences want to hear them, so there's no harm in doing that.

On the subject of Rick, there's a question I've wanted to ask for years: is Rick Wakeman in fact the funniest man ever to be in Yes?

He's funny, he's crazy, he's really off the wall! He's Monty Python and Benny Hill put together. He's a really good guy.

There have been rumors for a couple of years now about a joint project that you and Rick and Trevor Rabin were working on. Can you give us an update on that?

Well, I made the mistake of mentioning it once, and obviously a lot of people want to know what's happening, and it was just one period of time about a year and half ago or so when I was seeing Trevor quite a lot and we'd been writing a couple of songs and we talked about maybe working with Rick. It's funny because you spend time talking ideas and then six months later you've stopped talking about them, and then Rick's busy and

Trevor's doing another movie and I'm on tour. It was very hard to bring it together, and at the moment we're sort of in limbo.

Shifting gears again, I'm curious what your thoughts are about the relationship between a popular artist like yourself and the fans. People like Neil Peart of Rush have written songs about the strangeness of that relationship; his line [in "Limelight"] was that he couldn't "pretend a stranger is a long-lost friend." Have you had any particularly interesting experiences in bridging that gap between performer and fan?

The thing about fans is, we're all the same people, we're all connected on so many different levels. We're all connected through music, and when I meet somebody in the street, or in a store, I'm always very happy to meet them and always happy to make them feel good and relaxed, because I know what it's like.

I was over in Australia just now and there was Paul Simon, and it was very hard to even say hello. It's Paul Simon, you know? And I said hello, and he shook my hand, and I said how are you doing, and he said fine. It was lovely, but it was very brief. I've been in that situation where I've met somebody that I really admire and it's daunting! So, whenever I meet any fan, whatever age they are, I'm always happy to make them feel at ease and I say to them, "I'm a fan too." I love what we've done in Yes, I'm so proud of what we've done, and why not?

That's a wonderful story about Paul Simon, knowing that you guys covered "America," and what that must have meant to you to meet him.

Yeah, it was a trip! If he'd stopped and we'd started talking, I wouldn't have been able to say very much, because, you know, it's PAUL SIMON!

You've been asked many times over the past few years about the possibility of working with Chris [Squire] and Steve [Howe] and Alan [White] again in Yes, and you've said again and again that you are open to it and would welcome it. And I don't want to ask that question again, because you've answered it. But I wondered if maybe you could tell us this: if it was entirely up to you—and of course we know it isn't, but I'm just speaking hypothetically—if it was entirely up to you, what would your ideal scenario be for working with them again?

82

To work with Rick and the band—well, I said to Chris the other month, if Geoff [Downes] and Jon [Davison] are in the band too, I don't mind, you know, we can all work together. I'm very open. I think the music is more important, and the fans are more important than all that "I want the band to be my way" business. I was never into that. And I'm always very open for things to work out okay.

Rick is a very important part of the group. He was part of the special development musically of the band and I think that it's important that he should be involved as well.

And I spoke to Alan a couple of weeks ago. So we're in touch, and when the time comes, when the stars align, we'll probably be able to get together and perform together. I don't see myself going on crazy tours for months on end, I don't see the point in that—we're all a lot older, and I hope a lot wiser. We should do shows here and there and we should make sure the shows are very important and very, very well produced, something we can look back on and say, well, we really did it.

There was one other statement I wanted to try out on you and maybe you could just react to this. With all due respect to every one of the musicians who has been a part of Yes over the years, my personal feeling is that the band has almost always felt like it's greater than the sum of its parts, and that whoever has been in the band at any given point has done some of the best work of their career as part of Yes. I'm wondering if it feels to you like there's something about being in Yes that challenges people to raise their game to the highest level.

My whole feeling about the band is that we are very talented people, we are very lucky to do what we do, and we should work really hard to put on a great show, because the audiences deserve it. And the music should never be restricted to trying to have a hit record, because that's for other people to do. Yes music has its own energy, its own style, it's a unique, one-off thing. There's not many bands that can do Yes' kind of music; I don't actually know anybody that does the kind of music that Yes has done over the years. It's been very adventurous and very progressive music, and I think that's fun to look back on, especially now, and say that we did certain things that were really daring, that we took the road less traveled.

4

Crushes 1969-2001

AS I WAS SAYING: THERE ARE the albums that everyone loves, and then there are the albums that you love.

The former are widely familiar and have been even more widely reviewed. You may feel inspired to add a few words of your own for completeness' sake, but there really aren't any trails left to be blazed in reviewing such an album; you're treading well-worn paths traveled by multitudes of writers and listeners before you. You might feel an intense bond with the music, but there is nothing especially unique about your passion for it, no screaming headlines to report in the relationship you have established with it.

So, while I've often enjoyed the challenge of finding something new to say about a classic album, it's not generally what I'd call fun. It's a lot more fun, and challenging, to try to explore and explain the deep connections I feel with music that's less obvious, less *common*.

Which isn't to say this is a chapter of reviews of albums by relative unknowns—we'll get there soon enough, but not yet. No, this chapter is about my not-so-secret crushes, albums I fell in love with that might not feel as obvious in terms of choices as what's preceded them. You might have heard the artist's name (Quincy Jones), but not the album reviewed here (*Walking in Space*). You might recognize the artist immediately (The Kinks), but you might never guess the name of my favorite album in their extensive catalogue (*Misfits*). You might have heard the album's Big Single roughly a zillion times ("Closing Time"), but never heard any of the rest of the superb album it was taken from (Semisonic's stellar 1998 release *Feeling Strangely Fine*).

In a couple of cases, I've chosen to file well-known and extensively-reviewed albums under "crushes" because, in the opinion of many, they're the second-best album by that particular artist, thereby bumping them from the "classics" category, at least for our purposes here. Finally, convention be damned, two greatest hits albums appear in this chapter, because they're great collections of great music that inspired me to write about them. 'Nuff said.

As anyone who's ever been an adolescent can testify, crushes are powerful things. Their magnetic pull can overwhelm your normal defenses, as happened with several albums here that didn't leave the CD player in my primary listening room—a.k.a. my car—for weeks on end. When you're in the grip of a crush, your senses heighten and amplify, making everything—every word, every instrument, every note or beat—more intensely felt. Even after your crushes pass (and, news flash: they always do), the memory of them is often long-lasting, and may be fuel for later bouts of nostalgia. The good news about musical crushes is, you can enjoy the company of as many as you want, whenever you want, and none of the others will mind.

My myriad musical crushes have been broken into two groups for our purposes here. The first set spans 1969 through 2001, while the second runs from 2002 up through 2014. In between the two, we'll delve into the darker side of reviewing, with a batch of albums that were pretty much the opposite of crushes. For now, though, I hope you'll join me in basking in the glow of some absolutely terrific music.

*

Quincy Jones
Walking in Space
A & M, 1969
[Published on *The Daily Vault* 3/21/2007]

"Dead End," the opening cut on *Walking in Space*, kicks off with a finger-snapping little electric piano-bass figure that feels like late-night roadhouse boogie. Then a sassy muted trumpet comes in, lending an air of bebop sophistication. And then the full horn section blasts you with a one-two punch that leaves you feeling like the guy in the chair in the old Maxell tape ads, getting his hair blown back by the music pumping out of his speakers. Just as suddenly, everything but the bass and piano drops out and the electric guitar arrives to layer nimble fusion-esque solos on top.

Yes indeed, it's finger-snapping, floppy-hatted, narrow-tied, cooler-than-*Shaft* orchestral-gospel-soul-funk-jazz-fusion. Or something like that.

By 1969, musical renaissance man Jones had already played for Dizzy Gillespie and Lionel Hampton, arranged for Count Basie and Ray Charles, led a series of jazz big bands of his own, become the first African American to be named a senior executive of an American record label (Mercury), scored movie soundtracks and been recruited to work with Frank Sinatra. *Walking in Space* gave Jones the opportunity to fold all of these experiences into a single, expansive musical vision embracing big-band jazz, fusion, r&b, film scores and even pop influences.

The cast of players, as one might expect for a bandleader with Quincy's web of connections, is fairly spectacular—including Ray Brown on bass, Freddie Hubbard on trumpet, Bob James on electric piano, Eric Gale and Toots Thielemans on electric guitar, and Hubert Laws on flute and sax—and the results are everything you could hope for.

This disc's twelve-minute title track—like "Dead End," taken from the contemporary musical *Hair*—is the most experimental piece here, wandering through cinematic string-and-horn backdrops decorated with soaring background vocals, interspersed with extended solos on flute, trumpet, electric piano, muted trumpet, electric guitar, and probably a few I missed.

"Killer Joe," like the title track, has a sweeping, cinematic feel and features chorused female background vocals vamping "Killer Joe / Don't you go / Hurt me slow / Please Joe" off and on through the track. The track once again builds off a steady, sturdy jazz bassline and throws the kitchen sink at it—flute solos, trumpet solos, subtle little electric guitar riffing, a catchy chorus of "Cool Joe, mean Joe" over a snappy trumpet line—you name it. Just keep those toes tapping…

"Love and Peace" is a kind of orchestral blues, featuring a fat horn section over a slumbering rhythm section, segueing into a tasty, rather B.B. King-like guitar solo. Bigger and badder yet is the closing "Oh Happy Day," a giddy, heart-full-of-soul take on Edwin Hawkins' contemporary gospel hit that would make anyone with a pulse want to shake your hands in the air and sing along.

This frothy hybrid manages to be all over the map and yet cohesive for one simple reason: every single track sounds like the players were having the time of their lives. There is genuine joy in these grooves, and it shows. Jones' tastes as an artist and a producer would range farther and farther afield from jazz in the years that followed, but as a milestone along the path of a musical icon, *Walking in Space* is a major statement, and a memorable one.

Rating: A-

*

Pink Floyd
Wish You Were Here
EMI Records, 1975
[Published on *The Daily Vault* 7/18/2005]

The Dark Side of the Moon was an amazing, landmark album with a spectacular chart run. *The Wall* spawned a string of hit singles and awe-inspiring live shows. But *Wish You Were Here* remains, to this day, my favorite album by Pink Floyd.

I've concluded it must be the emotional context. *Dark Side* and *The Wall* are filled with angry, cynical tunes, amplified by expansive, often wildly creative music and electronic effects. But virtually every song on those two albums is a semi-autobiographical expression of bassist/lyricist Roger Waters' feelings of pain and alienation, making them ultimately a rather grandiose exercise in sustained self-pity. (Not that we don't all have our moments of feeling sorry for the fellow in the mirror, but it does get old after a while.)

Wish You Were Here has its angry, cynical moments, of course—"Have a Cigar" and "Welcome to the Machine" are two of the harshest, most devastating critiques ever of the swallow-them-whole-and-spit-out-the-bones nature of the music industry that was busy being born at the time this album was issued. But the essence of the album, as heard in the multi-part opus "Shine on You Crazy Diamond," as well as the title track, is a kind of eulogy for a living friend—lost soul Syd Barrett, the man who launched Pink Floyd before launching his mind off on an interstellar journey from which it would never return. The longing and regret the group associates with their absent friend is palpable on these tracks, and quite moving. There's even a hint of guilt for succeeding so well without the person who got them started.

Every song on this disc also features superb performances from the band of Waters, David Gilmour (guitar & vocals), Richard Wright (keys) and Nick Mason (drums). Favorite moments include Gilmour's slicing, stabbing solo in "Have a Cigar," complemented beautifully by Wright's swirling, menacing synths and the rhythm section's chunky, lurching pattern. "Wish You Were Here," for its part, is one of the most moving songs the band ever created, Gilmour's sublime acoustic guitar and Wright's plaintive piano and synth work casting a spell of deepest melancholy. Closing out the album, the second half of the "Shine On You Crazy Diamond' suite is simply spectacular, with Wright deploying some of his eeriest keyboard effects and tones as the song picks up a melodic idea, then mutates, then mutates again, moving near the finish into a superb funk segment where Wright gives his clavinet a workout over Gilmour's distorted r & b guitar lines as the synths continue to paint otherworldly textures in the background.

Wish You Were Here is a remarkable piece of work, a concept album that reaches the pinnacle of the genre: a thematically whole, emotionally engaging, musically diverse and sonically spectacular epic.

Rating: A

*

The Kinks
Misfits
Arista, 1978
[Published on *The Daily Vault* 9/16/2013]

The '70s were a rough road for the Kinks. Their early proto-metal chord-crunching (see "You Really Got Me" and "All Day and All of the Night") had given way later in the '60s to an operatic, witty, nostalgic, and distinctly British vision that saw the group delivering one expansive concept album after another under the leadership of frontman / chief songwriter Ray Davies and brother / lead guitarist Dave Davies.

By the mid-'70s, though, after dabbling in country and music-hall stylings and delivering three straight rock operas, it seemed the band, among the most resilient of the original British Invasion era, had worn out its welcome with both the record-buying public and the group's label. After being dropped by RCA, the boys landed a new contract with Arista on the condition that they put their artsy pretensions behind them and get back to basics.

Their first album for RCA, 1977's *Sleepwalker*, was tighter, poppier, heavier and—let's be frank—noticeably less challenging than what had preceded it. Ironically, it scored a minor hit with Ray's "Juke Box Music," a bitter lament dismissing his own life's work as "only juke box music." Once he began to emerge from his sulk, though, things got interesting again.

With 1978's *Misfits*, the Kinks commenced a mid-career renaissance that was at once startlingly successful and deeply ironic. Even as Ray Davies mocked his own artistic compromises and the narrowness of the public's tastes, the songs he produced grew more focused and harder-hitting, and the broad audience he was often in the process of insulting lapped up his every snarling word.

The essential argument of *Misfits* is that only weirdos and freaks really care about rock and roll—and by the way, they're also delusional and self-destructive. At least, that initially appears to be the message of the plaintive title track and the cautionary "A Rock 'n' Roll Fantasy," but there's more. In the end, "Misfits" evolves into a gentle call to action: "This is your chance, this is your time / So don't throw it away / You can have your day." And while he spends much of "Fantasy" deriding a unnamed third party's life of illusion, this one also finishes with a call to action, this time for Davies himself: "Don't want to spend my life, living in a rock 'n' roll fantasy / Don't want to spend my life, living on the edge of reality."

This album, too, is where Davies begins to figure out how to fold his penchant for odd, witty character studies into a more straightforward rock format. Yes, "Hay Fever" is ridiculous—but it *rocks*. Davies takes aim at insecure trend-chasers, and scores a bullseye, with "Permanent Waves." And the narrator of the jaunty road song "In a Foreign Land" runs away to dodge taxes and ends up "all out of jack and I can't go back" but seems more content to have said "goodbye to the champagne and caviar set" anyway.

Never one to back away from touchy subjects, Davies imagines a "Black Messiah" designed to jar the sensibilities of his audience and then, having long since introduced us to "Lola," pulls off another brilliant ode to transvestism with the playful, matter-of-fact "Out of the Wardrobe."

Still, the two cuts that got this teenaged rocker's blood pumping were the fiery, propulsive "Live Life," a bracing reminder to live in the moment and carry on through hard times, and rollicking closer "Get Up," the musical antidote to the album's despairing opener, in which Davies grabs the listener by the lapels and exhorts: "Somebody gotta get up and shout / Somebody gotta give us some clout / You're the ones who can make it all work out / It all depends on you."

As a child of the '70s—I was 15 when this one came out—*Misfits* was in fact my point of entry for The Kinks, and earned my loyal admiration through several years and albums to follow (true confession: a creature of my times, I was startled to learn in 1978 after falling hard for *Van Halen* that "You Really Got Me" was an old Kinks song).

Misfits is the moment where Ray Davies figured out how to channel the muscular brio and cutting wit that had earned the Kinks a record contract in the first place into a punchy, modern sound. Yes, he compromised in terms of musical approach, but he never gave an inch when it came to the subject matter of his songs or the passion with which he delivered them. *Misfits* is a testament to the power of change to both reinvent and rejuvenate an artist.

Rating: A-

*

Ronnie Montrose
Open Fire
Warner Brothers Records, 1978
[Published on *The Daily Vault* 2/3/1998]

The worst thing I can say about guitarist Ronnie Montrose's moody, inventive 1978 solo debut is that it's too damn short. At just under 36 minutes, *Open Fire* invariably leaves me wanting more.

Fresh from the second of three incarnations he's attempted of the Zeppelin-ish rock band bearing his last name (the first time around in '73-'74 having been Sammy Hagar's big break), Ronnie went into the studio to make *Open Fire* with former Montrose players Jim Alcivar and Alan Fitzgerald in tow and old pal Edgar Winter in the producer's chair. (Montrose himself had his own big break on Winter's huge *They Only Come Out At Night* album.) Stepping completely outside of the hard-rock formula he'd been locked into up to that point, Montrose created in *Open Fire* one of the truly memorable instrumental albums in rock history.

A lot of talented guitar players have tried and failed to make all-instrumental albums that sustain the listener's interest all the way through. I inevitably groove hard to two or three tracks on every Joe Satriani and Eric Johnson album—but the rest usually feels like a waste of my time and their considerable talent. Even the likes of Stevie Ray Vaughan conceded he needed some words to go with those awe-inspiring solos.

Montrose succeeded where so many have failed by defying expectations from start to finish, and doing it with as much subtlety as flash. After five years spent seemingly begging to be compared with Jimmy Page, playing virtually nothing but huge, pounding, angular riffs, Montrose opened his solo debut with an *orchestral* piece.

And not just some cheesy "See how hard I'm trying to be different?" snippet, either, but a driving, dynamic horns-and-strings piece ("Openers") that sounds like nothing so much as the soundtrack to a downhill skiing movie (Montrose would later contribute to just such an album, 1991's *Born to Ski*). At the climax, Montrose cleverly and almost seamlessly segues into the next track, with a theremin taking over the melody as the orchestra peaks out until the song is broken open by the ripping good electric riff that propels you into "Open Fire," theremin thrumming away underneath the entire time. It's a hell of a ride, and it's only the beginning.

Next up comes probably the album's highlight and as unique a sound as I've ever heard achieved. "Mandolinia" is a three-ring circus of layered, cascading mandolins and mandocellos, the impossibly sweet high notes bouncing off Winter's swirling, pulsating bass synthesizer, with occasional, precise guitar fills unobtrusively occupying the middle ground. I don't use the word "masterpiece" often, but here, it applies.

"Town Without Pity" is the one song that got any airplay off the album, a number borrowed from the soundtrack of the old movie of the same name. Straightforward as it basically is, Montrose sells it by incorporating the orchestra's horn section and wringing the drama out of every sweeping note of his solos.

The album also features two very enjoyable fusion pieces—"Heads Up" and "Rocky Road"—and two wonderful acoustic numbers, the circling, hypnotic "Leo Rising" and the almost pastoral "My Little Mystery," featuring Winter on harpsichord.

Open Fire closes with a minor opus, the shifting, startling six-minute "No Beginning/No End." After a solid minute or so of bizarre sizzling/shearing studio effects, it without warning cuts into a sublime acoustic guitar meditation that builds over the course of the next three minutes into a series of gently soaring electric solos. It is, like the album it caps off, utterly unique and masterful.

If you play guitar—or even if, like me, you just love music that's got real spark and creativity behind it—your music library is not complete without this album.

Rating: A

*

Bruce Springsteen
Tunnel of Love
Columbia Records, 1987
[Published on *The Daily Vault* 2/12/2004]

Whether or not this is in fact the loneliest album ever recorded—an arguable point—*Tunnel of Love* is without a doubt the loneliest album of Bruce Springsteen's brotherhood-anthem-filled career.

Lonelier than *Nebraska*, you ask, where he sang solo over his own acoustic guitar about the solitary lives of highway patrolmen, Atlantic City desperadoes and stone cold killers? Yes. Because there's no lonelier feeling in the world than feeling alone inside the one relationship you're counting on the most—your own marriage.

Some background is necessary. Bachelor Bruce had finally succumbed to marriage in 1985, toward the tail end of the biggest commercial explosion of his career. The monster album *Born in the USA*, wall-to-wall video coverage on MTV, and a sold-out, global stadium tour had put Springsteen's name on the lips of half the developed world (while the other half—notably President Reagan's re-election campaign staff—were still trying to figure out who he was).

Somewhere along the road, he had hooked up with—of all choices for a New Jersey street rat—a Hollywood actress, Julianne Phillips. The tabloids jumped on the case and before you knew it, they were everywhere you looked. (The Rock Star and the Actress—yeah, that moves papers.) The whole thing took on an inevitable momentum, and pretty soon their wedding was the headline in *The Star* et al. A couple of years later, all the same papers were headlining the messy dissolution of the marriage. (Calling these folks vultures seems entirely too kind…)

In between these two events, this disc arrived, an album confessing in brutal and courageous detail every misstep in a doomed relationship.

The sense of isolation and alienation is pervasive. In *Nebraska*, Springsteen sang in the voice of characters he was creating, second identities that immediately made the room feel crowded; here, his narrators are all either him or thinly-disguised mirror-images. Even the music betrays his sense of isolation—spare, mostly acoustic guitars and synth textures, with the sparsest E Street Band presence of any album other than *Nebraska*.

For the sake of contrast, Springsteen starts out on a relatively light note, parodying the mixture of exasperation, amusement and resentment inspired by his sudden fame in the autobiographical narrative of "Ain't Got You": "I been around the world and all across the seven seas / Been paid a king's ransom for doin' what comes naturally / But I'm still the biggest fool, honey, this world ever knew / 'Cause the only thing I ain't got, baby, I ain't got you." None of the hoopla matters, because inside it all, Springsteen feels more alone than ever.

This sense of isolation and self-doubt weaves its way through the remainder of the album, from the self-flagellating ballads "Two Faces" and "One Step Up" to the brutally pragmatic, roadhouse-rocking story-song "Spare Parts" ("Took her wedding dress, tied that ring up in its sash / Went straight down to the pawn shop man and walked out with some good cold cash"). Even in the album's two love songs—the stately, passionate "Tougher Than the Rest" and the countrified, romantic "All That Heaven Will Allow"—it's made clear that the relationships are struggling to win out against heavy odds.

This makes for rough going, but also for spectacular songwriting.

"Cautious Man" is a tale full of allegory, about a guy who can't let go of his demons, and instead carries them right into his marriage, where he knows "in a restless heart the seeds of betrayal lay." Eventually the narrator's nameless desperation leads him to bolt from his marriage bed into the night, but when he reaches the highway, he finds "nothing but road." So he returns, to fight the battle within himself once more.

My personal favorite on this disc, though, is the remarkable "Brilliant Disguise." I don't think there's ever been a more perceptive or fearless examination of the disintegration of a relationship in song. The essential theme is how the corrosion of trust can eat away at a couple's intimacy until you're left with nothing but a hollow, false facade. The song—steady-building and intense, featuring acoustic guitar, bass, piano, organ and percussion—also nails other relationship truths such as the way self-doubt can spawn larger doubts, and the fact that trying too hard almost always makes things worse. Chills, every time.

This album is full of striking images, dead-on allegories, and a deep sense of revelation, but one image in particular is central. The Cautious Man—in a nod to the movie *Cape Fear*—has tattoos on both sets of knuckles: "On his right hand Billy'd tattooed the word love and on his left hand was the word fear / And in which hand he held his fate was never clear." And there it is. The opposite of love isn't hate, it's fear. Fear prevents intimacy and love, and creates suspicion and resentment. You can't truly love until you let go of the fear. (A message Springsteen repeats in the title track—"Then the lights go out and it's just the three of us / You, me and all that stuff we're so scared of...")

Tunnel of Love is one of the clearest and frankest views an artist has ever offered of what a crumbling relationship looks like from the inside. This album isn't an easy listen, but it's full of moody, evocative music and superb lyrics that tell hard, lonely truths.

Rating: A

*

Gin Blossoms
New Miserable Experience
A & M Records, 1992
[Published on *The Daily Vault*: 10/21/1997]

Does stress concentrate the creative mind? Is angst the fount of all great art? Or is it just (un)happy coincidence that so many great songs and albums have been produced during times of intense personal turmoil for their creators (to name just a handful: Clapton's "Layla," Fleetwood Mac's *Rumours*, Bruce Springsteen's *Tunnel Of Love*)?

The occasion for this question popping up yet again (hey, there's nothing I can't overanalyze) is the passing into history of what I've come to believe is/was one of the '90s' best young bands, the Gin Blossoms. After an eight-year odyssey that took them from the Tempe, Arizona bar circuit to the top of the charts—with several years of relentless touring and the suicide of a key founding member in between—the Blossoms are by most accounts done for the moment (although to their credit they haven't formally "broken up," which these days seems mostly to be a publicity primer for the inevitable reunion) *[And indeed, the Blossoms reunited for good in 2002.—JW]*. Lead vocalist Robin Wilson and drummer Philip Rhodes on the one hand, and guitarist/vocalist Jesse Valenzuela and guitarist Scott Johnson on the other are rehearsing and gigging with new bandmates, while bassist Bill Leen hasn't been heard from yet as to his plans.

New Miserable Experience, the band's breakout album, brims with the kind of energy and propulsive guitar work that keeps the term "rock and roll" from becoming an anachronism. Yet it also puts on wide display the fundamental paradox of the Blossoms: downbeat, borderline mournful lyrics juxtaposed with rich, bouncy guitar hooks. A musical oxymoron, in other words—one echoed in their album titles (*New Miserable Experience*, 1996's *Congratulations, I'm Sorry* and their initial 1991 EP, *Up and Crumbling*).

This album—recorded before songwriter/guitarist Doug Hopkins' alcoholism and depression led to his departure (and subsequent suicide), but released after Johnson had replaced him—now seems ready to join the ranks of albums with a dangerously high internal-chaos-to-musical-quality correlation. The band's breakout album opens with two largely autobiographical Hopkins songs, "Lost Horizons" and "Hey Jealousy," both driving, insistently catchy tunes awash in references to drinking, floundering relationships and loneliness ("If I hadn't blown the whole thing years ago / I might not be alone").

These and other tensions inside the band only seemed to fuel the creative fire, though. Valenzuela's "Mrs. Rita" effectively alternates a driving riff with a Byrds-like jangly melody, while the lyrics offer a little more hope than most of Hopkins'. Dense rockers like "Hands Are Tied" and "Hold Me Down" are balanced nicely by more spacious numbers like "Found Out About You" and "Allison Road," the band's harmonies and Wilson's tambourine work effectively lightening things up whenever the twin-guitar assault threatens to become too heavy. Finally, "Cheatin'" shows off the band's versatility with a dead-on country sound complete with a goofy-on-the-edge-of-hilarious chorus ("You can't call it cheatin'— she reminds me of you").

So here it is—another great album created as the house was falling down around its creators. It's enough to make you want your life to be a living hell just long enough for you to create something truly memorable.

Rating: A

*

U2
Achtung Baby
Island Records, 1991
[Published on *The Daily Vault* 11/17/2004]

Berlin had to be a heady place to be recording a new album in 1990-91. The Wall had just fallen. East and West Germans were mixing and partying and rediscovering one another's cultures for the first time in a generation. And U2 needed a hit.

They needed a hit because the arc of fame and admiration/adulation that had risen through *War* and *The Unforgettable Fire* and *The Joshua Tree* had leveled, perhaps even slid a bit, in the wake of the somewhat bloated and self-indulgent *Rattle and Hum* album and movie. The whispers were out that the band that had been plastered across the cover of *Time* magazine as global icons was growing out of touch, maybe even threatening to become irrelevant.

If that malady was the disease, *Achtung Baby* was the cure.

This disc is the sound of U2 catching fire yet again, of a band that had already reinvented itself from angry post-punks to earnest, majestic rock and rollers going through yet another metamorphosis. Exit bombastic dabblers in American r&b and gospel, enter Euro-hip purveyors of brash experimental rock.

The one thing that's absolutely consistent here with the music that came before it is that this band simply oozes charisma. From the purposefully startling harsh industrial opening of kickoff track "Zoo Station" to the frequently distorted riffs to the complex rhythm patterns and dense layers of percussion to the refocusing of the lyrics on relationships rather than larger concepts, the band finds a host of new ways on this disc to simply demand listeners' attention.

And let's face it, it's pretty tough to accuse a band of irrelevance when they throw off the kind of sparks emitted by powerhouse tracks like "Even Better Than the Real Thing," "Until the End of the World" and "Mysterious Ways." "Real Thing" is a sharply arranged track featuring stinging, almost otherworldly guitar licks slicing through the middle of Bono's lushly layered vocals. "Until the End..." starts out with a dose of tribal thump from Larry Mullen Jr. and Adam Clayton before the Edge brings it hard, slamming down an appropriately apocalyptic riff that bludgeons you silly. This is super-sized rock and roll—and the lyrics aren't half bad either, a batch of surrealistic poetry with memorable lines like "In my dream I was drowning my sorrows / but my sorrows, they learned to swim."

Ah, but they're just the appetizer for "Mysterious Ways," one of the band's greatest creations, turbo-charged by a simply monstrous, throbbing Jimi Hendrix-meets-George Clinton riff laid down over a brilliantly propulsive bass line, dense percussion and Bono's ecstatic vocals. The bridge/breakdown/solo section is a thrill ride all by itself. "Kiss the sky," indeed—Jimi would smile at this one, I think.

Other memorable tracks like "Who's Gonna Ride Your Wild Horses" and "Tryin' to Throw Your Arms Around the World" seduce with melody.

"Ultra Violet (Light My Way)" sounds a bit more like *Unforgettable Fire* material except that it's once again relationship-focused.

And then there's "One," a track that I've been startled to hear played at more than one wedding. Although the "We've got to carry each other / One love" refrain is on the mark, I keep wondering if these people actually listened to the verses, which describe a tortured affair in which the two lovers/victims are in an utterly miserable state of emotional co-dependence. Whatever gets you to the altar, I guess...!

In the end, "The Fly" may encapsulate what I love most about this album, though, with its combination of dirty, raucous guitar and Bono doing his best Earth Wind & Fire imitation on the "Love, we shine like a burnin' star" harmony vocals. This is the sound of a band at the height of its creative and musical powers, cutting loose and having a blast.

That's a beautiful thing, and also, not coincidentally, the stuff hit albums are made of. "Achtung, world!" said this album — U2 is back on top.

Rating: A

*

Mary Chapin Carpenter
Stones in the Road
Columbia Records, 1994
[Published on *The Daily Vault* 11/17/1997]

Mary Chapin Carpenter's long-time musical collaborator / co-producer / guitarist John Jennings has called her voice "an invitation to intimacy." Not physical intimacy, he's quick to add, but the emotional kind. And truly, her honey-sweet tone and masterful phrasing on everything from the stillest of her ballads to her hardest-rocking flirtations suggest he's zeroed on one of the keys to her appeal.

What amazes me as a listener on this particular album, however, is not so much the skill of the singer as it is the power of the songs. Truly, this album is one of the *wisest* I've ever heard; every single lyric is infused with an intelligence and emotional maturity that's by turns startling and engrossing.

"In this world there's a whole lot of trouble baby / In this world there's a whole lot of pain / In this world there's a whole lot of trouble but / A whole lot of ground to gain," Carpenter begins, establishing the theme of resiliency that echoes through this entire album, even as the song's country-gospel sound—anchored by piano, fiddle and a chorus of background vocalists—reinforces its spiritual undercurrents.

As if constructing a novel, she moves then from establishing her principal theme to a bit of character history, illustrating in the steadily-rocking "House of Cards," a possibly autobiographical vision of a suburban childhood where "On the surface it looked so safe / But it was perilous underneath." In the title tune that follows, the search for emotional connections that ring true extends from the family out into the broader society. A folkish hymn to lost innocence, "Stones in the Road" places on the table the idealism of a generation that admired Martin Luther King and Bobby Kennedy—and then carves up the self-satisfaction it has degenerated into: "We pencil in, we cancel out, we crave the corner suite / We kiss your ass, we make you hold, we doctor the receipt... A thousand points of light or shame / Baby, I don't know."

Turning inward once again, Carpenter then steers us through a melodic, fully-realized series of life lessons. First "Tender When I Want to Be" makes a rippling plea for breaking down emotional barriers ("Don't ever let me hesitate / To be tender when I want to be"). Then "A Keeper for Every Flame" offers a sharp little fable about the way romantic longing sometimes overpowers realism ("I thought my heart was broken but it was just a little bruised / I thought love had spoken, guess I was just confused"). Soon after, the title of "The Last Word" serves as the unsung punchline to a stark, compelling retelling of two lovers' final confrontation: "I finally realized / You need it more than you need me / You can have it, I don't want it, and when you've got it, I'll be gone."

Leavening the mix smack in the middle of the album is "Shut Up and Kiss Me," a rollicking come-on that nonetheless has wisdom aplenty of its own to impart: "There's something about the silent type / Attracting me to you / All business baby, none of the hype / That no talker can live up to." Some juicy slide guitar from Lee Roy Parnell and Trisha Yearwood's background vocals round out this five minute party/intermission, before it's back to business with several more well-crafted looks at the ways we constantly search for connections (including the remarkable "John Doe No. 24," with its soaring Branford Marsalis sax work).

Finally, Carpenter falls back, as if spent, to the core of her argument: the key to resiliency is love—but not necessarily romantic love. The purest love, she argues in the closing "This is Love," is less about passion and romance than it is about a fundamental commitment to the other person's emotional well-being. It is a love that, in the end, grants you peace by being able to overcome even the hardest of hard feelings, and forgive (a theme Don Henley hit a career peak on with "The Heart of the Matter"). Listen in for a minute as the piano rolls to a steadily ascending beat, crowned by the last line:

> And I see you still and there's this catch in my throat and
> I just swallow hard 'til it leaves me
> There's nothing in this world that can change what we know
> Still I know I am here if you ever need me
> And this is love

For anyone who's ever experienced any real turbulence in their relationships, these lines are likely to carry the power of well-delivered two-by-four. Love hurts, Carpenter seems to say, but when we succeed in riding that pain out and returning to our eternal search for connection, we win the only battle we'll ever really need to in our lifetime. To me, the thirteen exceptionally well-written and played songs on *Stones in the Road* speak wisdom of a quality that is as rare in popular music as true love is in life itself.

Rating: A

*

Stevie Ray Vaughan & Double Trouble
Greatest Hits
Epic Records, 1995
[Published on *The Daily Vault* 1/20/1999]

Was Stevie Ray Vaughan the greatest blues guitarist who ever lived?

The question is impossible to answer, in part because Vaughan, surely the finest blues guitarist of the 1980s, died in an August 1990 helicopter crash. He was 35 then, at the height of his skills—and a young pup by the standards of the blues. How much better might he have become? You might as well ask how high the sky is.

The die-hard fan needs all of Vaughan's albums. His skill as an interpreter of anything from traditional electric blues to the work of his idol, Jimi Hendrix, is incredible to hear. But for the newcomer, *Greatest Hits* makes an excellent starting point.

The one—and only—fault I can find with this album is sequencing. Starting off with the familiar—but in Vaughan's hands, utterly transformed—Beatles track "Taxman" is bound to lead the casual listener astray in terms of expectations. The song is the only cover of a mainstream pop-rock song on the whole album, and Vaughan's rumbly barroom-shouter vocals here are a far cry from George Harrison's sweet tenor.

Still, the guitar, as you might expect, is fairly spectacular. Vaughan punctuates the beat with gunshot riffs that positively leap out of the mix. The one thing the song certainly accomplishes is to introduce his remarkable ability to play both rhythm and lead at the same time. There is only one guitarist playing here, and no overdubs, and yet there isn't an empty beat to be found as Vaughan leaps seamlessly from holding up the rhythm to banging out tight little lead riffs.

"Texas Flood" might have made a more logical opener. Taken from Vaughan's debut album of the same name, it's a classic "hard blues" track, the rhythm section slumbering along behind Vaughan's raw, steamy vocals, interrupted mid-song by a slow-burning solo that warms your ears up for what's to come.

"The House is Rockin'" picks up the pace with a tight, fun little roadhouse blues romp that pretty much forces you to tap your feet. "Pride and Joy," next up, introduces Vaughan's bread-and-butter genre, a mid-tempo blues that spotlights his rhythm-to-lead abilities, chugging along fervently from chorus to chorus and tearing through the solos between. Toward the end of the disc, "Change It," "Cold Shot" and "Couldn't Stand the Weather" fall in this same potent vein.

Among the best of Vaughan's originals is "Tightrope," a topical number addressing his battle with alcohol and substance abuse. Written and recorded just after he successfully completed a 12-step program, the lyric addresses how delicate sobriety is to maintain once you've had to battle to achieve it. That said, there's no mistaking the glorious relief Vaughan invests in the minute-long mid-song solo here. It is a total emotional release that just goes and goes, building and swerving and building once again until you're left standing there in your living room shaking your head with your jaw halfway to the floor.

And then, 60 seconds later, over the fade, he rips out another, completely different but in every way equal solo.

The only appropriate response is "DAMN."

But—and this is where you just have to laugh, because, I mean, if you're a player yourself, what the hell else can you do?—this is just part one of the trilogy that lies at the heart of this album.

No player that I've heard has ever come closer than Vaughan to matching both Jimi Hendrix's unique tonal style and his astonishing passion with his instrument. On this disc, Vaughan is heard covering Hendrix's "Little Wing" as an instrumental and investing himself 110 percent in every note. The movements in the song range from deathly quiet picking down low and up high on the frets to a pair of searing solos that sound like he's channeling Hendrix himself.

This tune's quiet finish leads directly into the one Vaughan cut that received substantial play on AOR stations. "Crossfire" was actually written by Vaughan's band, Double Trouble, and as you might expect it's very strong rhythmically, building off a driving bass line and muscular organ, and allowing Vaughan to concentrate on playing pure lead guitar. Vaughan produces one of his strongest vocals, a high, sweet, mid-song solo, and a closing solo that, well, DAMN. "Awesome" might cover the first ten seconds of it. It lasts thirty.

The answer to whether Stevie Ray Vaughan was the greatest blues guitarist of all time is that there isn't really an answer. There never can be; questions like this are inherently subjective. But there is a story, retold plainly and without false modesty in the excellent liner notes included on *Greatest Hits* (thank you, Dan Forte), that is worth repeating.

Vaughan's final concert was an all-star jam including sets from blues luminaries Buddy Guy, Robert Cray and Eric Clapton. Vaughan ripped it up that night, leaving the crowd breathlessly cheering his departure from the stage, and leaving Clapton with the unenviable task of following him. Clapton, whose prodigious playing was once hailed with the immortal phrase "Clapton is God," remembers his state of mind stepping onto the stage that night very clearly. "It had gone past the point of being envious or depressed," he recalls with an ironic laugh, "because no one could possibly expect me to be *that* good."

Was Vaughan the greatest? Who knows? But for one night at least, he was better than God.

Rating: A

*

Jimi Hendrix
Experience Hendrix: The Best of Jimi Hendrix
MCA Records, 1998
[Published on *The Daily Vault* 5/24/1999]

The world of the arts is littered with people who, metaphorically speaking, color inside the lines.

Most gifted artists begin by learning from those who went before them—observing styles, techniques, basic avenues of expression. Most then settle into a niche—maybe an interesting or quirky one that skirts the edges of the current scene, but for the most part, a niche that still lies within the boundaries of their own learning and experience. They find the lines they're most comfortable with, and they color inside them.

What the truly landmark artistic figures do is to say "Those lines are good, those lines are valuable, and I respect them—but now I'm drawing my own."

For four incredible and all-too-quickly-gone years, Jimi Hendrix drew lines that changed the world of popular music forever.

A true rock and roll devotee probably needs all three of the studio albums Hendrix completed during his lifetime; each is a remarkable accomplishment that shattered untold barriers in its day. But for the Hendrix beginner (which I'm not, but I'm hardly an expert), *Experience Hendrix: The Best of Jimi Hendrix* is a great place to start.

Hendrix's music is, at its core, blues music. In the early '60s he had served his apprenticeship as a sideman for rhythm and blues acts that included Little Richard and the Isley Brothers. He could draw inside those lines like a master, but his prowess with a guitar was so far beyond what was asked of him that neither he nor the acts he worked with were comfortable with his role.

When Animals bassist and fledgling producer Chas Chandler came across Hendrix, he was a barely-known solo club artist blowing away small crowds in New York with his virtuoso playing. Distortion, feedback, bizarre amp settings, behind-the-back playing, lightning runs on the fretboard, astonishing shifts in tempo and mood—all were part of his mainly self-taught repertoire before he ever recorded a song of his own.

Moving to London in 1966 at Chandler's behest, Hendrix recorded the first of his three studio albums, 1967's *Are You Experienced?* Seven cuts from that astonishing debut are featured on this 20-track compilation, seven cuts that grabbed the music world by the lapels and shook it until it was dizzy.

The jagged, angular hook that kicks off "Purple Haze" was like nothing ever heard before in popular music—the banshee wail of an incredibly potent new voice being born. It and its companion "Manic Depression" are arguably the first heavy metal songs in music history, all pounding backbeat under grinding guitar pyrotechnics that would turn

Jimmy Page, Tony Iommi and a thousand others on to the bone-shaking power of the fully amped, thoroughly unleashed electric guitar. (Even one of the chief themes of heavy metal is established here—how far is it, really, from "Manic Depression" to a "Communication Breakdown" that leaves you "Paranoid"?)

Still, "Hey Joe" was the first single, and here Hendrix's blues roots are on wide display. His gruff, sometimes shaky vocals aren't yet a match at this point for the sensitivity and fire of his playing, but the total effect remains remarkable. The same goes for "The Wind Cries Mary," another of the gentler, bluesy numbers that helped Hendrix break out as a singles artist. They came out of a recognizable genre, yet made it over with panache.

The songs that propel the first part of this disc, though—and the ones I personally could listen to for days on end—are the pulsating Chuck Berry-on-acid numbers "Fire" and "Stone Free." The combination of a driving backbeat and some of Hendrix's most aggressively rhythmic playing and singing is stunningly powerful. These thunderously amped soul grooves would ultimately offer inspiration to artists as diverse as Led Zeppelin and Parliament-Funkadelic, Stevie Ray Vaughan and Frank Zappa. They were the template for a new vision of music that erased all boundaries between blues, soul, pop and rock, and threw open the doors of invention for all those who followed.

Highlights from Hendrix's other two complete studio albums are also featured here, four tracks from *Axis: Bold As Love* (1967) and three from *Electric Ladyland* (1968). Both albums saw Hendrix's musical palette expanding still further, bringing exceptionally creative arrangements and experimentation of all sorts into the picture.

Take for example "Crosstown Traffic," one of Hendrix's deceptively simple compositions that's actually dense with inventive touches when you break it down—clever lyrics, call-and-answer vocals (featuring guest Dave Mason of Traffic fame), a stuttering, dynamic beat, and a guitar line that he doubles on, yes, a kazoo. And it works. Other memorable tracks include the terrific blues ballad "Little Wing," the uncharacteristically playful "Foxey Lady," and the delirious psychedelic jazz-funk jam "If 6 Was 9."

Among Hendrix's crowning achievements, though, has to be his adaptation of Bob Dylan's gritty, soulful "All Along the Watchtower" into a hurricane of churning acoustic rhythm guitar (Mason again) and simply astounding electric soloing. To admire a seminal artist is one thing, to

103

cover his work and top him at it is testament to the reach of Hendrix's talent.

Be prepared to collect your jaw off the floor a few more times before your 73 minutes are up, though, because this 20-track collection never lets up. Near the 3/4 mark, just as you begin to fear the highlights of Hendrix's all-too-brief catalogue may be about to peter out, a fresh burst of energy kicks in, beginning with the smoldering "Voodoo Chile (Slight Return)." Oft-cited by those who would know as the electric guitarist's ultimate challenge, the solos Hendrix shreds here are so consistently unpredictable and staggeringly complex as to defy description.

The next four cuts comprise the heart of the album Hendrix was working on at the time of his death, to have been titled *First Rays of the New Rising Sun*, and they belong right here with his best work.

"Freedom" is a driving R&B number that puts the rhythm section in a killer groove even as the lyrics take their inspiration from both 1970 socio-political currents and traditional African-American spirituals. "Night Bird Flying," by contrast, has an almost country-rock feel to it, as if Hendrix had invited the Gram Parsons-era Byrds to sit in. Both feature more exceptional soloing. Meanwhile, the striking ballad "Angel" is awash in the dreamy tones created by another of Hendrix's sonic experiments—amping his guitar through a Leslie organ speaker.

The set closes, appropriately enough, at Woodstock, with Hendrix's immortal kamikaze assault on "The Star Spangled Banner." While this wasn't his finest moment artistically, the out-of-control passion he invests in this rendition helped to seal his legend, and thus it belongs here beyond a doubt.

A review of this disc would not be complete without mentioning the excellent packaging and liner notes. Every song is fully annotated with just the right amount of background on its composition and recording, and the photos and design are top-notch.

All in all, this is a package in every way worthy of the artist it celebrates, an artist whose vision exceeded everything he saw around him, and who dared to make his vision real—to draw his own lines.

Rating: A

*

Semisonic
Feeling Strangely Fine
MCA Records, 1998
[Published on *The Daily Vault* 8/26/1998]

Forty years into this thing called rock 'n roll, is there an original sound left? It's a fair question when you hear an abundantly talented but indisputably familiar-sounding band like Semisonic.

On *Feeling Strangely Fine*, their second album, this versatile trio offers up hooks aplenty amid subtly complex arrangements. The grabber is right up front where their A&R guy obviously wanted it—the thunderously catchy end-of-the-night, pair-'em-up-and-head-'em-out anthem "Closing Time." Interspersing a gently urgent piano melody with crunching power chords, the track effectively showcases the band's skill at creating music that sounds much bigger than you'd expect from a trio. Dan Wilson is on lead vocals and guitars, John Munson on bass and vocals, and Jacob Slichter on drums and vocals, but here and elsewhere everyone contributes keyboards, extra guitars and string arrangements to fatten the band's sound.

It's a method trios like Rush have used to their advantage, but it does present some problems trying to pull off live versions of these tunes. Thing is, despite the late night, smoky club graphics and lyrics on this album, Semisonic has the aura of a great studio band that may not translate as well live. They simply pack too many sonic tricks and extras into songs like "Never You Mind," with its distorted, slowed-down bridge and "Singing in My Sleep,' with its manipulated, effects-laden intro and fadeout.

Still, the studio sound is a very strong, if familiar one. Drawing from a variety of classic rock influences, Semisonic incorporates some Hall & Oates-ish blue-eyed soul ("Secret Smile"); baroque Queen vocal arrangements and guitar tones (the bridge and quickie solos dotting "Never You Mind"); and a U2 homage that's so complete you think you're hearing a lost track from the *Achtung Baby* sessions ("Made to Last"). Beatlesque harmonies abound.

Which isn't to say Semisonic has no identity of its own. Lyrically, this album is a thoughtful and sometimes refreshingly earthy look at relationships. The lounge-y, orgasmic romp "Completely Pleased" is bound to make you smile, as is the intentionally pathetic rant "This Will Be My Year." The acoustic tunes are where lead voice Dan Wilson gets down to business and really shines, though. The all at once raw, sweet and seductive "DND," and the smartly written, arranged and sung "California" and "Gone to the Movies" reveal a sinuous, expressive songwriter coming into his own before your ears.

And if "California" also shapes up suspiciously like a lost U2 track, oh hell, what're you gonna do? A band could surely choose worse sounds to shoot for. For a group sometimes awash in influences, Semisonic does a terrific job of making it all sound fresh and worthwhile. *Feeling Strangely Fine* is sounding suspiciously like one of my favorite albums of 1998.

Rating: A-

*

The Jayhawks
Smile
American Recordings, 2000
[Published on *The Daily Vault* 11/15/2000]

Smile started out feeling like a long-overdue exploratory journey to me. I'd heard a fair amount about the Jayhawks before: a smart alt-country collective with a pair of gifted songwriters/lead voices, one of whom (Mark Olson) left the band a few years back. Named one of the most influential bands of the decade by *Rolling Stone,* made a "classic" album a ways back (1991's *Hollywood Town Hall),* critics' darlings, etc. etc.

In other words, one of those bands I kept telling myself I ought to know more about... but didn't. I'd never heard a single song by them before picking up this album a month ago.

The opening title tune was all it took for me to know I was in for something special. Dreamy lyrics, densely layered male-female harmony vocals, and rock instrumentation filled out with an assertive string section. I could hear the "alt," but where was the "country"? Of course, the end result was probably just what the band was going for in the case of rookie listeners like me: from that point forward, I cast aside all expectations and just drank in this remarkable album.

The Jayhawks draw deeply from influences ranging from Gram Parsons to R.E.M. and everything in between, while managing to put their unique stamp on every tune. They'll drill out a letter-perfect slice of Byrds/Tom Petty jangle-rock like "I'm Gonna Make You Love Me," yet imbue it with a completely unique (and in this case, decidedly off-center) point of view. Then they'll grab onto a sleepy acoustic riff like the one that anchors "What Led Me to This Town" and convince you they're about to serve up a straightforward country ballad, right up until the song blossoms into its striking, hauntingly beautiful chorus.

The latter track also gives you another taste of the rich harmonies between lead singer Gary Louris and keyboard player/harmony vocalist Karen Grotberg (who departed for maternity leave just prior to the album's completion, to be replaced by Jen Gunderman). It's a gorgeous effect used numerous times on this smartly arranged album, without ever coming close to wearing out its welcome.

At this point, it seems like track four could be just about anything. And it is... "Somewhere in Ohio" kicks off with a simple acoustic strum and a single looping keyboard tone layered over a techno-flavored beat. Louris croons two elusive, vaguely threatening opening verses ("You were feeling like a bomb without a target")... the music slowly builds... and then the electric guitars kick in with a stunning crunch, upping the ante a good 50 decibels. From there, the song falls back and surges again and again, coloring the basic rhythm track with guitars that range from Jangle 101 to feedback-laden power chords, plus an incredibly infectious "Ba-ba-ba-ba-ba-ba-ba-ba" pop chorus. It's a little of this, a little of that, and a knockout all the way.

Playing it smart, the Jayhawks then bring it back home with the simply stunning countrified ballad "A Break in the Clouds." Some actual slide guitar soars over Grotberg's artful piano melodies as she and Louris offer up another achingly pretty chorus-in-harmony: "Every time that I see your face / It's like cool, cool water running down my back."

It's tempting at this point to simply end the review with "etc., etc.," because the rest of the disc is equally rangy, gutsy, smart and beautiful. Veering from airy pop ("Queen of the World," "Mr. Wilson") to melodic heavy rock ("Life Floats By," "Pretty Thing"), to the plaintive, enigmatic ballad "Broken Harpoon," the Jayhawks just keep surprising you. Double-time techno beats are paired with distorted guitars and soaring pop choruses ("Wildest Dreams"), sounding somehow right at home alongside Dylanesque laments ("Better Days").

With Olson's departure, Louris is now the band's principal songwriter, but many of the best songs here are the results of his collaborations with Grotberg, bassist Marc Perlman, and drummer Tim O'Reagan. Perlman and O'Reagan's influence is especially evident in the strong rhythm tracks that characterize the whole album—a trademark also of producer Bob Ezrin (of The Wall fame), who clearly encouraged the band to push its limits.

Going for the big exit, the Jayhawks finish *Smile* with the brash, epic "Baby, Baby, Baby," in which Louris adopts the role of a fellow whose sudden, spectacular demise may somehow redeem his betrayal of his lover. (Is this Shakespeare or rock and roll?) A delicately modulated, almost tuneful wail of feedback closes things out with panache.

What the Jayhawks have accomplished is what the best bands strive to: use their influences as a launching point rather than a template. There are references to Parsons/McGuinn, Buck/Stipe, Jagger/Richards and '70s heavy metal sprinkled throughout *Smile*. Yet the music and lyrics are sparklingly original start to finish. Call it roots rock, call it "y'allternative," call it new traditionalist ... call it whatever you want. It's thoroughly modern music that respects the past; carefully conceived music that ignores boundaries; smartly imagined music that aims high, dares much and succeeds brilliantly.

Rating: A

*

Ben Folds
Rockin' the Suburbs
Epic Records, 2001
[Published on *The Daily Vault* 5/12/2004]

It will come as no surprise to longtime readers of *The Daily Vault*—not to mention my wonderful, long-suffering spouse—that I can be a moron sometimes. Case in point: I didn't pick up Ben Folds' 2001 disc *Rockin' the Suburbs* until earlier this year.

I've been a Folds fan since the first time I heard "Brick," the achingly beautiful crisis-and-aftermath ballad off the Ben Folds Five's *Whatever and Ever Amen* album. After the Five's third disc appeared in 1999, however, Folds more or less simultaneously dissolved the group, got married and moved to Australia.

Rockin' the Suburbs is therefore Folds' unofficial solo debut (although his 1998 side project, Fear of Pop, was basically a solo album). And as much as I enjoyed the frenetic energy that the Five's Robert Sledge-Darren Jessee rhythm section brought to the music, I can't imagine Ben Folds making a better album at this point in his career than *RTS*. With all due respect to Joe Jackson and Randy Newman—clearly both influences of

Folds'—there hasn't been album of piano-based rock this good since Elton John's early-'70s heyday.

Rippling melodies and sharp-eyed lyrical detail populate this album with hummable, memorable cuts. Folds' piano playing is so instinctively rhythmic on tracks like "Annie Waits" and "Fired" that it makes me want to go back even farther and invoke the name of the Great One, Jerry Lee Lewis. Yet he also pulls off restrained and gorgeous on ballads like "Still Fighting It" and the soaring, touching "The Luckiest." And superbly arranged harmonies? Let's just say Brian Wilson would be very proud of "Zak and Sara."

But really, the achievement of this album lies in the unique perspective and fully-realized characters of tracks like "Fred Jones Part 2"—about a retiring newspaperman's last day—and "The Ascent of Stan"—about a "textbook hippy man" who's mainstreamed with age and "become all those things you've always run from." These are full-blown character sketches that draw you in and show you the world from a new angle; quality writing, set to superb music.

Folds—who's played piano, bass and drums in previous bands— plays all three here, bringing in no more than a handful of studio musicians to help out on a few cuts. One of these is the one place where Folds really cuts loose with his jabbing sense of humor—the title track, a brilliant and brutal deconstruction of angry suburban white-boy metal-heads everywhere. Here Folds ditches the piano and lays on the guitars, but they're all for effect, and arranged to snarky perfection.

One other note. Next to waiting so long to buy the album in the first place, my biggest mistake was playing it for my 16-year-old son after I'd only listened to it once myself. After a single spin he enthusiastically "borrowed" it, and I didn't hear it again—other than brief snatches while riding in his car—for almost three months.

The moral of the story? Don't be a moron—buy this album. And then don't let it out of your sight.

Rating: A

~Segue~

Interview: Jesse Valenzuela

[Published on *The Daily Vault* 5/8/2006]

If you think you've never heard a Jesse Valenzuela song, you're probably wrong.

Between his role as guitarist / harmony vocalist / songwriter and now co-producer for '90s power-pop icons the Gin Blossoms, his songwriting work for the likes of Stevie Nicks and the Rembrandts, steady TV and production work, occasional gigs with old friends the Zubia Brothers, and a raft of other projects including his 2002 solo disc Tunes Young People Will Enjoy, *Jesse Valenzuela has got to be one of the busiest guys in the music business. Based in Los Angeles, Valenzuela regularly travels to the Blossoms' Tempe, Arizona home base and all over the country with the band's steady touring schedule.*

Valenzuela's most recent disc is a collaboration with fellow roots-rocking singer-songwriter/guitarist/producer Craig Northey, a veteran of Canadian critics' darlings The Odds. Jesse and I—a Sacramento native and admitted Gin Blossoms fan who bemoaned the GBs' habit of skipping Sac-town on tour—got together by phone recently to discuss Northey Valenzuela, *the perils of writing sad songs, and the finer details of the Blossoms' long-awaited new album, due this summer.*

The Daily Vault: So, how did the *Northey Valenzuela* album come about?

Jesse Valenzuela: Craig and I have known each other a long time. And having written so many songs together, we eventually thought we should record them all in the same session, so they had the same sound, and put them out there. It's really that simple.

How did you guys first meet and start writing together?

It was the "big '80s" when I met Craig in Hollywood. We were both kind of semi-living there, in and out of town, and we just played a lot of gigs together, up and down the coast. I think we played Sacramento together, as a matter of fact. A place called The Boardwalk, kind of a tough-guy, metal-bar place. I don't know how we got the gig. It was just a product of the usual hustle, just a couple of young guys trying to make some bucks.

There are some great performances on the album. It feels really loose, and I read where you guys cut most of the tracks in just a couple of takes. My reaction to the album, still, was that it's kind of a songwriting showcase. Is that how you see it?

I think that's an accurate impression, sure. We didn't write it to showcase any set kind of songs—we just kind of ended up with these. I don't know if people still make records like that, but—we did!

One of the things that really comes through on the album is that you guys are having a lot of fun.

Oh, it was a hoot. We had a week of laughs and it was just a good time. I wish we could do it every week!

Another thing I picked up on is that you guys write about some serious topics, but usually with a twist and some humor involved. For example, "Halfway to Happy" is about a pretty twisted relationship, but it has some funny lines. It seems like the best songwriters can find the humor in even the most difficult situation.

Well, that all goes back somewhere to guys like Randy Newman. And don't get me wrong—I love a good ol' dirge, too. I love a good sad song. "Halfway to Happy," you know, I think it caused a little concern in our household. My wife, after she started hearing some of those songs, said "Is everything okay? What's wrong with you these days?" Apparently Craig's wife said much the same. But that's just what came out when we were writing together.

I also read about you guys getting the song "Not a Lot Goin' On" placed as the theme song for a TV show (*Corner Gas*, on CTV). How did that come about?

We both do a lot of TV writing, and that song happened through a phone call from some people we know in the business. They called Craig and Craig called me, and we actually wrote the song over the phone. It's about sort of a hapless, loser guy, and I said, well, let's make it in the key of "E" and we just kind of went from there.

Were there particular groups or songwriters that you and Craig admired and maybe were trying to emulate with this record?

The classic songwriters like Spooner Oldham and Dan Penn, [David] Porter, [Isaac] Hayes—any of the guys who wrote the Memphis songs, the Stax stuff. We were working that vein—that was our inspiration.

You guys played a few shows together in February, but it looks like you have a pretty full touring schedule with the Gin Blossoms for the rest of the summer. Are there plans for more Northey Valenzuela shows?

We're talking about the fall, and I'm also hoping that Craig may come and do some shows with me and the Gin Blossoms. Craig and I are courting the Gin Blossoms about an opening slot. I hope it works out—it'd make my year. Playing with Craig is just a blast, and it sounds great. We bring it down to two acoustics, maybe a bass player, and it just kills. They're still putting together this summer's tour, so we'll have to see.

Did Craig guest at all on the new Gin Blossoms album?

Sadly, no. Craig lives up in Canada, so we don't get together that often. It's mostly by phone. It's too bad—if he lived here, we'd probably get a lot more work done! But we only need a couple of days to get a lot done because we're each pretty keyed in to how the other one writes. We work pretty fast.

Both the Odds [Northey's former group] and the Gin Blossoms have experienced more than their fair share of the perils of the music business. I was wondering, with the benefit of experience and hindsight, if you had any advice for bands trying to break into the business today?

Well, let's see. Where do I start?! I hate to see any young band sign production deals too early. There's a phenomenon in the music business, that's been there forever, which is for someone who's a little bit older and a little bit wiser to come along and find a very talented young group and sign them to a production deal. And then they pay what seems to a young band like the insurmountable amount of money they need to put together a demo. Paying that couple of thousand dollars, the producer gets a good piece of the company going forward. I hate to see bands do that, and it doesn't have to happen anymore, because of the new ProTools recording equipment that's available.

Just don't sell off your stuff too early—and don't do anything your mother wouldn't want you to do. (Laughter) It's a crapshoot, but I do highly recommend it—I think it's a great career, and if you have a good time and you love music, why not give it a try? There are a lot worse things you could do for a living.

No kidding. Now, about that new Gin Blossoms album—not to nag you or anything, but—when is it coming out??

(Laughter) Well, let me tell you about that. The single date is June 5. The record will be out as soon after that as we can make it happen. I've been mixing the record here in Los Angeles, and 10 of the songs are done, and there are two more to be mixed. I hope I'm done with that by the end of next week. Once I have that turned in, the rest is really up to the record company. If they've got a single set for June 5, I have to believe the record comes out about a month after that. That's traditionally how it's done.

Obviously we wish it would've been earlier, but we had to re-record. We originally recorded in Memphis, and it went okay, but the label wasn't completely satisfied, so they asked us to bring some stuff back to Los Angeles and work on it a little bit here. That's what I've been doing for the last four weeks, and it's been tough, because I have a lot of tour dates, as well as my regular recording/producing gig. I've been doing as much as I can with my schedule.

The band must be excited to get some new music out there after all this time.

Yeah! The guys seem genuinely excited about it, and I can't wait to see what happens.

On the new album, did you guys do any co-writing or are the songs mostly individually written?

I think it's pretty traditional Blossoms format. The Gin Blossoms have never really written together that much. Robin [GBs lead vocalist Robin Wilson] and I have written together a few times over the years, and on this record we did write two songs together. But generally everybody writes by themselves, and then we bring it in and it becomes a Gin Blossoms song.

How about the album title? You guys have had a couple of memorable ones in the past [*New Miserable Experience* and *Congratulations, I'm Sorry*], but I've heard this one is going to be self-titled.

Yeah, you know, we have this crazy Gin Blossoms site (www.ginblossoms.net) and on the message boards people were very upset that we weren't going to give it one of the wacky titles we're so well known for, and I thought gosh, we can't get away from that! We were just going to call it *The Gin Blossoms*, but now the record company says it would be better if we had a title. So everybody has their irony bone in overdrive and we're trying to figure out a good title for it.

It's hard to hear that and not go straight to the title of the single— "Learning the Hard Way." That sounds like the Gin Blossoms' autobiography!

That's funny, because the record company wanted to call it *Learning the Hard Way*! And it is the first single and all, but Robin didn't like that idea, so we're back to the drawing board.

Alright, well—that was my shot. (Laughter)

I know! But you're in good company, because all the record company guys thought that was perfect. It does make sense. It reminds me of an article written years ago about the Gin Blossoms in which [bassist] Bill Leen said "This band's been through hell." And the writer said, "If this band has been through hell, they've made their own travel plans." Very true! We just don't know any better, do we?

*

[Postscript: The Gin Blossoms issued Major Lodge Victory *in 2006, followed by* No Chocolate Cake *in 2010. They continue to tour regularly.]*

5

Rants

"MOST OF MY FAVORITE REVIEWS of yours are about albums you hated."

This is an actual quote from a colleague at *The Daily Vault*.

There are degrees of negative reviews, of course. But you won't find many Bs and Cs represented in this volume; those sorts of "pretty good / not bad / just missed it" reviews can be technically interesting, but don't tend to bring out the best in the writing, because in terms of emotional response to the music, there are no bright colors involved, just (to borrow a phrase) fifty shades of grey. The higher and lower grades are where emotion comes into greater play, and the writing begins to sing.

I've given relatively few bad reviews in the past 20 years. In fact, out of more than 700 reviews, I've given exactly one F, four D minuses, and nine Ds. There are good reasons for this.

First, I simply can't be bothered to spend the time required to listen repeatedly to and then analyze an album that doesn't provoke some kind of reaction from me. I have left countless reviews of poor-to-mediocre albums unwritten precisely because they simply weren't worth the effort that would have been required.

Second, with rare exceptions, I won't give a negative review to an unknown artist. What's the point? Someone is struggling along trying to find an audience for their art, and you, the reviewer who can't play a note, are going to come along and piss on their work, just because you can? How does a negative review of an unknown artist contribute anything to the situation, for either audience or artist? It's just mean, and I don't do mean.

So, what you'll find in the pages ahead are negative reviews of established artists. People who (in some cases) have achieved success without achieving self-awareness, perhaps by exploiting the lowest-common-denominator tastes of much of the music-buying public. People who (in some cases) may have gained some measure of fame without really earning it. People who, in the final analysis, really ought to know better.

Those are the artists worth criticizing. And as long as you're going there, I've always figured, you might as well have some fun.

*

A historical footnote: the first three of these reviews were all part of the same month-long retrospective on *The Daily Vault* in June 2006. Retrospectives were a feature we presented monthly for the better part of five years, highlighting either a notable artist's entire catalogue, or highlights from a particular genre or time period of music. In June 2006, our theme was Arena Rock.

Now, I don't have a particular grudge against arena rock—hell, I grew up on the stuff, and can still be found listening to Journey or Boston or Foreigner on occasion with barely a twinge of guilt or irony. But let's face it—as a genre, it was full of overinflated music made by overinflated egos (not to mention overinflated hair). If you're looking for a particular genre of popular music to mock, arena rock is what you might call a target-rich environment.

*

Foreigner
Foreigner
Atlantic, 1977
[Published on *The Daily Vault* 6/12/2006]

When you think of the bands that epitomize arena rock, Foreigner is simply inescapable. Big, simple guitar riffs; big, simple synthesizer melodies; big, simple lyrics; and one big, simple goal behind it all: sell some records, man. Get some chicks, buy some cars, party it up. Just... don't... think... too... hard. The end result is a band that's about as culturally significant as Ronald McDonald.

Foreigner formed around the musical partnership of British guitarist/producer Mick Jones (*not* the guy from The Clash) and American lead singer Lou Gramm, joined by an eclectic collection of supporting players consisting of ex-King Crimson sax player Ian McDonald, ex-Ian Hunter drummer Dennis Elliott, and New Yorkers Al Greenwood (keyboards) and Ed Gagliardi (bass).

With Jones and Gramm writing the songs, the band assembled this debut full of chest-thumping rockers and woe-is-me ballads so musically uncomplicated and frankly commercial as to make their immediate success feel inevitable. Of course the ringing, buoyant "Feels Like The First Time" and the sharp, angry "Cold As Ice" were hits—they're like cartoon cut-outs of rock songs. Opening riff goes here, repeat twice, verse, chorus, flashy bridge, verse, chorus, and close it out with a swelling chorus of collagen-injected background vocals.

To be fair, though, looking back from decades later, this album isn't completely without merit. The main riffs are workmanlike and "Long Long Way From Home" is a standout, with genuine drive and creative incorporation of horns. "The Damage is Done," after a plodding start, actually blossoms nicely mid-song, showing some imagination in its changes. The otherwise pedestrian "Fool for You Anyway" features Gramm's best vocal here, adding a little Motown flavor to his typical cinch-it-up-and-shout delivery.

The sinkhole into which this album ultimately falls, though, is dug by the lyrics, which I'm thinking must have been Jack Black's model for Tenacious D. I mean, how do you keep a straight face singing a line like "I am the captain of this body of mine / I send fear into the enemy lines"? And has there ever been a more put-upon, passive-aggressive, self-pitying pair of wannabe macho men than Jones and Gramm? "Woman oh woman / Don't bury me alive / Just make me feel like I've the right to survive." I dunno, maybe that's what too many meetings with A&R guys does to a musician's self-esteem. All of this of course makes "I Need You" the perfect closer, a sort of co-dependents' national anthem: "Yes I need you / Say you need me too." (Not until you get down on your knees and beg!)

Foreigner would go on to issue several more albums' worth of sad-sack, paint-by-numbers music with Big Rock Riffs Embedded For Your Listening Pleasure, but never managed to top this stupendously mediocre outing. At least when Loverboy issued this same album again a couple of years later, they had a little fun with it.

Rating: C-

*

REO Speedwagon
Hi Infidelity
Epic, 1980
[Published on *The Daily Vault* 6/19/2006]

I've always thought archaeology would be an interesting line of work, and not just because of that Indiana Jones guy. The digging and sifting might get old after a while, but I'm fascinated by the idea of using artifacts to try to understand how a culture evolved.

All of which occurred to me as I attempted to solve the following historical puzzle: just how in the holy hell did this album become a multi-platinum phenomenon?

Let me be clear—I'm not here to bash REO Speedwagon as a band. They put out a respectable amount of respectably good material over the years. But *Hi Infidelity* was unquestionably their commercial pinnacle and, as a prototypical slab of arena rock, the clear pick for our current retrospective. And it's really, really, really, cringe-inducingly bad.

REO started out as a Midwestern college band in 1968 whose early lineup formed around keyboardist Neal Doughty, drummer Alan Gratzer and guitarist Gary Richrath. Their first three albums saw the group burn through three different lead singers, including Kevin Cronin, who was dumped after a single outing for the long-since-forgotten Mike Murphy. Three albums later, Cronin was invited back for 1976's *REO* and the group's fortunes took off. The success of 1977's double-live *You Get What You Play For*, featuring a blazing live version of "Ridin' the Storm Out," set the table for the next studio album, which would also be the first to feature longtime bassist-vocalist Bruce Hall. Their platinum 1978 disc *You Can Tune a Piano, But You Can't Tuna Fish* may have suffered under the weight of a dubious title, but the music sparkled with melody, led by the surging "Roll With the Changes," still a personal favorite from the REO catalog.

Engine thus primed, the Speedwagon came out of the curve and floored it down the straightaway with this album full of Top Ten singles. Top Ten singles... in the year 1980 (you've been warned).

Big Single #1 "Don't Let Him Go" has some drive and drama to it, but also features some of the most godawful bleepity-blip tones ever regurgitated by an '80s keyboard. Following right on its heels, Big Single #2 "Keep on Lovin' You" is a candidate for the ultimate power ballad—for a Spinal Tap fan. Piano, bells, melodramatic lead vocals, big-as-the-sky production values and steroidal background vocals, all coalescing around one of the most brain-dead lyrics ever recorded. "You played dead, but you never bled / Instead you laid (sic) still in the grass all coiled up and hissin'."

Look, it rhymes with "listen," see? Whaddya want here, Robert Frost?

Big Single #3 was "Take It on the Run," whose sturdy descending chorus hook supports a lyric that seems lifted straight out of the Foreigner songbook of Victimized Men Who Really Need to Quit Whining and Get on With Their Lives. As non-violent a person as I normally am, listening to this song makes me want to hit things.

To REO's credit, they aren't a one-trick pony; they do their best to work in a little variety. "In Your Letter" is a sincere if rather limp Brill Building pastiche. "Shakin' It Loose" shoots for rockabilly swagger, though Richrath's fiery leads are undermined by Cronin's airy vocals. "Follow My Heart" starts promisingly, laying down a nice hard-blues groove under the first verse, but then you discover that's all there is — within 30 seconds you're into the Painfully Obvious Chorus (an unfortunate REO specialty), which is repeated enough times to qualify as torture under the Geneva Convention. And ultimately, there's just no redeeming a disc with a song as monumentally dopey and weak-kneed as "Rough Guys" on it.

This album is, in sum, a thundering mediocrity, popular enough in its day to ensure that Cronin, Doughty, Hall and a pair of hired hands are still playing state fairs 25 years later, an artifact of an earlier time whose mores and values we are still struggling to comprehend.

Rating: D+

*

Asia
Asia
Geffen, 1982
[Published on *The Daily Vault* 6/22/2006]

The *Daily Vault* panel has developed a kind of rhythm in recent months when it comes to greeting new recruits. As the new writer gets acclimated and joins our e-mail discussion list, two or three folks on the panel will wish them well—and then, with perfect comic timing, Jeff Clutterbuck will chime in with this tongue-in-cheek piece of advice: "Just leave your soul at the door and everything will be fine."

I have no idea what Geffen Records' A&R rep said to the four guys in Asia when he signed them, but "leave your souls at the door" seems like a decent guess.

Asia's inaugural lineup of guitarist Steve Howe (Yes), drummer Carl Palmer (ELP), keyboard player Geoff Downes (Buggles/Yes) and bassist/lead vocalist John Wetton (King Crimson, Roxy Music, UK) collectively constituted one of the premier assemblages of pure musical talent ever convened. With those pedigrees, fans had every right to anticipate a brilliant set of complex, multilayered progressive rock.

Except.

Except these four players had by 1982 all apparently tired of slugging it out in the cerebral, musically challenging prog bands that had fallen out of favor during the punk/new wave era. They'd been in the music business long enough to understand how the game worked, and what it might take to get back on the radio.

Thus was born Asia, a group that sounds like Yes, King Crimson and ELP teaming up to record a Survivor tribute album.

To give them credit, they nailed their demographic. Spandexed arena rock fanboys and girls flicked their lighters by the thousands to "Heat of the Moment" and "Only Time Will Tell," turning a quartet of aging prog-rockers into 1982's Next Big Thing. If only there was one single redeeming feature about this album after you get past the Roger Dean cover.

Alright, there may be one or two things. Numbers like "Time Again" and "Cutting It Fine" do offer little teases of a more complex prog approach to the music before lapsing into lame Top 40 schlock. And while I've said some pretty harsh things over the years about Steve Howe's willingness to take this ride, after listening to this disc again I'm willing to offer this mea culpa: Howe's nimble runs on the fretboard are actually the highlight of the album.

That said, it amounts to lipstick on a pig. This album is as creatively bankrupt as they come, full of trite lyrics, bland melodies and melodramatic arrangements that only amplify the stench this stuff is letting off. Bombast works when the music is actually grand; here it sounds like nothing quite so much as musical reputations crumbling before your ears.

If you want specifics, we could go into excruciating detail about the utter saccharin pretentiousness of "Only Time Will Tell" and "One Step Closer," Wetton's awful can't-hit-the-note singing on numbers like "Sole Survivor," and the truly embarrassing "we fight / for king / and country" chorused background vocals on "Wildest Dreams"—but frankly, I don't get paid enough for that.

Rating: D

*

Starship
Greatest Hits (Ten Years And Change 1979-1991)
BMG, 1991
[Published on *The Daily Vault* 12/18/2007]

Like the musical acts who create them, some albums need to exist and some just plain don't.

Starship is a group that should have ceased to exist in 1988, if it should ever have existed at all. And yet here in Northern California, every year I continue to see nightclub and casino ads listing "Starship featuring Mickey Thomas" among their future shows. Therein lies the story of this album.

Starship came into being in 1985, when Paul Kantner finally decamped what remained of the group he had founded as Jefferson Airplane in the '60s and continued as Jefferson Starship through the late '70s and early '80s. The catch was, the rest of the then-current lineup still wanted to stay together. One lawsuit and one settlement later, Kantner walked off into the sunset with the name Jefferson Starship in his pocket, while the remainder of the band—which by then consisted of Mickey Thomas (vocals) Craig Chaquico (guitars), Pete Sears (bass), Donny Baldwin (drums) and longtime Kantner foil Grace Slick (vocals)—forged onward known simply as Starship.

A reasonable solution in theory. The problem is, from that point forward the band continued to disintegrate album by album until by 1991 you had Mickey Thomas recording under the name Starship with no one but himself left who had ever been in Jefferson Starship. Grace Slick—who after the settlement held a 51 percent interest in the name Starship—could have stopped the madness when she left in 1988, but for whatever reason, she opted not to play the heavy.

Among other things, her failure to act resulted in this 1991 travesty of a greatest hits album. Basically, this album highlights the "Mickey Thomas years"—like there was any great groundswell of demand for that to happen—of the two different groups for which he was male lead vocalist between 1979 and 1991.

The first five cuts here are taken from the final three releases issued by the 1978-1984 edition of Jefferson Starship, *Freedom At Point Zero*, *Modern Times* and *Nuclear Furniture*. This opening salvo includes hit singles "Jane" and "Find Your Way Back," cuts which still sparkle with a guilty-pleasure arena-rock sheen almost 30 years later, making them the clear highlights of the Thomas years. Chaquico in particular shines, banging out muscular leads and shearing solos that contrast markedly with his later reinvention as an acoustic New Age artist.

Ah, but it's all downhill from there. The minute Kantner left, any balance or tension between his iconoclastic vision and Thomas' distinctly Top 40 mindset ended, as did any attempt by the band at writing its own songs. The result was a series of increasingly slick, soulless, empty-headed singles like the over-caffeinated synth-pop anthem "We Built This City"—once named the Worst Song Ever by *Blender* magazine—and the sickeningly syrupy power ballad "Sara." Both of which went to number one, of course, but if ever there was proof that quantity doesn't equal quality, these two songs and the flaccid, Diane Warren-penned schlock-fest "Nothing's Gonna Stop Us Now" would do it. Hard to imagine, but if you survive that trio, the music actually gets worse after that.

As you move through the four latest songs here, from 1987, '89, '90 and '91, the band sheds one member after another, with drummer Donny Baldwin's 1989 departure being the most notable other than Grace Slick's, in that it followed a physical confrontation between him and Thomas that landed the latter in the hospital. (Hey, if my drums sounded as processed-cheese-y as Baldwin's did by then, I'd probably want to hit something, too…)

By the last track, the credits list Thomas and a cadre of hired hands, including "We Built This City" co-composers Peter Wolf (the Zappa keyboard player, not the J. Geils Band frontman) and Martin Page. As each member leaves you can feel the foundation crumbling out from under what had already become an empty shell. Closer "Good Heart," recorded for this disc in 1991, is unintentionally ironic; if the guy singing it had one, he would have long since shut things down and moved on.

Greatest Hits is neither the greatest hits of Jefferson Starship—since it doesn't include any pre-Mickey Thomas JS singles like "Miracles" or "Play on Love"—nor the greatest hits of Starship, since they didn't issue enough material post-Kantner to rate a hits collection all their own. Instead, this album was the musical equivalent of *Weekend at Bernie's*—Mickey Thomas and the group's label propping up the corpse of a long-departed band and trying to con people into believing it was still alive.

Rating: D+

*

Yes
Big Generator
Atco, 1987
[Published on *The Daily Vault* 7/2/2008]

Ever watched a scene in a movie or TV show that in hindsight you really wish you'd fast-forwarded through? It can be like that with albums, too.

After a 21-year holdout, I decided the other night while browsing through the used section of my local music emporium that my life as a Yes fan simply was not complete without a full listen to *Big Generator*. I of course had heard the singles on the radio and had them plus an album track or two in my musical library thanks to the band's two boxed sets. But I'd never heard the full album in sequence, or heard a couple of its more obscure cuts at all.

And so, I thought to myself, how bad could it be? I mean, I made it through *Tormato*. I survived *Union*. It's the same lineup—Jon Anderson, Trevor Rabin, Chris Squire, Tony Kaye and Alan White—that made *90125*, which, well, didn't suck. For seven bucks used, why not give it a shot?

How many reasons do you want?

There are moments of not-suck-ness, granted. Leadoff cut "Rhythm of Love" is the obvious analog to *90125's* big hit "Owner of a Lonely Heart," a slick but appealing slab of arena rock with layered harmonies and little stabbing orchestral flourishes dressing the edges. The airy, intriguing "Shoot High Aim Low" features perhaps the best arrangement ever of the Anderson-Rabin dueling lead vocals that characterized this era of Yes. And Rabin's solo composition "Love Will Find a Way" is obvious commercial AOR fodder, even if it doesn't really seem to have much to do with Yes.

But! The rest of this shambling disaster of an album verges on unlistenable. "Big Generator" sounds like a lost episode of *Jon Anderson Sings the Night Ranger Songbook*; I would rather have my ears chewed off by rabid squirrels than be forced to listen to this song again. "Almost Like Love" has all the jittering musicality of a caffeine-induced seizure; there's no word for it but embarrassing. And "I'm Running" shoots for epic but comes off like a complete psychotic break, a blithering flood of incomprehensible lyrics over a neck-snapping barrage of musical snippets that seem related only in their artificiality and triteness.

As for the Anderson closer "Holy Lamb (Song for Harmonic Convergence)," one can imagine the dialogue in the studio as they argued. Anderson: "Trevor got a song that was all his own, so I get one too." Squire: "Yes, Jon, alright, fair enough, but does it have to be THAT one?" Rabin: "You've got to be frigging kidding me." If this song were any more fingernails-on-the-chalkboard twee, it would simply curl up and vanish in a puff of smoke.

Three passable songs are not nearly enough to rescue this sinkhole of an album. The idea that the group that released this disc is in any way related to the group that issued *Close to the Edge* seems preposterous—and the fact that it is, merely sad.

Nothing to see here, folks. Move along. Nothing to see.

Rating: D

*

Bruce Hornsby
Harbor Lights
BMG Music, 1993
[Published on *The Daily Vault* 10/13/1998]

I always try to give an artist the benefit of the doubt when they decide to try something new. For many casual fans, a change in approach makes them lose interest; I've always tried to be more flexible, and, I suppose, loyal to someone whose work I've enjoyed in the past. I guess I figure once they've given me a certain amount of pleasure, they've earned the right to test my patience a little.

For example: I'm not crazy about Bruce Springsteen's *Nebraska* album, but I admire its audacity. I thought U2's *Pop* was downright annoying musically, but admit the lyrics are as good as anything they've ever done. And then there's Yes, a band that seems to virtually alternate between great and terrible albums... and yet, I keep buying them.

But five years later, I still haven't managed to forgive Bruce Hornsby for *Harbor Lights*.

Hornsby's 1986 debut *The Way It Is* was an overdue breath of fresh air in the plasticized '80s—the rich, rolling acoustic piano melodies; the evocative lyrics, full of images of small-town life along the Virginia coast; the seamless construction of the songs; and the precision of Hornsby's tight band, The Range. The follow-up *Scenes From the Southside* was, if anything, even better, a hugely engaging and resonant song cycle of life in the South in the late 1980s. 1990's *A Night On the Town* took the band toward a looser sound, with less care spent on the lyrics and more on the solos, and represented a step down on the quality scale in my mind.

Then, with *Harbor Lights*, Hornsby took a swan dive off the platform.

Apparently, at some point Hornsby decided simply playing sweet melodies within the confines of well-constructed songs didn't allow him enough room to display his notable prowess on the keyboard. So, he seems to have said to himself, the hell with structure, the hell with melody, the hell with the fans and even the hell with the band... let's just stick a rhythm section in the back to keep the beat and I'll start playing my frigging fingers off, and for fun maybe invite in a few guests like fusion guitarist Pat Metheny and my old pal Jerry Garcia to jam along with me.

To Hornsby, I suspect *Harbor Lights* felt like a declaration of independence. You know, "I scored my hits, got the multi-album deal from the label, and now I'm going to do whatever I damn well please musically." Well, what he does on *Lights* may have pleased him (it must have, since he's followed that musical path ever since), but for a fan of the likes of "Mandolin Rain" and "The Valley Road," there's precious little to cheer about here.

The gorgeous, flowing piano lines and tight folk-pop arrangements of his first two albums are banished almost completely; in their place is a fragmented, painfully self-conscious style that seems to be trying to cram juking, atonal jazz rhythms and wandering instrumental passages into his old song structure. As Hornsby himself confesses in the liner notes, on this album "no one ever accused us of playing one note when five would do."

In places it's almost interesting, watching Hornsby stretch. The title song has its moments early on, when he lets the band play like they mean it, building up momentum into the initial choruses. But just when you think it's about time to wrap up and get out, he blows the whole deal by veering off into first a horribly off-key piano bridge and then an aimless two-minute instrumental break where he trades pretty but irrelevant solos with Metheny.

Next up, "Talk of the Town" reveals a change in Hornsby's approach to singing that's as unwelcome as the change in his approach to the songs themselves. Rather than employing the soaring vocal energy that brought his first two albums to life, he plays laid-back soul man, burying what could have been a meaningful pop tune about an interracial romance in a unwieldy jazz-singer pose full of staccato rhythms and sing-song spoken vocals, a style that brutally wastes his voice's capabilities.

The rest of the album amounts to more of the same. "China Doll" resembles the title track in that it starts off strong but then runs off the tracks into a series of purposeless instrumental breaks. Here his herky-jerky piano fills and two-handed "Aren't I something?" solos are nothing short of grating, and Metheny's patched-in guitar run is sharp but thoroughly out of place.

"Fields of Gray" shows the most promise, building up a nice head of steam melody-wise—until he hands the solo off to a string quartet. I mean, why stop there? Why not throw in the frigging USC Marching Band (with all due apologies to Fleetwood Mac)? The six-and-a-half-minute, unintentionally ironic "Pastures of Plenty" closes the album, its three-minute lyric all but obliterated by a series of bloated, chronically self-indulgent solos from Hornsby and special guest noodler Garcia.

Overall, *Harbor Lights* shows Hornsby turning his back on everything that made him such a pleasure to listen to on his first two albums. The songs lack resonance, the solos lack restraint, and the entire exercise lacks the kind of polished craftsmanship that made his early music such a pleasurable listen. Instead, you get Hornsby and his pals swinging, jiving, jamming and overplaying to their hearts' content, satisfying no one but themselves.

Rating: D

*

Pat Boone
In A Metal Mood: No More Mr. Nice Guy
Hip-O Records, 1997
[Published on *The Daily Vault* 11/30/1998]

Lock up your children and round up some supplies for the old bomb shelter, because I think the televangelists might just get their wish this time—if Pat Boone remaking "Stairway to Heaven" as a big band jazz waltz isn't a sure sign of impending Armageddon, I can't imagine what would be.

That said, this album is actually amazing in a couple of respects beyond its mere existence. First, because Boone himself takes the whole thing deadly seriously throughout—his liner notes on the project run to a couple of thousand words, including all manner of earnest suggestions to the effect that "this unprecedented mix of milk and metal may win over a whole new audience for these very worthy songs."

And second, because, whether with tongue in cheek or not (it's hard to tell), some well-known metal-heads actually appear in the studio to egg Boone on. Ritchie Blackmore himself shows up to pound out a few chords of his immortal head-banging lead guitar on Deep Purple's "Smoke on the Water"—at least before Pat carries the whole thing down into a fearsome netherworld of breathless William Shatner-like emoting.

The liner notes also reference at length the grand time Boone had swapping stories on a tour bus with Alice Cooper, author of the title tune. (Can't you just hear them now? Pat: "Oh, yeah, I know just what you mean, I had to bait a rat in my garage once..." Alice: "No, not bait. I ate a rat. On stage. A live one.")

A quick run-through of the lowlights: Ozzy Osbourne's "Crazy Train" is made over as a gentle trombone and trumpet swing that breaks into what could only be termed a spastic staccato beat at the unintentionally hilarious chorus; Hendrix's classic "The Wind Cries Mary" gets a surreal, horn-heavy lounge jazz treatment, with nary an electric guitar in earshot; and in one of the most bizarre moments in musical history, Boone attempts to transform the Guns N' Roses stomper "Paradise City" into a double-time big band scat, inspiring visions of Axl Rose in a torn-up tux chasing Boone across the stage with a meat cleaver.

I'm pretty sure it was midway through AC/DC's "It's a Long Way to the Top (If You Wanna Rock'n'Roll)"—somewhere between "Gettin' drunk, gettin' stoned / gettin' beat up, broken boned" and "If you think it's easy doin' one night stands / try playin' in a rock'n'roll band"—when I first started laughing hysterically.

Still, my favorite moment was definitely deep in the heart of Van Halen's "Panama" (redone in classic big band fashion, loaded with horns and a chorus of female background vocalists), when our man Pat goes into David Lee Roth's mid-song, famously lascivious spoken break. Here was the big test: "I can barely see the road from the heat comin' off of it... think I'll just reach down here... ease the seat back... fasten my seat belt..."

Okay, I guess maybe we can call off Armageddon. But just imagine if Pat Boone had actually said "I reach dooooown betweeeeeen my leeeegs...

(pregnant pause) ...and ease the seat back. Ahhhhhh." Why, the earth would surely have split open right there and then.

Rating: F

*

John Mayer
Battle Studies
Columbia, 2009
[Published on *The Daily Vault* 3/2/2011]

"I've gone from being a musician to being a celebrity. And when people do that, their work usually suffers."
-- John Mayer, Playboy interview, March 2010

Dear John,

You seemed like a decent enough guy until we really got to know you.

Sure, I ripped your folk-pop debut *Room for Squares*, but then you made writers like me eat crow when you followed it with the considerably more muscular and insightful *Heavier Things*, and I ended up heaping praise on the superb and remarkably mature *Continuum*. You recommitted yourself to the music, integrated Clapton-style blues-pop into your songwriting, and the results were damned impressive.

Unfortunately, in the wake of *Continuum*, your life outside of music descended into tabloid hell. Suddenly you were more famous for who you were dating than what you were singing. And the infamous *Playboy* interview from which the above quote is taken surely didn't help. Publicly announcing that "My biggest dream is to write pornography," declaring your preference for masturbation, and dropping the n-word while discussing why your penis prefers white women? If (as you also mention in the interview), you don't like having people assume that you're a douchebag, why act like one?

But what about the music? In that same TMI-peppered interview you also talked about how you've devoted yourself to music since age 13 with a pure and relentless intention that makes it all the more remarkable that you would allow something as ephemeral as fame to not just interfere with your creative life, but hijack it. The musical end result of this tumultuous period in your life, *Battle Studies*, is a stunning contradiction, a musically

128

rich and sophisticated album that is at its core a Hollywood-blockbuster-scale pity party, so full of both self-regard and self-pity as to verge on parody.

If only you were kidding.

The melodramatic, endlessly self-referential album-opener "Heartbreak Warfare" informs your audience, fresh from reading of your latest dalliance with the latest nubile knockout in your life, that you "Dream of ways to make you understand my pain." Really? This, from a guy who says in the *Playboy* interview that "There have probably been days when I saw 300 vaginas before I got out of bed"? Dude. Listen to yourself.

And yet you can't let your victim complex go, and deploy every tool in your considerable musical toolbox to hammer home your points. Much like "Heartbreak Warfare," the weepy "All We Ever Do is Say Goodbye" is catchy as hell, a crisp, clean, beautifully arranged and produced ballad with lyrics that make me nauseous, if only because of the inescapable context surrounding them.

That at times overwhelming meta-ness only accelerates when Taylor Swift guests on "Half of My Heart," a song that at least demonstrates frank self-knowledge when you declare that "Half of my heart is the part of me that's never truly loved anything." (A diagnosis that I dare say young Dr. Swift would agree with; the only thing she seems to have gotten out of her dalliance with you is songwriting material.)

But the worst is yet to come. In this album's alleged single, you ask "Who says I can't get stoned / Call up a girl that I used to know / Fake love for an hour or so / Who says I can't get stoned." Who says, John? Well, for one, YOUR CONSCIENCE—if you still have one.

What kills me, though, John, is the way you manage to back even the most self-worshipping lyric on the entire album—the thoroughly regrettable "Perfectly Lonely"—with deliciously sharp and sophisticated blues-pop, supported once again by ace sidemen Steve Jordan (drums/production) and Pino Palladino (bass). "Had a little love but I spread it thin / Falling in her arms and out again / Made a bad name for my game 'round town / Tore out my heart, shut it down." There it is, the essence of this album: poor John, making the best of it after being victimized by the unreasonable expectations of these women who inexplicably get upset when you sleep with them and then toss them aside like used Kleenex.

Let's play devil's advocate for a moment, though, John. Willful disregard for the consequences of your actions is not the same thing as actually asking for the tabloids to overexpose you and make it impossible for the listener to separate your art from your life. But honestly, what did you expect? You can't go out with Hollywood stars, incessantly tweet and serially overshare, and then ask people to pity you for all the scrutiny you've received as a result. You bear as much responsibility as they do.

You didn't really cross the line from embarrassingly self-indulgent to creepy, though, John, until you got to "Assassin." "Little did I know the girl was an assassin too" you sing, equating a failed attempt to forge a relationship with trying to kill each other. Not that you're likely to experience a successful relationship anytime soon, given that you can't even seem to tolerate the thought of spending the night: "You get in, you get done, and then you get gone / You never leave a trace or show your face, you get gone."

I'll give you this, though. You did a great job taking on Hendrix's "Axis of Love" on *Continuum*, and your version of the Robert Johnson classic "Crossroads," made famous by your acknowledged idol Mr. Clapton, is rich and soulful, even if that renders it out of sync tonally with everything else on this album.

I wonder, John, did you see this album as your opportunity to respond to your critics? If so, how does a line like this one from "Edge of Desire" — "I want you so bad, I go back on the things I believe" — help your case? Though I suppose as long as you're coming to the realization that you're a hypocrite with no real core values, you might as well own it.

And the titles, John… the titles. *Battle Studies*? "Heartbreak Warfare"? "Assassin"? "War of My Life"? Did it never occur to you that America has been in a real-life shooting war for the past decade and that comparing your travails in the bedroom to armed conflict in which people are dying every day might be just a wee bit disrespectful?

What I'm left with in the end, John, is the strong impression that *Continuum* was just a feint, a momentary façade of maturity that masked the truth revealed by *Battle Studies*: that underneath you remain at heart an immature narcissist, a doe-eyed, Grammy-winning, platinum-selling, star-bedding lothario who we should all feel sorry for because you're so, you know, misunderstood.

Musically, *Battle Studies* is smartly crafted, beautifully arranged and expertly produced. All it lacks is a soul, a conscience, and a reason to care. Two words, John: grow up.

Rating: C

*

Dream Theater
Awake
EastWest Records, 1994
[Published on *The Daily Vault* 4/1/2004]

One of the fun parts of the music reviewer gig is learning about artists I've never listened to from my fellow writers. On a regular basis I sit up and take notice as one of my colleagues waxes eloquent about a band or disc that's completely new to me. Sometimes I even go out and buy it, or another disc by the artist in question. Sometimes I even find myself very glad at having done so.

And sometimes not. (Can't win 'em all.)

Dream Theater is considered a paragon of a genre that I really ought to enjoy, prog-metal. I mean, I love both Yes (the progressive stuff, anyway) and old-guard heavy metal bands like Led Zeppelin and Montrose. So, upon spotting *Awake* in the bargain bin at my local music emporium (the bricks-and-mortar kind, 'member those?), I decided to go for it.

In some ways, it was just what I was looking for. This is, beyond a doubt, a very talented group. John Petrucci (guitars), John Myung (bass), Kevin Moore (keys) and Mike Portnoy (drums) each proved to me in the first three minutes of opener "6:00" that they are technically proficient musicians. The playing is tight and fast and frequently impressive. Trevor Rabin would be very proud. (Classic Yes fans who know me are grinning already.)

Indeed, the musicianship is quite notable. It's the music itself that makes me want to cover every bodily orifice I possess in hopes that no sound will get in.

If this is the best I can expect from prog-metal, thanks but no thanks. Quality prog music takes a series of musical themes and twists them into sonic taffy, varying, embellishing and extrapolating on them. The best heavy metal meshes brawn and melody into an immeasurably potent blast. *Awake*, however, doesn't evidence any of the elements I enjoy in either of the referenced genres. Instead, it combines the worst aspects of both—the self-indulgent instrumental excesses of the weakest prog, paired with the disjointed lyrics and tone-deaf vocals of the worst heavy metal.

Awake, it must be said, is wankery of the first order. This isn't music; this is musicians showing off. Virtually every song here is from the "Hey look at me!" school of composition, full of overblown chords and time and tempo shifts that serve the ego, not the song. As if that wasn't bad enough, this disc features some of the lamest lead vocals I've heard in years.

"Innocence Faded" in particular sounds like bad pop-metal with progressive pretensions, sort of like a merger between the lowest ebbs of Kansas, Poison and Toto, with one of the seventeen utterly forgettable Rainbow vocalists who followed Ronnie James Dio sitting in. Except, not that good.

As for the other tracks, I'd seriously consider trying to use the throbby/screechy opening section of "The Mirror" to scare the aggressive neighbor cat out of our yard tonight, if I wasn't concerned about the neighbors calling the cops on me. If the mindlessly repeating chords didn't get him, the really-bad-Dio-imitation vocals surely would.

Oops, almost forgot to mention the lyrics, and that would be a mistake given the presence of gems like "Love is an act of blood and I'm bleeding / a pool in the shape of a heart" and "Mother Mary quite contrary / Kiss the boys and make them wary." The annual fake Hemingway writing contest has nothing on these guys.

Awake is empirical proof that putting a group of technically skilled musicians in a well-equipped studio is no guarantee of getting worthwhile results. Shallow, pompous and strangely passion-free, this album is, quite simply, a waste of time and talent.

Rating: D

*

Angie Aparo
The American
Melisma Records, 2000
[Published on *The Daily Vault* 2/13/2003]

Sometimes artists whose songs get turned into hits by others are underappreciated geniuses (e.g. John Hiatt, Matraca Berg). And sometimes they just get mind-bendingly, two-time Lotto-winner lucky.

One more piece of evidence for the latter arrived over the holidays, in the form of Angie Aparo's 2000 release *The American*. My friend Dave, something of a country fan, took note of the fact that Faith Hill's mega-hit "Cry" was written by Aparo and first appeared on this album. That, plus the fact it was produced by Matchbox Twenty producer-in-residence Matt Serletic seemed to offer enough promise to make it a gift.

Indeed, the opening "Green and Gold" has its intriguing moments, matching Serletic's trademark crystal-clear sound, textured loop effects and fat guitar hooks with a moderately ambitious environmentalist lyric. Aparo's vocals are nothing if not powerful as he demonstrates strong range and some nice phrasing in the quieter moments.

And that's the album in a nutshell. Superbly clear, slightly gimmicky production, fat guitars and dramatic vocals. (Oh, God, you're really going to make me finish this, aren't you? Fine, but first I have to apologize to Dave. I know you meant well, and I swear I gave it several tries. But...)

Alrighty, then. After listening to this entire album several times, I have come to the inescapable conclusion that Mr. Aparo should thank his lucky stars that Faith Hill liked his song. Because, while the guy has a boomer of a voice, what he does with it alarms as often as it impresses.

One of his biggest handicaps is that, as a lyricist, he's a heck of singer. "A spaceship landed by the mall / There was a big parade / Everybody got laid / And they burned all the books and the Chevrolets." No, really, that's straight off the lyric sheet. Hey, buddy, you getting any oxygen in that vocal booth?

Well, then, let's cut straight to the prime point of curiosity about this album—how does "Cry" sound done by the original (male) artist? Mostly, it gives you a good idea what the song would sound like done by Michael Bolton, or maybe even Cher. If Aparo's delivery was any farther over the top he'd fall off the other side. (Never mind that the song itself is a creepy little jab of self-pity and resentment.)

The Foreigner-circa-1979 synth solo on "Third Time Around" is at least a laughable distraction from Aparo's continuous over-emoting. But we aren't so lucky on "Free Man," where Aparo blasts right through the walls of common sense and lets loose with his own version of the infamous Neil Diamond bray. If I had a dog, this is about when it would likely have run whimpering from the room.

Speaking of old Neil, ever had a hankering to hear him try sing-songy rapping? That's roughly what the verses of "Beautiful" sound like. It's almost enough to distract you from lyrics as awful as "Suzy burned for the admiration / And the cocaine urn Social Confirmation / On the water bed / Staring at the ceiling while her halo bled." Please, someone, make it stop.

The production is, well, just what you'd expect from Mr. Matchbox Twenty. And in truth, I have no argument with crafting dramatic soundscapes—swelling synths, chirpy loops, beefy guitars, etc.—if they're put into service backing a strong song. In the context of these songs, though, the production feels overdone as a charcoaled steak.

Interestingly, there's one other passable track here, the (nominally) hidden title cut. "The American" features Aparo giving a relatively restrained performance over acoustic guitar, piano and strings. He still slips into Diamond-isms in a few places, and the lyric is somewhat muddled, but it's a decent listen that makes you wonder what he might sound like with a stripped-down sound and some help with lyrics.

So, better luck next time, Angie Aparo. My advice is to work on the songs, modulate the delivery, say goodbye to Matchbox-boy, and keep sending Faith Hill roses until Tim McGraw makes you stop.

Rating: D-

*

Maroon 5
Overexposed
A&M/Octone, 2012
[Published on *The Daily Vault* 7/4/2012]

First things first: auto-tune should be effing illegal. If I want to listen to someone singing like a freaking robot, I'll put on an old Kraftwerk album.

If only that were the extent of the problems with *Overexposed*, the fourth studio album—well, kinda sorta, you'll see—from once-upon-a-time neo-soul prodigies Maroon 5. Back in 2002, this quintet came along with a fresh sound—poppy to be sure, but full of the groove and genuine emotion evidenced on early hits like "Harder to Breathe" and "She Will Be Loved." Frontman Adam Levine in particular had an outstanding voice capable of swerving effortlessly between a pleasant tenor and a soaring falsetto.

As the years have worn on, though, the band has begun to founder. First drummer Ryan Dusick left, then Levine distanced himself from the group a bit by joining the panel of *American Idol* knockoff *The Voice*. Most recently founding keyboardist Jesse Carmichael, co-composer with Levine of the bulk of the group's songbook up until now, took a leave of absence for this album.

This album which, in the final analysis, isn't really a Maroon 5 album at all, but rather an Adam Levine solo disc. It's hard to come to any other conclusion after listening to a series of tracks where everyone in the group other than Levine is barely present. "One More Night" and "Payphone" might feature solid beats and a certain shiny appeal—marred in the latter case by a head-shaking amount of entirely gratuitous profanity—but these songs have virtually nothing to do with Maroon 5. They're densely produced synth-pop numbers populated with drum machines and programming, devoid of any of the sharp ensemble playing the group manifested on earlier albums, and in fact bereft of the very things that made Maroon 5 appealing in the first place: soul, emotion, sincerity.

His voice auto-tuned just shy of Alvin the Chipmunk territory, Levine for much of this album literally sounds like he's singing through a circuit board. On most of these tracks it's impossible to even detect an organic instrument or voice; it's heavily processed electronic drums plus densely layered synthesizers plus heavily processed vocals equals 100 percent sheen.

Even when you can detect (barely) actual non-synthesized instruments, as on the driving "Lucky Strike," there isn't a single note that hasn't been tweaked to death by a computer. "The Man Who Never Lied" is worse yet, a paint-by-numbers songwriting crapfest with less originality than your average used car commercial. (By this point I was taking careful notes on the thundering herds of co-writers and producers deployed on these tracks to make sure I never purchase another album on which they are featured.)

When M5 finally do step off the dance floor and away from the auto-tune, it's for a limp, forgettable piano ballad aptly named "Sad." Even that awkward respite is a brief one, though; the next two tracks are pure formula songwriting, piling the "enough of dancing in this club, let's go home and get busy" clichés to the ceiling. At least closer "Beautiful Goodbye" isn't another formulaic dance tune; it's simply an innocuous, lightweight pop ballad with all the substance of a snowflake.

Overexposed is the first album on which Maroon 5 sounds more like a brand than a band—just another faceless, homogenized, computerized, plasticized pop machine. Ten years ago, Adam Levine was a terrific white-soul singer with a hot band and a promising debut album under his belt. Ten years from now, he'll be that cheesy "Moves Like Jagger" guy who used to be on *The Voice*. Apparently he thinks that's trading up. "Sad," indeed.

Rating: D-

*

Styx
Regeneration Volume I & II
Eagle Records, 2011
[Published on *The Daily Vault* 10/5/2011]

"Give me a job, give me security / Give me a chance to survive"
-- *"Blue Collar Man"*

If forced to select a single word to describe this album, I would choose "unnecessary."

It's hard to know what to think these days about the raft of surviving '70s and '80s bands, chugging along mining the nostalgia circuit—the current triple bill of Journey, Foreigner and Night Ranger being a prime example. I mean, everybody's got to make a living, and it surely hasn't gotten any easier in recent years, whether you're located inside or outside of the shambling ruin that is the modern music industry. While it can be strange and sometimes disheartening to watch longtime bands become increasingly hollow shells, gate-collecting jukeboxes churning out the hits with two or three or four original members conspicuously absent, it's a perfectly rational decision to make if you're straddling sixty with no other marketable talents.

So what you get, more and more, is bands with just enough of the original juice left to keep soaking their fans' wallets a little longer. Increasingly, these patched-together groups have resorted to re-recording the old hits that have kept them viable for the past 25 years with their current lineup, as if to prove to the world they can still make that same familiar sound even though X or Y or Z (or all three) are no longer with the band. (And not incidentally, so that the current lineup can benefit from whatever album sales they may be able to eke out.)

Styx is a Chicago band from way back, having formed in 1972 around the rhythm section of brothers Chuck and John Panozzo and lead vocalist/keyboardist Dennis DeYoung. Help soon arrived in the form of guitarist/vocalists James "JY" Young and John Curulewski, and this five-man lineup persisted three moderately successful years until Curulewski abruptly exited and was replaced by Tommy Shaw. The band's classic lineup then produced a string of hit singles ("Babe," "Come Sail Away," "Crystal Ball," "Renegade") and albums (*The Grand Illusion, Pieces of Eight, Paradise Theater*) that virtually created the template for arena rock, tempering the group's initial prog leanings in favor of soaring power ballads and thundering, mostly predictable rockers.

136

The ensuing internal drama provided abundant material for one of the best episodes of *Behind the Music* in the show's history, so I won't belabor it, but suffice it to say that 1983 was the last time DeYoung and Shaw managed to tolerate being in the group at the same time for more than a brief reunion or two. Since 2003, Shaw and Young have anchored a lineup that includes latter-day tap-ins Lawrence Gowan (a DeYoung soundalike) on keys and vocals, Ricky Phillips on bass, and Todd Sucherman on drums. Founding bassist Chuck Panozzo also sits in from time to time on tour, and on this album (brother John passed away in 1996). The group's one-sheet proudly notes that the current quintet plus one has now "been together longer than any other lineup in the band's 40-year existence"—a declaration of victory of sorts for the Shaw-Young camp. Whatever, guys.

Regeneration, Volumes I & II is an album consisting primarily of re-recordings of Styx classics by the current lineup—basically a replication of their current live set in the studio. I would compare the results to an omelet made with fake eggs; it kind of looks the same, kind of smells the same, and kind of tastes the same, but it's definitely not the same. It's not that these re-recordings are in any way sub-par. They are professionally done and in most cases remarkably similar to the originals. For exactly that reason, they are fundamentally unnecessary. The best recordings ever issued of "The Grand Illusion," "Fooling Yourself (The Angry Young Man)," "Lorelei," "Sing For the Day," "Blue Collar Man," "Too Much Time on My Hands" and all the rest already exist, and these aren't them.

There is exactly one new song to be found here, "Difference in the World," and it does nothing to promote the idea of Styx returning to a recording studio anytime soon. The only other "new" content consists of Styx versions of two Tommy Shaw tunes that he carried back from his early '90s band Damn Yankees; I wish he hadn't. "Coming of Age" is generic, dated arena rock, and "High Enough" is a power ballad so flaccid a double-dose of Viagra couldn't help it.

Does this album succeed in demonstrating that the current touring lineup can reproduce the sound of classic Styx accurately and professionally? Indeed it does. Will this album help Shaw, Young et al to sell concert tickets as they continue the stretch drive to top off their retirement savings accounts? Indeed it will. Is there any other conceivable reason for this album to exist? Not really.

Rating: D

~Segue~

Interview: Billy Sherwood

[Published on *The Daily Vault* 9/17/2007)

Progressive rock fans—and perhaps especially Yes fans—are a breed apart. Deeply devoted and often just as deeply opinionated, they have a tendency to put the fan in "fanatic." But what happens when you put two lifelong Yes fans on the phone, one a music writer and the other a longtime prog musician and—to his own lasting amazement and pride—former member of Yes?

The topic at hand was the new album by Circa, a fresh conglomeration of Yes associates past and present that includes Billy Sherwood on bass and vocals, Tony Kaye on keyboards, Alan White on drums and Jimmy Haun on guitars. The group sprang from a collaboration between interviewee Sherwood—multi-instrumentalist, singer-songwriter, producer and longtime Yes collaborator—and founding member of Yes Kaye. And while we covered a lot of ground related to Circa, Billy also took the time to share stories from his time in Yes, delve into the mechanics of record-making in the digital age, and release his inner prog fan long enough to wonder at the places his musical path has taken him. A good time was had by all!

The Daily Vault: There's sort of an obvious question here to start off with. With all four members of Circa having played on Yes albums at one time or another, three of you having been in the band, and Tony Kaye having been a founding member, it seems impossible to talk about Circa without talking about Yes, too. And my sense is that you're all fine with that, that you really welcome people drawing (pardon the pun) parallels between Circa and Yes.

Billy Sherwood: Well, as you said, we all lived in that band for years, and so it's natural that when you get this mix of people together, it's going to generate that kind of music. It's not meant to be Yes, it's meant to be Circa, but obviously the music we make together has a very Yes flavor. And that's fine with us, because that's who we are and where we've been and it's in all of our souls to make this kind of music.

Yes fans have been hoping to hear some new music from the band since 2002, and I think most of them are pretty excited to hear Circa.

So far it's been very well received, and the die-hard Yes fans have accepted it and dig it and it's our goal to remain this particular lineup and carry on and make records and hopefully tour and just continue on, pushing down that musical road.

Getting into the origins of the group a little more, you and Jimmy Haun had played together off and on for a long time, and you knew Alan White and Tony Kaye from your time working with Yes. But how did this particular lineup and set of songs come together?

I had just completed *Back Against the Wall*, which was a remake of [Pink Floyd's] *The Wall* that I did with a bunch of great "prog icon" guys, and Tony was among them, as was Alan. So at some point I said to Tony, because he lives near me, "Hey, we're local and we're friends, maybe we should get together and make some music."

Through that process we started working up this material, and after a while I said maybe we should talk to Alan and see if he wants to jump in and play on some of this stuff, because it sounds like something he'd be able to enhance and make his own and make it even better. So we gave Alan a buzz, he came down and played on the stuff, and all of a sudden it started sounding like more of a band thing than a project.

Even though I play a lot of instruments, on this project I just wanted to play bass and sing. So we needed a guitar player. Jimmy had been a friend of all of ours for ages and he's a dear friend of mine, plus he's a great player and I knew he would fit like a glove, so I called him and that's how we put it all together.

Speaking of your bass playing, it definitely feels like you were focusing on that in this lineup. Your approach on "Cut the Ties" in particular struck me as very evocative of *Fragile*-era Chris Squire playing, very big and aggressive and melodic. Just curious—were you just kind of playing what felt right there or were you thinking "Wow, Chris would really get into this"?

Well, Chris has been a huge influence on my bass playing, and when I started I used to play along to Yes records to learn how to play. As I evolved as a player I took on other influences like Jaco [Pastorius] and various other bass players. But Chris' influence on me was big, playing with a pick and trying to get that kind of aggressive tone. It isn't like I sat in the studio and thought "This is what Chris would do," I just did my thing, which is highly influenced by that kind of playing. It fits in that style of music, and when you do it in that style of music, it tends to sound like that kind of "Squire-y" tone and approach. I don't mind the comparison at all because Chris is a great bass player and I'm happy to be compared to someone who plays that well! I guess the thing that starts making it sound less like a standard bass and more like kind of a Squire or Geddy Lee approach is when the bass is moving around at a hundred miles an hour and there's eight million notes and everything. That's kind of breaking the mold of the traditional session bass player! (Laughter) So it starts immediately fitting into a different kind of model and that's a model I'm very comfortable working with.

I know you guys played a live show in Southern California recently. With Yes on hiatus, this seems like a great time to get out and play. Are you guys working on putting some more shows together?

We played the Coach House in San Juan Capistrano last month and filmed it and recorded it and I'm actually working on getting the mixing together now and talking to a few different people about trying to get the band booked. We would love nothing more than to play a bunch of shows. Hopefully there's an agent out there who sees the same vision we do and is willing to help us along. At the moment, there's nothing scheduled, but we're pursuing a lot of different avenues, looking to plug someone in who can help us get it to the next level. So, stay tuned.

Will do. I caught the cell phone video that's up on YouTube of you guys at that show, and the sound is poor, but you can tell the crowd's having a great time and I thought I caught snippets of "Roundabout" and "Close To the Edge."

Yeah! We captured that show on 11 cameras, three of which were high-definition cameras, and the raw footage looks amazing to me. I'm really picky and personally not very big on filmed concerts, but what I saw was really impressive, so I'm pretty excited about trying to get this live DVD done.

That sounds great. I know it's early, but do you have any sort of timeline on that project yet?

I'm working on it right now. It's an arduous task to mix a live show because you've got microphones everywhere and to try to get some clarity out of the mix is a daunting task. It's not going to happen overnight. I would imagine in a couple of months' time I might have something together, but it's going to take a while. That'll be the next Circa release for sure, a live DVD, and we're talking about maybe making it a triple-disc set, one disc being the Circa material, the second being the Yes medley, and the third being bonus footage, background goofing-around kind of stuff.

On the Circa album, I really got into "Brotherhood of Man" in particular, which to me comes closer to the feel of a Classic Yes epic than anything the band itself has done since probably *Going for the One*. Were you guys aiming to create a new epic, or was it just one of those songs that kept stretching out and going new directions?

Tony Kaye was very influential in pushing that song in that direction and wanting a big, epic-y piece. It's one thing to say, "Let's write something long," and it's another to be ten minutes down the pipe and going "Um, is this any good… or is this just long?" [laughter] I was actually quite happy with the way that track came out. Tony Kaye's influence on the whole production really benefited the making of this record in a big way, and he had a big role in getting that song into that kind of shape.

I see from the liner notes that Trevor Rabin got a co-writing credit with the band on a couple of tracks ["Don't Let Go" and "Look Inside"]. I'm assuming he's heard the finished product by now. What was his reaction?

He dug it! After the *Talk* tour in 1995 I said to him, hey, we should write some tunes. We had a great time hanging out on the road on that tour, so it just kind of evolved. He gave me a DAT tape with five musical ideas on it with no melody and lyric, and I took it and wrote lyrics and melody over the top, and we both dug what we had come up with, and said we were going to do something with it, but time and scheduling got in the way and it never happened. So then flash forward to about a year and a half ago or so, and I'm looking at that material again and saying "Man, this is really cool, let me mess around with this." And so I started sketching it out and then presented a couple of those ideas to Tony and said "What do you think about this?" and "Maybe we can develop it for this project." He really dug what he heard and we took it, reshaped it, and turned it into a Circa-sounding thing. But you still hear Rabin's stamp [on those two tracks] big-time.

Here's a question that, as a Yes fan myself, I've got to ask. You grew up a Yes fan and ended up first playing with and then producing and finally joining the band. I've read about how you and Jimmy got together as teenagers and played Yes songs in the back room for many, many years. Stepping back from who you are today for a minute and imagining yourself as that teenaged Yes fan again, how amazing has this path you've taken been?

During the gig we just did Jimmy and I were tripping, because it was like, God, we did this when we were fourteen and we used to pretend that was Alan White behind the drums—and now it is! (Laughter)

It trips me out to think about it. There's a certain amount of fate involved in my life that I used to wonder about that I don't even question any more, I just wake up and go with it. My time in Yes is just one of those things. For me, it was an amazing thing to grow up loving a band that much and ending up working with them and then even more amazing to end up joining and having a say and all that kind of stuff.

It was a mind-blower on many levels—musically, business-wise, personally. I mean, that was my dream and I achieved it, you know? It's an amazing thing and I wouldn't trade any of that for the world, even though part of it was magical and exciting and fun, and then there was part that was really rough and tumble and all about business and sometimes in your face, too. But I'm a big boy and I dealt with both sides and just kind of put it in context.

All these years later, I wouldn't change it for the world, I'm very proud of having been a part of Yes and been able to help it along. A lot of people when I joined were asking "How did he get in there? What a lucky guy, overnight he just joined Yes!" They didn't realize the history that led up to that point. I'd been involved with those guys since about 1990 behind the scenes.

There was an evolution; once I met them, and knew them and was working with them, the magic part of "Oh my God, I've finally met these guys!" starts to go away, and you just begin having regular relationships and you realize these are just people with families. And then you meet their families, and you become part of the family. It was a magical thing.

I have other dreams, I'd love to play with Genesis and Pink Floyd, but I don't think it's going to happen in the same way that it did with Yes! And the good news is, out of all the bands that I could have joined, Yes was my number one all-time favorite. So I can't really complain. (Laughter)

Well, I get the sense the internal politics in Pink Floyd put Yes' to shame!

Yeah, probably! I mean, there's probably a lot more money on the line with Pink Floyd. It can get intense, but you know, it comes with the territory, and when I was in the thick of it, as rough as it might have been sometimes, you couldn't really match the feeling of being able to play "Awaken" on stage with the band. And I got to play it so many times that it really sunk in just how cool it was.

That story made me remember when I picked up *Yesyears*, the 1991 boxed set, and saw that last song on there, "Love Conquers All," and looked at the credits and said to myself "Who's this Billy Sherwood guy, and why's he writing songs with Chris Squire?"

Exactly! (Laughter) It took many years for people to figure out the history and how it evolved. Yes is a very precious thing to the fans—the super-fans—and I know, because I'm part of that guild! And people wanted to know "Who's this stranger in Yes?" But after all this time, I think the people who may have been skeptics have realized what I did and that my participation, good, bad or indifferent, at least continued to propel the band through the late '90s.

Absolutely. I hadn't seen Yes live in almost 20 years when I caught a couple of those shows on the *Open Your Eyes* and *Ladder* tours, and it

was a different configuration and a different chemistry, but it was still Yes and I loved it.

I thought it was really, really good and the band was playing great. It was my goal when I joined the band to get Yes back on the radar, because it was fading out, and I really didn't want to see that happen to my favorite band. At the time I joined, Rick [Wakeman] had just quit, the *Keys to Ascension* cycle was done because there was no tour, and the band was splintering off and heading into the abyss. And for whatever reason, I just decided "I can't watch this happen, I've got to try to motivate these cats to get back on the radar and get in the game." And I did. And then when I turned around and looked, it was like, "Wait a minute. Why am I getting such grief for this?"

But over time that's evolved into acceptance and now a lot of people who might have been nay-sayers about my joining the band at the time seem like they've realized things were different than they thought or assumed. It is what it is, it's all good. I just wanted to motivate the band to keep making music together—that was my main reason to be there.

It's definitely taken time for some fans to come around and understand that. But as one myself, I appreciate it.

Right on. I'm happy to have done it. You know, I tell this story a lot now because I've gotten involved on a lot of forums online, just saying hello and interacting with a lot of people. I'm a computer junkie myself, so I figured why not jump in? But when I first joined the band, I'd call my wife from wherever I was on the road and she'd say "Whatever you do, don't read the forum!" (Laughter)

And I'd say "Why? What the hell did *I* do?" That's turned around now because, as I said, I think with time people have gained a little more context. At the time, the context was kind of confusing because of the *Keys to Ascension – Open Your Eyes* thing. A lot of people thought that when I joined I somehow physically stopped *Keys to Ascension 2* from coming out. But the reality was, *Keys 2* was dead in the water, the label had told the band it wasn't going to release it, and there was nothing happening. So after we got *Open Your Eyes* rolling, once we got momentum, then the label that was NOT going to put out *Keys to Ascension 2* suddenly decided "Now's the *perfect* time to put out *Keys to Ascension 2!*"

And of course that created confusion because the Yes fans thought "Well, hang on a minute, why do we have this version [the *Open Your Eyes* lineup with Sherwood and keyboardist Igor Khoroshev] and that version [the classic-era lineup with Rick Wakeman on keyboards]? We want that version and not this version!" It was a crazy, crazy time, but again, I wouldn't change it for anything. I did what I did out of respect and honor for the band and I took a lot of hits for it, but I really don't care because I've gotta do what I've gotta do.

Didn't you co-produce that second *Keys to Ascension* album?

Yeah, I produced the studio stuff with the guys, "Mind Drive," "Foot Prints" and all that stuff.

Those are great songs!

Yeah! I worked very closely with the classic lineup in my studio—where we made *Open Your Eyes* shortly after that—and I watched it all dissolving. I've explained this before, but it was actually happening right there in my studio, I was watching everyone fighting and the group disbanding. Had I not taken some initiative—I'm not saying Yes would have been over, but who knows when and where it would have done something again, and I decided in my hearts of hearts that I couldn't just watch that happening right in front of me. I had to take some initiative. And that's what I did.

Having spent quite a bit of time in the various Yes forums myself, I'm curious to hear more of your take on them. There are a lot of, ah, characters out there...

Well, it's interesting, because on a forum you're free to say whatever the hell you want and you don't really think there'll be any repercussions. And usually there aren't, but I've noticed a change now that I'm there. It's like my wife says: "Are you sure you want to do that? It's almost like Dad's in the room and the kids can't play!" (Laughter) But whatever the consequences, I'm goin' in, and I entered as Billy Sherwood, I'm not going to hide behind a screen name. I am who I am and I don't fear that interaction.

Everyone said the same thing when I joined—"I hope you've got a thick skin, because it's gonna be nasty in here!" And I said "Yeah, I do, so don't worry about it," and the reality is, it's been a very pleasant experience. I've had a lot of interesting conversations with a lot of cool people, and maybe it's because "Dad's in the room" or whatever, but the anti-Billy rhetoric has kind of chilled out. I don't know if that's just because these people who might have been nay-sayers are now in direct contact with me and realize "Oh, wait, he's a human being"—I don't know. But I'm quite happy to be involved with it, and as I said I'm a computer junkie, so what the hell...

That's so true. I think people do have a tendency to shoot from the hip when they're just sitting at the screen writing and it doesn't seem like they're having a real conversation about real people—I know I've done that!—but the minute they think the person they're writing about might actually read their words—

Yeah! It changes things. And you know, I've seen comments on the forums that make me think "I should really engage with this guy," but then it's like "Nah, I don't want to bum him out and ruin his world, he's enjoying taking the piss out of me, so just let him." [Laughter]

But when Circa developed, we decided to go about it in a different way and use the Internet as a tool, so it felt like the right time to jump in and make direct contact. I'm on all kinds of forums now talking with all kinds of people, not to mention our 11,000 friends on MySpace. And I'm quite happy to answer anyone who takes the time to write to me. I'm not Mick Jagger; I'm not going to get eight million e-mails and not be able to respond! I can actually take the time and have conversations with people if they want to interact, and I'm quite happy to do that.

That's a great tool for any musician in this day and age, but progressive rock in general and Yes in particular have always had a very active Internet fan base.

I think that's because the whole prog movement, which we're obviously a part of, all grew up with computers. I'm sure a lot of us owned a TRS-80 from Radio Shack when it first came out, because it was the coolest thing to have! (Laughter) Here in 2007, I don't know any prog rock fan or musician who isn't net-savvy—I've never met one. And I think MySpace has helped a lot of prog rock fans and musicians find each other and interact.

It looks like you and Circa are primarily marketing the album over the 'net—how's that going?

Very well! We've sold over 1,000 records in our first month with zero promotion and zero press, with me just out there shaking hands and saying hello, digitally speaking. For us, it's really good and we're happy about the pace. We're not looking for some landslide of 100,000 records sold, we're quite happy to just have a slow steady momentum and just keep climbing that hill.

People ask me, "What are the advantages or disadvantages of the do-it-yourself approach?" At the moment, with the business collapsing in on itself everywhere you turn, and record stores dying—I mean, when Tower Records on Sunset closes, that's the shot heard around the world! It means that all of a sudden retail is a different ballgame, and that being able to do this on the Internet is a very cool thing.

One thing that really sticks in my mind, having done this so many times with record companies, is attention span. Usually your record comes out after you work on it for a year or a year and a half, you hand it over to the label and they say great, we're going to press this thing and put it out and we're going to work it. And you're excited and it comes out and you get about six to eight weeks in the spotlight. But if it doesn't catch fire in that timeframe, they move on to the next thing. Your record doesn't get any more attention, and you don't get it back for seven or eight years.

In our situation with Circa, we own the record for the rest of our lives. I could work this album slowly over the next ten years, and it's as new tomorrow as it was yesterday to people who don't know about it. So there's more of a chance for the music to surface and find an audience over the long term, as opposed to just giving it to a label right now that's going to move ten thousand copies in a hurry, and then it's over. For us, that advantage far supersedes any deal that we could get in 2007. And frankly there really aren't that many deals out there for our kind of genre and our kind of music.

It's also a way for us to make the kind of music we want to make, because I don't think you could get this kind of music past a record company these days. I don't think they're interested and I don't think they think it would be worth investing their money in. And it may sound cliché, but I'm not doing this for the money—I go in there and I make the music I like to make. And when I'm done, we have an incredibly uncommercial record on our hands! (Laughter)

So anyone who says we're doing what we're doing for the money, I'm like "Really?!" For us, long term, it's just beneficial to be able to hold onto our work, to own it and distribute it at our pace, which is the world's pace. If the world decides it wants 30,000 records, we can service that; that's not an issue. The existence of the record over the long term has really become the issue for us, and so, by not putting it out through traditional means, we end up doing ourselves a service.

Here's an example of what I'm talking about. I've got people constantly on MySpace telling me "Where do I find *No Comment*, where do I find *The Big Peace*?" [Billy's two solo albums to date.] Well, I really can't even answer them, because I don't know if the label pressed up enough to service anybody. And that's frustrating, because those are my solo records that a label said they'd take and work for me, but if they are, why am I getting strangers telling me they can't find it?

The good news is, people who want Circa, know where to get Circa. As far as I'm concerned, the Internet is the new frontier. We're not the first to do this, but I think we're among the first, and I definitely don't think we'll be the last. I think you're going to see a lot of artists switching tracks as the business side of the music world continues to evolve.

*

[Postscript: Since this interview took place in 2007, the ever-prolific Billy Sherwood has issued five solo albums and six albums (two live) with Circa, along with his work on numerous other projects, including mixing recent CD and DVD releases from Yes. In spring 2015, Billy's friend Chris Squire asked him to play bass and sing with Yes on the band's summer tour because Squire was too ill to perform. After Squire's passing in June 2015, Billy was invited to rejoin Yes.]

6

Crushes 2002-2015

THE FIRST SET OF CRUSHES PRESENTED in Chapter 4 were albums that fired my imagination for one reason or another. This next set of more recent crushes, covering the years 2002 to 2015, in many ways represents faith restored.

Having grown up through the tail end of 20th century popular music's golden age, experiencing the Beatles as a child and disco as a teenager, as a young adult I was confronted by the soul-sucking commercialism of the '80s. I flat-out hated that musical decade; the soulless synthesizers, the electronic drums, the cool detachment and overproduced melodrama. The raw passion of rock n' roll that had attracted me in the first place seemed to have been shunted off into the punk ghetto, turning emotional release into a novelty. The combination of raw energy and rich melodies that attracted me to music in the first place seemed to go missing for much of the decade.

As a result, when I started writing about music in the '90s, the first obstacle I faced was overcoming my own prejudices about the seeming dearth of new music worth celebrating. It took time, but the focus on and access to new releases that reviewing offered propelled me into a fresh appreciation for modern music. This continuing voyage of discovery— now 20 years on—was fueled in significant part by albums like the ones found in this chapter, both hidden gems and gaudy, custom-cut stones.

This chapter features some of my favorite releases of the past 15 years, albums of new music that I've listened to again and again until they've become old friends. I hope you'll enjoy meeting them as much as I did.

*

Sheryl Crow
C'mon C'mon
A & M Records, 2002
[Published on *The Daily Vault* 5/7/2002]

There's something I need to get off my chest. While bright little pockets of hope remain here and there for the venerable institution of rock and roll—I'm thinking particularly of the young and surging Jimmy Eat World, and the reformed and resurgent Gin Blossoms—they remain oases in an often-barren musical wasteland. Never mind the scorched earth that is modern pop; even the harder stuff feels pathetically faceless today. I mean really, if I have to listen to one more overprivileged white kid growl over lumbering post-grunge power chords about how much the world sucks, I may puke on my keyboard. Boys: get over it.

It's springtime and, despite abundant evidence of man's fallibility (not to mention the destructive nature of blind faith in anything), the world does not appear to be coming to an end anytime soon—and if it does, it certainly won't be because some pouty suburban rap-metal singer's girlfriend dumped him. More likely, it will be because the world's musicians and poets and painters and actors all forgot how to create a frank, engaging, well-crafted and fundamentally human work of art like *C'mon C'mon*.

Sheryl Crow's fourth album is a musical coming-of-age in the truest sense. At 40, she's twice the age of most of her competition at the top of the charts, but she has used her time so well, honing her craft and earning a compelling body of self-knowledge, that she's finally ready to deliver a real musical statement.

C'mon C'mon, it has been said elsewhere, feels at times like a throwback to the classic summer albums of the '70s, shot through with sunny optimism and images of the road and the wind in your hair and a belief in life's possibilities. And that's true in places, especially on the opening ignition-blastoff one-two punch of the raucous, airy "Steve McQueen" (complete with patented Steve Miller Band "woo-hoo"s) and the witty, bouncy "Soak Up the Sun." But this emotionally complex and often soul-searching album falls about as far thematically from the lightweight, homogeneous pap dominating the charts as you could possibly ask for. It's tempting to say *C'mon C'mon* harks back to the summer of '78 or so, but a truer comparison might be U2's *All That You Can't Leave Behind*. It's that rare bird: an album of stirring, yet undeniably mature rock and roll.

One of the keys is that, after following the raw, sardonic pop of *Tuesday Night Music Club* with the aggressively retro *Sheryl Crow* and the almost studious classic rock of *The Globe Sessions*, Crow has rediscovered her sense of humor. Her wise, acerbic wit shines again and again here: "We've got rock stars in the White House / All our pop stars look like porn"... "I don't have digital / I don't have diddley squat / It's not having what you want / It's wanting what you've got"... "I, I've got a hole in my pocket / You give me love and I drop it / I just throw it away."

But the sense of playfulness that Crow has reintroduced is just one of a wide range of emotional shadings she achieves here. Every song carries with it both a memorable melody and an unmistakable purpose—you won't find any wasted effort or throwaway tracks here. There's the serious stuff: chiefly the urgent, timelessly melodic folk-rock of the title track (featuring harmony vocals from pal Stevie Nicks), and the shimmering, transcendent optimism of "Diamond Road." And the not-so-serious, as in the sizzling rocker "Lucky Kid" and the irresistibly hooky nugget "Hole in My Pocket." Want more? How about a pair of gorgeous country-rock ballads, the comfortable-as-an-old-pair-of-shoes "It's Only Love" (featuring Crow mentor Don Henley) and the keening, note-perfect "Abilene" (featuring Dixie Chicks' Natalie Maines). Or a little musical contrast—Crow goes for heavy, shiny funk with fellow retrophile Lenny Kravitz on "You're an Original," but sounds just as natural dueting with the angelic Emmylou Harris on the meditative closing ballad "Weather Channel."

In a concession to modern fashion, Crow (who produced the album herself, in addition to writing or co-writing every song) tops off these songs with a magician's bag of sonic flourishes. The proof of her mastery comes in the fact that these loops, backbeats, sonic squiggles and electronic tones consistently embellish without becoming obtrusive, filling out the songs' palette rather than interfering with their flow. The album's multiple guest vocalists are used to similar effect—not as stunt-casting, but as complements to the most expressive singing of Crow's career.

C'mon C'mon is one of those special albums that manages to hit all the right notes, on which every track has something a little bit unique to offer, while the package as a whole brims with both raw energy and careful attention to detail. There are a lot of labels you could slap on a piece of work of this caliber, but I'd rather just call it what it is—the best rock and roll album of 2002, so far.

Rating: A

*

Josh Joplin Group
The Future That Was
Artemis Records, 2002
[Published on *The Daily Vault* 1/15/2003]

Back when I was in high school, long before the turn of the century—and yes, ha ha, I mean the 21st—there was this really unique guy. He was clearly smart verging on genius, in all the advanced classes and treated with some awe by many of the teachers. But he was undeniably odd, sitting silently in class for weeks at a time before, out of the blue, piping up with a two-minute dissertation covering five brilliant points that hadn't even occurred to the rest of the class yet. The penetrating nature of his observations made us all uncomfortable, though he seemed to take them in stride, even chuckling sometimes at our startled expressions.

I don't think I went to high school with Josh Joplin. But the possibility, however remote, occurred to me after listening to *The Future That Was*, because it is just so damned intelligent, and yet so willfully, candidly out there. The only thing I can compare it to is an album the Barenaked Ladies might make with a young, pissed-off Elvis Costello sitting in.

The Josh Joplin Group's 2000 major label debut, *Useful Music*, was an intriguing introduction to the band, a serious-minded song cycle full of oddball characters and upbeat melodies. Even the radio-friendly single "Camera One," with its beefed-up production and mainstreamed alt-rock guitar crunch, reeked of an intelligence rarely found on the pop charts. It's hard not to be cynical about the result, though: perhaps the most thoughtful *and* melodic rock single of the year went nowhere. My local modern rock station tried it out for a couple of weeks and then dumped it for extra helpings of Creed and Third Eye Blind (yawn).

The 2002 model of the JJG confronts head-on the conundrum of making non-conformist, daringly literate rock and roll in an era that likes its pop-culture icons dumb and cute—confronts it and says, with a slightly snarky grin, "Whatever." Sure, the kick-off track "Must Be You" offers a pleasantly repetitive chorus and generous harmony vocals, but lines like "Well let the people stare I can't tell them what to do" clue you in that you're dealing with someone just a little off-center. "The Wonderful Ones" offers an equally melodic base for a bullseye skewering of American celebrity culture ("Everybody knows us, we're the wonderful ones").

But that's just the entree to an album filled with geek-rock as clever and esoteric as any you're ever likely to find. How else to describe a song like "Siddharthas of Suburbia," an upbeat, piano-based tune that casts suburban materialism as a shallow culture's desperate response to Buddhism's core tenet, the inevitability of human suffering. (No, really.) As if to up the ante even further, the JJG follows the philosophical "Siddhartha" with "It's Only Entertainment," a twelve-gauge blast of garage-rock that manages to cram *To Kill a Mockingbird*, Pat Boone and a penis-envy punchline into the same three-minute diatribe.

Don't let this confuse you, though, for "I am not the only cowboy in this one horse metaphor." Uh, okay. Ridiculously well-rhymed spoken-word verses with a sung chorus supported by a string section and rich harmonies. Gah. Somebody call Shawn Mullins, this guy's out of control! But wait, he's not done yet: "Some people wish they could be like Moses / And get their information from burning bushes / Well I tried but the neighbors complained / I set their lawns aflame."

Okay. Let's try to regroup here.

The JJG's basic sound is stripped-down, quirky pop-rock, with Joplin's voice clearly the focus. On the instrumental side, Joplin's guitar shares space effectively with Allen Broyles' piano and organ. The rhythm section of Geoff Melkonian (bass) and Eric Taylor (drums) keeps it simple but shows versatility as the group slides easily between steady backbeats and more contemplative tracks like "Listening," "Fire" and the dreamy/sad closer "Wonder Wheel." The JJG is nothing if not musically economical; the majority of these thirteen songs run right around three minutes, yet they all feel complete.

The beauty of Joplin's approach is that there's nothing and no one he's afraid to target with his devastating critiques. In the rocking "Happy at Last," he takes a disarmingly frank look at his own life: "I sound like Michael Stipe and I dream like Carl Jung... And I don't know where I'm going and / I'm running out of cash / I may not be well off but I'm happy at last." (And yes, he often sounds eerily like Stipe. Deal with it.)

Enough blabbering. Here's the essential information: *The Future That Was* is a brilliant album. That's the only word for it, really, that encompasses its hyperactive wit, its deadpan wisdom, its merciless exposure of flaws within and without. Buy two and share it with a friend—just make sure they have a sense of humor and a decent encyclopedia.

Rating: A

*

Fountains of Wayne
Welcome Interstate Managers
S-Curve/Virgin Records, 2003
[Published on *The Daily Vault* 10/2/2003]

I have a long history of falling in love with things—girls, cars, food, bands. When I like something right away, I typically like it a LOT. This has, at times, resulted in acute embarrassment when I've later come to my senses and gained some perspective.

With that in mind, I'd like to introduce you to my new crush—Fountains of Wayne's third and latest disc, *Welcome Interstate Managers*—and tell you that it's utterly brilliant, the best thing I've heard all year, maybe all decade. This densely packed, musically diverse set from Jersey legends-in-the-making FOW is filled with intelligent, nuanced songs that carry real emotional heft.

Even breakout single "Stacy's Mom," a four-minute blast of pop-rock novelty-song cheekiness, has a wistful undercurrent that gives it texture and resonance. Clever, bouncy and catchy as hell, this track also manages to capture perfectly the tortured longing for the unattainable that is the essence of male adolescent angst. The narrator may be slightly delusional, lusting after his friend's mom and imagining she's more than flirting in return, but the mixture of desire and tenderness ("since your dad walked out, your mom could use a guy like me") rings true and suggests one of those earnest, vulnerable types who always get their hearts broken.

"Mom" is paired perfectly here with "Hackensack," a melancholy mid-tempo tune about pining for a girl who's long since moved upward and onward. Thematically, though, this album is less about romantic longing than it is a slice of alienated twenty-something life. As adept at building a narrative as masters like the Kinks, as witty and sardonic as contemporaries like Josh Joplin, songwriters Chris Collingwood (lead vocals, guitar) and Adam Schlesinger (bass, guitar, keyboards, vocals) inhabit one intriguing character after another, most of them struggling to find their place in a world that resolutely fails to care.

This theme runs through a whole string of songs touching on the soul-sucking drudgery of the workplace, from the throbbing, sarcastic power-pop of "Bright Future in Sales" to the airy folk-rock of "Hey Julie," and provides the lyrical connective tissue that binds together an album that's musically as diverse as you could ask for. There's jangle-rock with terrific electronic accents ("No Better Place"); Ramones-y punk-pop ("Little Red Light" and "Bought for a Song"); lush pastoral harmonies ("Valley Winter Song"); and smile-inducing country-rock ("Hung Up on You"). Not to mention a four-minute song about a single momentum-shifting play in a football game (the dreamy, absurdly compelling "All Kinds of Time") and perhaps the ultimate ode to lousy table service (the witty "Halley's Waitress").

Collingwood and Schlesinger are joined by bandmates and fellow musical chameleons Jody Porter (guitar, vocals) and Brian Young (drums, percussion), as well as guests such as former Smashing Pumpkins guitarist James Iha and Ronnie Buttacavoli, who adds trumpet and flugelhorn to a couple of tracks, notably the spot-on Chicago homage on the bridge of "Fire Island." If there's a flaw here at all, it's simply that this album may actually offer too much of a good thing; at 16 tracks, it could probably lose a pair toward the end and only gain in potency.

Sprinkled with superb rhymes ("I saw you talkin' to Christopher Walken") and sparkling turns of phrase ("You're awake and trying not to be / Wrapped around your pillow like a prawn"), buoyed by its effortless musical range, this album towers over most of the commercial dreck being put out by the record industry today. Don't let your local corporate radio franchise's merciless flogging of "Stacy's Mom" deter you; it's the bright red cherry on top of a 15-scoop hot fudge sundae. *Welcome Interstate Managers* is a great album today, and I'm willing to bet whatever dignity I have left that it will still be a great album long after tomorrow, next month and even next year.

Rating: A

*

Death Cab for Cutie
Transatlanticism
Barsuk Records, 2003
[Published on *The Daily Vault* 5/4/2004]

One of the main side benefits of this gig is the opportunity to be introduced to new music. When *The Daily Vault*'s own Sean McCarthy put Death Cab For Cutie's *Transatlanticism* near the peak of his 2003 Top Ten, I paid attention, and after a few listens, there's no longer any puzzle as to why this disc made any number of Top Ten lists this January. It's a moody, airy, brilliant compendium of artfully crafted songs whose quality actually lives up to their pretensions.

For the record, Death Cab for Cutie is anchored by singer/songwriter Ben Gibbard and guitarist/producer Christopher Walla, with longtime cohort Nicholas Harmer on bass and new guy Jason McGerr on the drums. Gibbard and Walla also contribute keyboards and textures that fill out the atmospherics of many of these tracks.

The music itself is a mix of ethereal ballads sung with genuine sadness and powerful yet sleepy-eyed guitars-and-harmonies rock. The songs are a circular, yearning series of vignettes, little moments that blur into each other like an Impressionist painting. More sophisticated than Jimmy Eat World and wittier than Coldplay, with *Tranatlanticism* Death Cab For Cutie have created a true album, themed and flowing and progressive in its moods and expressiveness.

Which is not to say there aren't moments that stand out... the strange, beautiful passages and jams late in songs like "We Looked Like Giants"... the evocative lyrical detail of tracks like "Title and Registration" and "Tiny Vessels" ... the way "The Sound of Settling" juxtaposes sunny harmonies and ringing guitars with a profoundly downbeat lyric about surrendering dreams and settling for what you can get... and the way even the muscular passages of cuts like "Expo '86" manifest a kind of elegance and drama.

Most of the songs run the standard three or four minutes, with the notable exception of the title track. By contrast, "Transatlanticism" is given abundant room to build and build, and is thoroughly successful from its haunting opening chords to its crescendoing finish, almost eight minutes later. It's an opus that earns the space it's allowed.

It also distills the theme of this disc—the distance between people, even when they're close... maybe especially then. "I need you closer" sings Gibbard, again and again, with more and more longing and urgency in his expressive voice. Another example of this theme is the heartbreaking matter-of-factness with which Gibbard delivers the line "She's beautiful, but she don't mean a thing to me" in "Tiny Vessels." In this respect, as in many others, *Transatlanticism* harks back to Pink Floyd's original brand of dreamy despair and alienation. Death Cab forgoes Floyd's flashes of anger, though, in favor of a particularly poetic strain of resignation.

Elegance and drama, despair and resignation... yes, this is as British an album as has ever been recorded in Seattle. In the end, I'm not sure *Transatlanticism* is an album I'll listen to all that often—it's too sad. What I am sure of, is that it's one of the notable musical achievements of this young decade.

Rating: A

*

Jet
Get Born
Elektra, 2003
[Published on *The Daily Vault* 9/13/2005]

As if the world—not to mention my teenaged children—needed any more proof that I am hopelessly uncool and out of it, I *just* caught on to this disc.

Sure, I saw the memorable iPod commercial featuring "Are You Gonna Be My Girl," but it wasn't like I was going to buy an album based on an advertising jingle, even one with that much adrenalin and attitude.

No, it was the eventual second (or third? I dunno) single, the dreamy ballad "Look What You've Done," that made its way into my imagination and simply refused to leave. I would find myself humming the melody at the weirdest times, catching myself mid-chorus before I actually started singing out loud (an act which has been known to cause small birds to fall from nearby trees). As a firm believer in the "feed a fever" philosophy, I knew there was only one cure—retail therapy.

Jet is a gleefully retro quartet that combines the raunchy rock and roll swagger of the Stones and the Faces with the ecstatic riff-rocking of fellow Aussies AC/DC. Or at least that's the easy conclusion to come to after head-bobbing your way through thumping, propulsive, pure-pleasure rockers like "Last Chance," "Rollover DJ," "Get What You Need," "Get Me Outta Here" and of course "Are You Gonna Be My Girl," every last one of them complete with a grin-inducing main riff and shout-along chorus. "Take It or Leave It" even manages to find that same sweet spot ("hard rockabilly"?) between Chuck Berry and heavy metal that Led Zeppelin mined so well on "Rock And Roll." Dirty-sweet riffing, thundering beats and sassy flourishes (piano, studio noise, tambourine, stop-start dynamics)... yeah, this stuff is just plain fun.

And then they pull out their secret weapon.

Because Jet—brothers Nic Cester (lead vocals, guitar) and Chris Cester (drums, vocals), along with Cam Muncey (guitar, vocals) and Mark Wilson (bass, piano, vocals)—might be even better at ballads than rockers. In addition to the catchy-as-hell "Look What You've Done," they toss off terrific, straight-from-the-gut slow-burners like "Come Around Again," "Timothy" and the gorgeous "Move On." The latter's opening verse also places the band precisely where they aim to be musically, beautifully mimicking the quiet, close-miked wistfulness of the opening to the Stones' classic "You Can't Always Get What You Want." (There's also more than a little *Abbey Road*-era Beatles in the somewhat experimental "Lazy Gun.")

More than just a powerhouse debut, *Get Born* is a hell of a good time, one of those instant-party albums you throw in the player in your car and leave in for a week straight. Few higher compliments can be offered to an album of rock and roll music.

Rating: A-

*

Jimmy Eat World
Futures
Interscope Records, 2004
[Published on *The Daily Vault* 12/1/2004]

What's left to do once you've conquered the world?

It's a question that has troubled many a band over the years. It's all too common to see groups reacting to their big break by spending the next few years either trying too hard to repeat it, or trying too hard not to. Getting what you've been after all those years—success, acceptance, an audience—can be completely unnerving.

Three years ago Jimmy Eat World conquered the known rock and roll universe with the smash album *Bleed American* (retitled *Jimmy Eat World* post-9/11) and its Godzilla-sized hit single "The Middle." Coming on the heels of a series of setbacks that had seen the band dropped by Capitol Records, only to be re-signed by Dreamworks, the success (creative and commercial) of *Bleed American* had to be a tremendously satisfying personal triumph for the band.

The answer to the obvious question—what now?—is *Futures*. And it's a very, very good answer.

On their three-years-later follow-up, some things have changed for the boys of Jimmy—Jim Adkins on vocals and guitars, Rick Burch on bass, Zach Lind on drums, and Tom Linton on guitars and vocals—and some have stayed the same. The band remains a tremendously appealing combination of doe-eyed sincerity and heavy, hooky riffs. What they wisely don't try to do is recreate the epic undercurrents of many of the songs on *Bleed American*. No, there isn't a song as instantly memorable as "A Praise Chorus" here—but neither is there a song that strives as hard to *be* instantly memorable.

Instead what you get is a solid, impressive, steadily-grows-on-you set from a band that has experienced success without losing the earnestness that has always been at the core of its music. I mean, who else in this uber-cynical age could get away with opening an album with a declaration as optimistic as "I always believed in futures"? The surprisingly political title track also includes lines like "Believe your voice can mean something" in service of a searching, forward-looking attitude.

Yes, this band is growing up and the music is growing with them, with a number of songs here narrating transitions to adulthood, notably "23" and the luminous, melancholy, altogether wonderful "The World You Love." The theme doesn't end there, though; even relationship songs like "Work" and "Kill" show a recognition of consequences that is distinctly mature.

Other highlights include: "Night Drive," a well-crafted seduction piece full of potent images ("pierce my heart like a willing arm"); "Pain," with its dynamic production and hammering chorus of "It takes my pain away / It's a lie / A kiss with open eyes"; and "Polaris," a gorgeous track on which Tom Linton arguably does a better job of channeling the airy, epic mid-'80s U2 guitar sound than The Edge has in years. (For more of the latter, see also the solo on "Nothingwrong.")

The danger this band flirts with from time to time is that their earnestness will drag them down somewhat obvious lyrical paths, as on the rather maudlin "Drugs or Me." Thing is, they're so good at selling this kind of song with a fully committed performance that they can usually get away with it.

Futures is a terrific step forward for one of the best bands of the new century, an album brimming with youthful rock and roll energy that also manages to be wise beyond its years. It's an album that will make you believe, or at least want to. The world could use more of them.

Rating: A

*

The Redwalls
De Nova
Capitol Records, 2005
[Published on *The Daily Vault* 7/21/2005]

Either these four young guys from Deerfield, Illinois have got elephant balls, or they just don't know any better. P.S. I'm pretty sure they know better.

There have been hundreds and hundreds of bands over the past 35 years that have listened to, learned from, looked up to and/or longed to be more like the Beatles. They were, after all, the single most influential group in the history of rock and roll, and the originators of / inspirations for any number of musical trends and genres that followed in their wake, from power-pop to psychedelia.

But.

The Redwalls do not "sound like" or "pay homage to" or any other half-assed phrase one might use to try to relate their style to the Beatles. They freaking *channel* them like a million-megawatt radio / time machine. This album could be titled *Revolver II (The Next Generation)*, and no one would blink.

The British invasion wall-of-guitars, the playful three-part harmonies, the knowing nods to r&b rhythms, the occasional headlong dive into soulful blues-shouter vocals... even the detours into throbbing psychedelic pop, horns-and-strings accents and earnest political statements. It's all here, executed with a casual brilliance that boggles the mind, because not only are these four lads from the suburban Midwest, they're barely out of high school. Brothers Logan Baren (vocals & guitar) and Justin Baren (bass & vocals) are 22 and 19, respectively; best pal Andrew Langer (guitar & vocals) is 20; and new guy Ben Greeno (drums) is 21. (And they say you can't get a musical education in America today...!)

My favorite moments on this disc go by like a blur every time I listen. But here are just a few: the instantly memorable choruses of "Thank You" and "Building a Bridge"; the ebullient dare-you-not-to-dance drive of "Love Her" and "It's Alright"; the dead-on acoustic protest song vibe of "Glory of War"; and the truly glorious, wailing "Twist and Shout" vocals deployed by Baren on the blazing-fun closer "Rock and Roll."

The first time through you're dazzled by the audacity of the sound—the repeated Lennonisms in Baren's vocals, the note-perfect retro arrangements, the giddy rock numbers seasoned with Hammond organ and orchestral flourishes. Then on subsequent spins you start listening to the songs themselves and find out these guys really know what they're doing. They aren't imitators. They are a band that has adopted the Beatles' sonic template whole, and applied their own considerable writing talents to the task of making new music within it.

Nowhere is this clearer than on the one song where I really did get the chills the first time I heard it. "Front Page" opens with processed vocals that sound like Lennon speaking from beyond the grave, whereupon Baren moves steadily through a somber lyric ("As they talk about / Sixteen kids gone in a schoolyard / The papers read / She shakes her head") that sounds eerily like "A Day in the Life 2005." For that reason, part of me wanted to hate it, but I couldn't—it's too good.

As a general rule, I want artists to show me something fresh and new. Tribute bands just make me sad that the real thing isn't still around. And that's the crux of the musical dilemma posed by *De Nova*—is this album original? Not in the sense of creating something the likes of which has never been seen or heard before. But it certainly is original in the sense of accomplishing something I'm not sure I've ever seen done this well before—taking a familiar and very famous sound and breathing fresh new life and vibrancy into it. They won this somewhat jaded writer over to the point where all I have left to say is: Meet the Redwalls.

Rating: A-

*

Switchfoot
Nothing Is Sound
Columbia, 2005
[Published on *The Daily Vault* 1/4/2007]

It seems like every year now an album sneaks up on me. I catch something on the radio or TV or the 'net that sparks interest and I end up going back and finding an album that I completely missed that turns into an instant favorite. In 2004, it was Ian Hunter's *Rant* (2001); in 2005 it was Jet's *Get Born* (2003).

And in late 2006, it was Switchfoot's 2005 disc *Nothing Is Sound*.

The hook that initially reeled this fish in was "Stars"—not the familiar electrified album version, but one of those live-in-the-studio acoustic radio performances early last year. The sound and lyrics grabbed me right away—richly melodic, searching, philosophical, and ultimately optimistic.

The same could be said of most of Switchfoot's music, which could be shorthanded as sounding something like Bono fronting Jimmy Eat World or the Gin Blossoms. They write songs about big issues and ideas—philosophical, societal, spiritual—and then set them to even bigger guitars. They emerged out of the CCM camp, but you won't find any sermons on this lyric sheet; this is a Christian band that chooses to ask open-ended, thought-provoking questions about life and the universe rather than proselytize.

The electric version of "Stars" is one of the highlights here, launching with a heavy 45-second instrumental intro that sounds like Doug Hopkins channeling Jimmy Page (or vice versa), fat, angular riffs propelling the song forward like a slingshot. The verses are an often-clever rumination on feeling alone in the universe—"I've been thinking maybe I've been partly cloudy / Maybe I'm the chance of rain"—that erupts at the chorus into a spiritual affirmation— "When I look at the stars I see someone else / When I look at the stars I feel like myself."

Ironically, after twenty or so listens to this disc, the captivating "Stars" has dropped to fourth or fifth on my list of favorite songs here.

Tops is "The Shadow Proves the Sunshine," a hymn-like poem set to ringing, chiming guitars over echoey, martial drums, a stark, insightful, gorgeous cut that would fit seamlessly into *The Joshua Tree* (and that, sir, is quite a compliment). Not far behind are the thunderous opener "Lonely Nation," a spot-on screed against empty materialism ("We are slaves of what we want"), and the late-album stadium-sized singalong "We Are One Tonight."

To their credit, the band—Jonathan Foreman (vocals/guitar), Tim Foreman (bass), Chad Butler (drums), Jerome Fontamillas (keyboards) and Andrew Shirley (guitar)—put you through some changes between these big numbers. "Easier Than Love" goes for a bouncier, frothier sound, though ultimately there's a fairly heavy love-versus-sex message wrapped inside. "The Blues" is just what it sounds like, but surprisingly moving at that ("Does justice never find you? Do the wicked never lose? / Is there any honest song to sing besides these blues?"). And "Golden" is a suitably shimmering, jangly affirmation for a friend.

These songs—all written by Jon Foreman, with three co-written by brother Tim—manage to rock with authority without sacrificing an ounce

162

of meaning or purpose. The ability of adrenaline-fueled numbers like "Politicians" to make you think and head-bang at the same time is a pretty neat trick. My only possible criticism is that this album has been mixed so pristinely that the band's natural thunder feels actually scrubbed too clean in places.

That quibble aside, this is a terrifically entertaining and thought-provoking slab of guitar rock, and one that's already inspired me to dig deeper into Switchfoot's catalog. Highly recommended.

Rating: A

*

John Mayer
Continuum
Aware/Columbia Records, 2006
[Published on *The Daily Vault* 9/19/2006]

While John Mayer's 2003 sophomore disc *Heavier Things* was a step forward for the one-time folk-pop wunderkind with its mature songwriting and strong arrangements, few might have guessed at the phenomenal artistic growth curve Mayer was already in the process of accelerating into.

After schooling himself by playing sets with a series of blues masters and soaking up everything he could musically, Mayer re-emerged late last year with *Try!*, a completely unexpected and unexpectedly strong live album featuring him fronting a Cream-styled blues-rock trio with scene veterans Pino Palladino on bass and Steve Jordan on drums.

Well, that's a pretty neat trick, the critics and listening public seemed to say, but c'mon. Are you serious?

Continuum answers that question with an exclamation point the size of the Mississippi Delta. Not only is Mayer serious, he's graduated from the College of Blues and come out swinging for the fences. Not content just to record a credible blues album, Mayer here unveils 12 of the most potent, penetrating and relevant songs of his or anyone else's career. *Continuum* is nothing short of a triumph, easily among the best albums of 2006.

The challenge to the music industry and music-buying public will be whether they can catch up with Mayer's growth. Here's the former teen idol mixing silky r&b grooves with sparkling blues jams, employing decades-old musical idioms to express deeply felt ideas about love, war and faith that are more perceptive and powerful than 99.9 percent of the lyrics you'll find in your radio dial today.

Right out of the gate, Mayer tosses off the first song in years that actually feels like it captures the mood of a generation. "It's not that we don't care / We just know the fight ain't fair," goes a key line in the bittersweet "Waiting on the World to Change," as its slinky, gorgeous groove digs in before finishing you off with bells right out of a Motown dream.

Sophomore track "I Don't Trust Myself (With Loving You)" sets up this disc's main dichotomy, alternating tracks that have an outward focus with ones that zoom in on the messy interiors of our hearts. The groove Palladino and Jordan set here is, impossibly, even deeper, smoother and more irresistible than "Waiting."

"Belief" is where Mayer hits one not just over the fence but clean out of the park. Returning to worldly concerns, Mayer takes on as charged a subject as you could imagine—the dangers of religious fundamentalism—and crafts a musical statement that's simultaneously deft and devastating. "Belief is a beautiful armor," he sings, "But it makes for the heaviest sword," as a tight, lilting electric guitar figure propels the song, one minute weaving in flashes of electric soul, the next delving into Far Eastern chord progressions and bluesy soloing. Not since "What's Going On" has a song this meaningful met a groove this entrancing.

Traversing the middle three, "Gravity" is a spot-on, steady-building blues; "The Heart of Life" is a *Slowhand*-style shuffle with a superb, affirming chorus; and "Vultures" is a velvet hammer on the tabloid media's collective head. (You know an album's good when three songs this well-crafted only rate a passing mention.)

"Stop This Train" ups the ante again as Mayer goes acoustic while delivering an emotional bulls-eye of a lyric about growing up and growing older. At the core again lies a simple truth: "I'm so scared of getting old / I'm only good at being young." Right on its heels comes "Slow Dancing in a Burning Room," a contender for break-up song of the decade—emotionally nuanced, masterfully paced, as true as the tears in a lover's eyes. In short, brilliant.

Still, though, the ex-teen idol has all those commercial expectations on his shoulders, so… time to rein it in, right? Maybe bring it home with a couple of safe love ballads.

Not exactly. Three quarters of the way through this disc, Mayer has planted a small time bomb—a truly bold cover of Jimi Hendrix's "Bold as

Love" that is as heartfelt as it is impressive. Somewhere, Stevie Ray Vaughan is smiling.

After that, the final trio of songs passes in a kind of delirious haze. "Dreaming With a Broken Heart" is a piano-driven blues ballad that would land among the top three on a weaker album; "In Repair" is an introspective blues with more sweet Claptonesque soloing and superb flourishes from Jordan behind the kit; and "I'm Gonna Find Another You" closes things out in style, a tight little "2:00 a.m. and my woman done left me" weeper with a knockout horn section and a sweetly witty lyrical kicker.

Continuum—whose title cleverly implies more of a thread between his older and newer work than the change-averse among his longtime fans may find—is album three in a trilogy of growth for John Mayer, and marks his official arrival as not just a major mover of product, but a major musical artist. Modern corporate radio may have trouble figuring out what to do with an album full of world-class blues from a former teen idol, but you shouldn't.

Rating: A

*

Ian Hunter
Shrunken Heads
Yep Roc, 2007
[Published on *The Daily Vault* 10/1/2007]

Stones, schmones.

Everybody likes to hold the Rolling Stones up as some sort of amazing fountain of youth. "Man, they're in their sixties and they're still huge!" More accurate would be to say that they're in their sixties and still milking the media machine like the pros they've become. The Stones have been more about marketing than music for over half their career now.

Ian Hunter, by contrast, is of similar vintage to the Stones but just keeps getting better musically. Well into his sixties he is in fact making some of the best music of his long and storied career.

Hunter's early splash as frontman for legendary glam-rockers Mott the Hoople has been well-documented elsewhere. What has been less-chronicled is his exemplary solo career, starting with 1975's self-titled disc, through his 1979 commercial high-water mark *You're Never Alone With a*

Schizophrenic (remember "Cleveland Rocks"?) and all the way up through 2001's stirring, sharp-as-ever *Rant*.

If there's a secret to Hunter's gift it's in the mixture of raw honesty and cheeky British charm he brings to his incisive songs. Opener "Words (Big Mouth)" is a strong example of both, a self-deprecating confession that's both witty ("Words... nasty little lizards... grammatical bacteria... Yakety-yakety-yakety-yakety") and tinged with a wistful self-knowledge. The music here, as throughout this disc, is smartly-arranged roadhouse blues-rock, acoustic rhythm guitar embellished with punchy electric leads, organ, piano, and on "Words," Springsteen sidewoman Soozie Tyrell on violin.

In this typically rich and intelligent outing, Hunter skewers both designer materialism ("Brainwashed") and his own aging perspective on the world ("I Am What I Hated When I Was Young"), while also ripping out a hard-rocking yet nuanced ode to a troubled friend ("Stretch"). On *Shrunken Heads*, though, he saves his most potent verbal broadsides for the Bush Administration, lashing out with numbers like the rollicking "Fuss About Nothin'," the surprisingly poignant title track, and the thundering Hurricane Katrina response indictment "How's Your House?" Expatriate Englishman Hunter isn't about to concede his affection for his adopted homeland to anyone, though. On "Soul of America" he pounds out an anthemic love letter to the USA every bit as sincere and potent as any of Springsteen or Mellencamp's forays into similar territory.

Another of Hunter's underappreciated talents is pacing and sequencing. Yes, there are several angry, politically inclined songs on this disc, but they are interspersed with (and leavened by) a trio of Hunter's trademark heartfelt ballads, including the soaring, magnificent "When the World Was Round" and the stunning closer "Read 'Em and Weep," which deserves a place among the finest tunes he's ever written.

There isn't a weak moment to be found on *Shrunken Heads*, which has been nominated for Album of the Year by *Classic Rock Magazine*. The conclusion is unmistakable: leave the stunt-marketing to Mick and Keith, and leave the music to Ian Hunter.

Rating: A

*

Big Big Train
The Underfall Yard
English Electric Recordings, 2009
[Published on *The Daily Vault* 12/11/2009]

I haven't been to England in years—unless, that is, you count the trips I've taken recently while driving through California's Central Coast listening to Big Big Train's magnificent new album *The Underfall Yard*.

Of all the things that might strike me about these British progressive rockers' latest outing—the superb arrangements, the world-class musicianship, the depth of feeling poured into some of their most personal songs—the sense of place is what loomed largest in my mind as I sat down to write this review. It's quite simply one of the most British albums I've ever heard.

While it's true enough that most of the classic prog bands were/are British—and the music here feels like a charismatic melding of early Genesis and classic Yes, with more than little Floydian melancholy, reimagined with modern dynamics and sparkling production—it's the lyrics that cement the character of the music. This is an album grounded in history, with a literary quality to its lyrics about passing eras, the end of empires large and small, and the effects of societal change on those who can't or won't adapt.

The Underfall Yard is Big Big Train's sixth studio album, the follow-up to 2007's superb *The Difference Machine*, and their first with new vocalist David Longdon. Longdon joins founding members Greg Spawton (guitar, keys, songwriting) and Andy Poole (bass, production) as the core trio of a steadily evolving conglomeration of musicians that now includes Nick D'Virgilio (Spock's Beard) as a "permanent guest" on drums and background vocals. Dave Gregory of XTC also contributes guitar on five of these six tracks.

To call Longdon a "good fit" for Big Big Train would be an epic understatement. The newcomer to a band of avowed Genesis fans is not only at times a dead ringer vocally for Peter Gabriel, he actually worked with Tony Banks and Mike Rutherford for six months in 1996, competing for the lead vocal slot in the post-Phil Collins edition of Genesis that eventually featured D'Virgilio on drums and Ray Wilson at the mike.

The new lineup's debut outing opens with the instrumental "Evening Star," effectively the overture to an album about the end of eras of one sort of another, and the losses that pile up with the passage of time. Even the five-line narrative of the subsequent six-minute-plus "Master James Of St.

George" conveys a deep sense of loss; Master James "used to build castles of stone / Steel and blood / But lines get broken down."

The emotional core of the album resides the stunning "Victorian Brickwork," Spawton's elegy for his father, a navy man whose serial departures frayed the connection between father and son. Two minutes into this 12-minute track, the soft, pastoral opening gives way to a guitar-bass-drum-organ theme that frames the remainder of the song, a lively and complex motif that feels like an outtake from *The Yes Album*. The mid-song climax comes as Longdon/Spawton declares "Now I know who I am / I know what I mean / And I know where I came from / From the sea" before the music falls back into a long, dreamy jam that evolves into a gorgeous, soaring orchestral section where strings and horns build toward a magnificently sad crescendo, a segment that could easily be subtitled "Soundtrack to an Era Passing." The chorus then returns, this time as a gentle coda: "Lost in low light and ocean tides / The love you never meant to hide." Gorgeous and absolutely brilliant.

Next up are a couple of uniquely British tales. "Last Train" traces the literal "end of the line" for a railroad man whose branch line is being abandoned, and features especially fabulous Gregory guitar solos. And "Winchester Diver"—whose opening instrumental section has a rather Ian-Anderson-fronting-the-Alan-Parsons-Project feel—spins the tale of the lonely, impossibly dangerous work done in 1906 by a lone diver shoring up the foundations of Winchester Cathedral as worshippers and clergy continued about their business above.

The epic title track—22 minutes of turning, twisting, captivating prog—is a veritable all-star jam, with terrific, fully-integrated guest appearances by Jem Godfrey (Frost*), Francis Dunnery (It Bites) and Dave Gregory, and especially percussive flute work from Longdon. Favorite moments include the powerful jam between 6:30 and 7:20, where Godfrey duels the rhythm section to a draw, and the flowing, distinctly Greg Lake-ish acoustic guitar / analog synth section from around 15:05 through 15:35.

As wonderful as *The Difference Machine* was, *The Underfall Yard* is its equal and more. Longdon is a magically good fit for the group, and the addition of brass and strings to half these tracks lends extra weight and substance to the naturally-present orchestral elements of the music. Indeed, there is a distinctly British beauty to the music, which manages to be both reserved and passionate, stark and sophisticated, keenly aware of history while drawing a clear through-line to the present.

The best prog taps into the imagination and emotions in ways that carry the music beyond the scope of entertainment and into the realm of art. With *The Difference Machine* and now *The Underfall Yard*, Big Big Train has firmly established itself as one of the most impressive and affecting progressive rock acts working today.

Rating: A

*

The Black Keys
El Camino
Nonesuch, 2011
[Published on *The Daily Vault* 4/4/2012]

Saying you watch *The Colbert Report* for the music is kind of like saying you buy *Playboy* for the articles.

Regardless, it was The Black Keys' performance on *The Colbert Report* earlier this year that convinced me to give these guys a shot, and I'm not sorry.

The first thing that almost has to be said in any writer's initial Black Keys review is this: Dan Auerbach and Patrick Carney are not ripping off the White Stripes. Not even close. Yes, Auerbach sings and plays dirty guitar with flashes of Jimmy Page-like intensity, and yes, Carney plays nothing but drums and plays them big and loud. Both groups favor a decidedly low-fi, garage-y vibe. But where the Stripes were a virtual two-person Zeppelin tribute band with an avant-garde, artsy sensibility, the Keys mine earthier turn-of-the-'70s sounds, layering on analog synths and bass and digging a series of hard, greasy grooves that locate the undiscovered nexus between the MC5 and Marvin Gaye.

Opener/single "Lonely Boy" takes threads of garage rock, ZZ Top Texas boogie, low-fi DIY and glammy analog synths, adds double-time drumming and a chorus of female background vocals on the chorus, and builds a thundering engine of cool. By the time the boys finished powering through this one on *Colbert*, I knew this album was in my future.

Things get even more interesting right away, as "Dead and Gone" features a deep r&b groove, Motown bells and Hammond and airy background vocals, complemented by ragged garage guitar and Auerbach's desperate blues-shouter vocals. "Gold on the Ceiling" cements the impression of varied influences having their DNA recombined in fascinating ways with acoustic rhythm guitar, greasy T.Rex lead guitar, thrashy drums and seedy hipster-cool synths. The airy pre-chorus sets you up again and again for the gang-vocal chorus and tight, raging guitar solos that follow. Think Booker T & the MGs with Page sitting in, the Supremes singing backup, and everyone on acid.

"Little Black Submarines" is the one place where you really have to give a nod to the Zeppelin/Stripes influence, given that it's a virtual "Stairway to Heaven" homage, acoustic opening building to a huge chorus backed by thundering twenty-foot waves of guitar and drums. It's great tune, though, the longest on the album at 4:11, and yet it feels like it goes by in a flash.

From there you get variations on the same purposefully weird mélange of musical styles. "Money Maker" is a big, chugging rocker with menacing rhythms and a dash of talkbox at the crest of the wave. "Run Right Back" is wildman funk, full of the ramshackle exuberance that fuels the Keys' music. "Sister" makes me think of T. Rex, albeit with a shimmery Motown vibe behind the fat rock rhythm section and pseudo-hipster retro synths. "Stop Stop" features a loping rhythm, bells and falsetto "yeah yeah"s right out of the Berry Gordy playbook.

"Mind Eraser" close things out in suitably apocalyptic fashion, with Carney slamming away Bonham-style on the opening while Auerbach decorates the upper end with eerie, fat chords, before the track settles into a deep r&b groove.

Danger Mouse, who coproduced with Auerbach and Carney, gives *El Camino* a spacious feel that allows the individual instruments room to breathe and be heard, accentuating both the essential drive behind the music and the unique way these arrangements blend diverse influences. Low-fi savant Tchad Blake mixed most of the album, weaving Mouse's analog-funk keys over and under Auerbach's stabbing guitar lines and Carney's cavernous backbeats.

El Camino is a wild ride well worth taking, a headtrip into a musical parallel universe where Jimmy Page was obsessed with Motown and Texas boogie grooves instead of Willie Dixon and Howlin' Wolf. Thanks for taking me there, Stephen Colbert.

Rating: A-

*

Gary Clark Jr.
Blak and Blu
Warner Brothers, 2012
[Published on *The Daily Vault* 10/14/2013]

Some young black singers grow up wanting to be Smokey Robinson or Marvin Gaye or Gil-Scott Heron; some young black guitar players grow up wanting to be Chuck Berry or Albert King or Jimi Hendrix. Gary Clark Jr. apparently grew up wanting to be all of them — the difference being, this particular dreamer seems to have the talent needed to make all of those dreams come true.

After three well-received indie releases, Clark's major-label debut *Blak and Blu* opens in blistering style with "Ain't Messin' Around," a manifesto of sorts: "I don't believe in competition / Ain't nobody else like me around." The fact that this bravado comes wrapped up in a song that sounds like James Brown and Al Green strapped to a cruise missile, with Lenny Kravitz on lead guitar and a fat horn section providing the rocket fuel, makes it all the sweeter. "When My Train Pulls In" follows with a stinging blues jam that's stretched out by a series of increasingly expansive, psychedelic solos that would make either Jimi (Hendrix or Page) smile.

The title track finds Clark paying homage to both the great Gil Scott-Heron and Albert King, wrapping a smooth, soulful, very Marvin Gaye mid-tempo number ("Somewhere we got twisted / How do we get lifted?") around samples from Heron's "Pieces of a Man" and King's "As the Years Go Passing By." This kind of thing takes big cojones to try and bigger ones to pull off, both of which Clark clearly possesses, whatever his remarkable falsetto might imply to the contrary.

If you hadn't figured it out by now, Clark's range is astonishing and his knowledge of his musical forebears encyclopedic. After the steady, grinding blues "Bright Lights" gives way to the Berry-inspired roadhouse rock of "Travis County," "The Life" delivers hip-hop-inflected r&b on the way to the loud, dense psychedelic funk of "Glitter Ain't Gold (Jumpin' for Nothin')." No, seriously — and every track hits the mark, accenting the most appealing aspects of each style and executing them flawlessly in support of Clark's often-eloquent lyrics.

The even bigger and more distorted psychedelic blues "Numb" leads into the Smokey Robinson-inspired ballad "Please Come Home," which showcases both Clark's superb falsetto and a solo at the end that feels like it could be Hendrix before he went solo, back when he was an r&b

sideman. "Things Are Changin'" extends that Motown feel momentarily, before the homage goes from stage-whispered to shouted out loud. Covering either Hendrix's "Third Stone From The Sun" or Johnny Taylor's "If You Love Me Like You Say" is a gutsy move, but tying the two together into an interpolating medley? There are really only two ways to come out the other end of that decision; you're either going to look like a fool or a genius. By now you should be able to guess which Clark is. The guy is so good that it isn't even surprising when the closing jam feels like it might literally set the sky on fire.

"You Saved Me" demonstrates Clark's gift for musical alchemy yet again, a slow jam with big, fuzzed-out guitars behind his smooth r&b croon that erupts into a psychedelic solo at the end. The album closes on a quieter note with the back-porch acoustic slide blues number "Next Door Neighbor Blues."

Gary Clark Jr. is a rare talent in so many ways; a frontman who's exceptional on both guitar and vocals; a composer/arranger who draws from the past to create music that's nonetheless bold and innovative; a superb soul singer who can handle blues and rock and funk and rap with equal aplomb. A genuine musical Renaissance man, Clark gives you every reason on *Blak and Blu* to believe he's going to be a talent to watch for many years to come.

Rating: A

*

Elbow
The Take Off and Landing of Everything
Concord Music Group, 2014
[Published on *The Daily Vault* 5/15/2014]

Best-selling British quintet Elbow have described their music as "prog without the solos," which seems fair enough. Their music is all about esthetic, rather than any sort of flash—complex in the sense that they eschew pop formula to travel wherever the song takes them, but their hallmark is an often-spare intensity rather than the instrumental excess for which prog is known. Elbow is refined, restrained, precise (and urgent). By way of musical reference points, to "prog without the solos," I would add: Coldplay without the eagerness; Peter Gabriel without the flamboyance.

And indeed, it seems less than coincidental that the basic tracks for this album were recorded at Gabriel's own Real World Studios before the band moved on to their own studio to finish up. There is a haunting, beguiling aspect to these songs, which rarely accelerate past second gear; it's more post-rock than rock, but steadily rhythmic, with a measured sort of surge to it when the moment demands. The immensely complementary production courtesy of keyboardist Craig Potter reminds of Jeff Buckley's *Grace*, with soft echoes burnishing every note to a kind of gauzy shimmer, as if the whole thing was recorded in an old church.

"This Blue World" introduces the album smartly with frontman Guy Garvey's voice gently keening over the simplest of backings: a muted beat from drummer Richard Jupp with only the subtlest flourishes from bassist Pete Turner, guitarist Mark Potter, and keyboardist Potter decorating a hypnotic narrative. Over the course of the track's seven minutes, the arrangement builds in an unhurried way, gaining elements, gaining power, gaining beauty.

Sophomore track "Charge" is a deeply satisfying concoction with a thrumming organ figure at its core, accented by strings and soft, chunky, percussive guitar chords. These rhythm tracks pulse rather than pound, just the right accompaniment for a set of songs about love and loss and longing. "Fly Boy Blue / Lunette" adds another degree of intensity, with a weighty orchestral arrangement supporting a sturdy backbeat. Vocalist Garvey possesses a quiet charisma, his steady intensity convincing you over and over that he's just about to say something really interesting— again—and you don't want to miss it. The tension in Turner's bass line in the latter part of this cut is tremendous.

The first single off the album, "New York Morning" is ringing, engaging, and downright lovely, anchored by a simple, rhythmically repeating piano figure. The key line "Everybody owns the great ideas" is emphasized by the quietness of the music around it the first time, and cradled by its lift the second. The final stanza of the superb lyric opens with this poignant, richly alliterative triplet: "The way the day begins / Decides the shade of everything / But the way it ends depends on if you're home."

The memorable lines keep coming as Garvey assures his lover that "You never need fear a thing in this world / While I have a breath in me, blood in my veins" ("Real Life (Angel)"). (Now that's devotion.) Then things turn south and he declares "I cannot stay where all the broken plans were made" and departs, declaring that "I'll spin some lies to tell you upon / My return from the ends of the earth." All the while the band

173

thrums and chimes around him, piano and guitar functioning almost as rhythm instruments.

Melancholy has rarely sounded prettier than on "My Sad Captains," as Garvey sings of dissolution and "a perfect waste of time" while the horn section offers stately accents. The title track has an especially cinematic feel, with the title repeated over and over towards the end as the song achieves liftoff, a repeating keyboard figure, circular melody and lush vocal arrangement fueling its ascendance. "The Blanket of Night" is a rather strange and playful closer, carrying a bit of almost theatrical flavor to it before its abrupt finish.

The Take Off and Landing of Everything lives up to its overcomplicated title, delivering 57 minutes of yearning, enchanting and generally lovely music, with Garvey's Gabrielesque vocals up front and the band offering restrained but evocative accompaniment, rich with texture and mood. Some albums get your attention by shouting at you; *Take Off* takes the opposite tack, delivering a murmured invocation that nonetheless captivates, music to be savored rather than wolfed down and forgotten.

Rating: A-

~Segue~

Interview: Jon Foreman

[Published on *The Daily Vault* 12/8/2007]

San Diegans Jonathan Foreman, his brother Tim and their friend Chad Butler started Switchfoot while Tim was still in high school and the other two were at the University of California, San Diego. Their original format was the classic power trio with Jon on guitar and lead vocals, Tim on bass and background vocals, and Butler behind the drum kit. Older brother Jon was—and is—both a major Led Zeppelin fan and an avid surfer; Switchfoot is a surfing term.

The band issued three albums as a trio: The Legend Of Chin *(1997),* New Way To Be Human *(1999) and* Learning To Breathe *(2000), steadily building a following before signing with Columbia in 2002. During the same period, the group added longtime friend Jerome Fontamillas on keyboards and guitar, issuing 2003's* The Beautiful Letdown *as a quartet and scoring hit singles "Dare You to Move" and "Meant to Live." Over the course of the next two years, they added a fifth member, guitarist Drew Shirley, and delivered 2005's* Nothing Is Sound, *which featured the rather Zeppelinesque single "Stars." At Christmas 2006 they were back with the diverse* Oh! Gravity, *which stretched their sound in new directions. In 2007 the band toured behind* Oh! Gravity *early in the year, then left Columbia, started work on a new independent disc, and assembled a fall tour with co-headliners Relient K that benefitted Habitat For Humanity.*

In the midst of all this activity, Jon Foreman found time to record the first two of a series of four seasonally-themed, Internet-only solo EPs. Fall *came out in November via iTunes and Foreman's website. We caught up with Jon Foreman via e-mail just days before he boarded a plane to catch his boyhood idols' December 10, 2007 reunion concert in London.*

The Daily Vault: Please tell us about the Appetite for Construction tour and how it came about.

Jon Foreman: The idea came about one day when we were playing in Austin, Texas. We were hanging out by a river talking about how we could do the touring thing differently. We were looking back at three years of doing the Bro Am [an annual charity event Switchfoot sponsors in San

Diego] and we were thinking about how amazing it would be to dive into other communities as well.

We wanted to find a low-overhead organization that folks could get directly involved in on a local level. Habitat for Humanity was a perfect fit. Two things are needed for the job site: funding and personnel. This tour helped accomplish both—thousands of kids signed up to get involved and the tour and the song we wrote for the tour raised more than $100,000 for Habitat. It was such a dream to see it all come together!

I gather you've been friends with the guys in Relient K for a while. How would you describe them and their music to your own fans?

We've been friends with the RK boys for a while... They were the local opener on a tour we were on back in the day, so it's been great to see them evolve as a band and to be cheering them on. Matt is almost like a little brother to me and I have a ton of respect for him and his tunes. His music is extremely deceptive—happy-clappy pop-punk songs that have as much depth as you want to dive into. Witty, honest, darkly personal songs in a candy coated shell.

Back to Switchfoot. You guys fought your way through the indie world for years, signed the major-label deal that every independent band *used to be* shooting for, put out three albums with Columbia, and now you've turned around and gone back to the indie route. Tell us about how that all came to pass.

It's all about trust. We started this thing as a family—my brother, my friend and myself writing songs we believed in and playing 'em.

We found some folks that we really trusted over at Columbia and had an amazing time. But then the turnover at Sony got to be ridiculous—a new "family" every other week. There were decisions made by our label that didn't reflect our intentions.

So we decided to move on. No hard feelings, just wanting to protect the music we believe in.

The path you've traveled—which is getting more and more well-traveled—begs the question: are big labels obsolete?

I'm not sure, I can only speak from my perspective: there's got to be a deeper motivation than the bottom line for me to feel fulfilled by what I do. And that motivation is hard to find at the big labels nowadays...

A lot of artists see file sharing as a mixed blessing—great for initial exposure, but terrible over the long haul if you're trying to make a living playing music. What's your take on file sharing and especially its effects on independent artists?

Hmmm... We've always made a living by playing live music. We just played the biggest tour we've ever had with no new record around. Weird...

File sharing is our reality. It's like asking whether or not you feel clouds are good or bad: they're both good and bad, I suppose, but wishing them away ain't gonna help! I really love vinyl but I doubt we'll ever move back. The question for me has always which songs will change my world.

Switchfoot has been through a lot of changes over the years, building a mainstream audience, adding two members and expanding the scope of your sound. Looking back on it now, how do you see the evolution of the band having affected the music and you personally?

I feel like most of these changes have been attempts to arrive at an ever-changing destination. A lot of times, (like now for example!) we start a record hoping to go in one direction and finish the project with a completely different objective. That's why live music can be so fulfilling— because the goal and the attempt happen simultaneously.

I'm thankful for the songs, though. I feel like they have been gifts, it's a gift to be able to sing a song you believe in night after night. To get a chance to give birth to something that you really care about. That has been the constant within the changes.

You guys seem to be always recording, always pushing toward the next release. Anything you can tell us about the next band album yet?

The reason why I love music is because it has this intangible spark, this once-in-a-lifetime urgency that breathes down the neck of my soul and makes me cry or laugh or throw something. So you dive into music and begin to learn how things work, the mechanics, the rules. And suddenly it becomes math instead of magic.

I feel like the most dangerous place for us to be as a band is to be comfortable. The rule for this record is that if you've done it in the past you can't do it again. We want the music to move us. I heard somebody say — "If you ain't crying, why you playin' it?" I like that...

We recorded 14 songs with Charlie Peacock [producer of Switchfoot's initial trio of indie albums] this summer. Our first approach was to take a song and play it for an hour or two and then listen back to what we achieved and move forward from there. It's completely new for us—we've never "jammed" before.

There is a searching quality to your songs; they ask the questions at the core of every human's experience: why am I here? Does my life have a purpose? What does it mean to be a good person in this world? In your music, you guys approach spirituality in an open-ended way, making it mostly about asking the questions rather than preaching a particular set of answers. Was that a conscious choice, or more of a natural outcome of how you approach your own life?

I've never possessed the ability to write good songs where I am not emotionally involved. The questions that I'm asking are not rhetorical. The songs are my vehicles to try and understand the world. Often I find that I can be far more honest in a song than in real life. I'm working on trying to figure that out...

A lot of your lyrics focus on spiritual issues, and you're also frontman for a rock band. One thing spiritual leaders and rock stars have always had in common is a tendency to attract some pretty intense followers, people who have a really deep-seated need to believe in someone. How would you describe your experiences with so-called "superfans"?

For the most part, I feel incredibly honored when I think about the folks that listen to our songs. Most of them are amazing people that inspire me... When someone tells me that one of our tunes helped encourage them to join the Peace Corps I'm blown away. And that type of thing happens all the time. People who treat us strangely simply don't understand our tunes… Seldom do I run into folks that love the music that don't understand who we are.

A columnist in the *New York Times* wrote recently about the fragmentation of music, how it's all genre-driven now and there are no more universal acts like the Beatles or Led Zeppelin or U2 that everyone listens to. To me that argument both rang true and paralleled your lyric in "Lonely Nation." The more choices we have, the more we're able to customize the world we come in contact with, the lonelier we get, because we're no longer sharing experiences in a communal way. How do you react to that idea?

If I understand the comment correctly, I feel like the columnist got it wrong in some ways. With the death of radio and the birth of the iPod, nothing is genre driven—what's the difference between rock, or alternative or indie? James Taylor is in the rock section at iTunes. Most big "indie" bands are on a major. And alternative is even more confusing. Everyone listens to everything; it's all Jack.fm.

I do feel like the universal experience is dying, however. There are too many options to have an Elvis come on the scene. I suppose hip-hop is the closest thing to universal. And yet community is a huge part of the human experience. Even in cyberspace we're searching to belong somewhere, looking for community. But often things are moving too fast. Even in music, too many choices can lead to mediocrity. Every good record was made by the restrictions placed around the music, i.e. time, budget, ability, ambition.

Aside from life expectancy, who's to say that our modern human existence is fundamentally better now than it was two thousand years past. War, famine, disease, greed, murder… machines do many things, but they cannot save us from ourselves. And I haven't found one that cures loneliness. We have created a modern day serfdom of sorts: we slave away, chaining ourselves to our devices and giving the first fruits to the global corporations.

Many people see a gulf in American society today between the faithful and the secular. People on both sides of that continuum seem to have become more rigid in their views of each other. I've read about ardent Christians grousing because you guys don't just write worship songs,

and also about ardent secularists being put off by the spiritual messages your lyrics contain. And then there are people like me—a spiritually seeking agnostic who's somewhere in the broad middle, and who finds your music resonates deeply with me precisely because it's spiritual but not dogmatic. What do you make of that?

I think people throw rocks at the things they don't understand. We've always attempted to make music for thinking people. Some of these folks are Christian, or Jewish, or Taoist, or determinist, or dentists, or plumbers… It's absurdly close-minded to think that we should all only listen to and fraternize with folks who think like we do. That's the way fascism grows! I love people that I disagree with. I listen to them. They listen to me. Sometimes we never see eye to eye, but we still hang out, we still care for each other. If you don't love people you disagree with, you won't have many friends!

I feel like music is one of the few areas in our rigid world where tolerance is still found. To box it up into something more organized would be many a journalist's dream and many a music lover's nightmare!

You're planning to release four solo EPs of six songs each over the next 12 months. How did that idea develop?

I had these personal songs that didn't belong on a Switchfoot record and yet they kept coming to me. I just kept recording them at home every night never thinking that they would ever see the light of day.

Everything felt very natural, very honest—I paid for everything myself, and recorded most of it on my own. For most of the project I had no idea that people outside my family and friends would actually ever hear these songs, maybe that's why they're so personal. I am so excited to get these tunes out, it's a dream come true in many ways.

The EP format felt like the right way to go: no real fanfare, just a continuous yearly flow of 24 honest songs created for the moment. Every song gets the attention it deserves and there are no singles.

I've listened to *Fall* and my initial take is that the songs are both quieter and more personal and specific to you than the average Switchfoot

song. They're almost like hymns you might sing to yourself. How do you see these songs?

These songs reflect the hours and they were made and the purpose they had. I wrote and recorded these songs late at night at my house after the world was sleeping. For the most part they were written as a personal consolation for pain.

In my first listen I caught some strings and horns and other fresh textures in the music. Do you have some guest players with you on some of the EP tracks?

Yes. After I got the basic tracking done I flew to Nashville and had some friends and friends of friends lay some things down. I wanted textures that took the songs away from the "singer-songwriter demo" feel and yet I was careful that the soul of the song remained intact.

Let's see... Jeff Coffin of Flecktones fame was amazing... Charlie Peacock played and helped with direction overall. Keith Tutt was the secret weapon on the cello. Tim [Foreman] and Jerome [Fontamillas] from the Foot helped me in a few spots too... Stacy DuPree from Eisley sang on *Winter*...

Anything else you'd like to tell folks about future plans for the EPs?

Winter beat *Fall* for me... which is unfortunate because fall is my favorite season. I haven't started on spring or summer and I really have very little direction at this point. I want the mood to change for those disks to represent the seasons but I still want the honesty... I'm trying to employ the production and the song selection to get there.

 Finally, a three-part random bonus question: Any secret musical vices? What's your favorite '80s metal band? What was the first album you ever bought?

Vices, hmmm... I'm not sure what you mean, a vice as a weakness of musical character? Well, I need a good crowd to play a good show. I wish I were a bit less caring, like Dylan or something... but my experience onstage is often far too influenced by what type of crowd we have. I play from their perspective.

I think it's Chuck Klosterman who has some good stuff to say about guilty pleasures. Something like: a guilty pleasure is something that you like that you think you shouldn't like. But who's to say you shouldn't like it? Who's to say that someone else's opinion should mean more to you than yours? In the end, why should you be embarrassed about something that brings you joy?!

I guess I don't really have a favorite '80s metal band. I was too into Zeppelin and surfing in junior high... the leather pants and the makeup scared me off. But I loved the lighter stuff, "Pour Some Sugar on Me" was the best thing I had ever heard...

I can't remember what record I bought first, but the first tape I got was a birthday gift from my elementary school friend: Whitesnake... "I'm going down the only road I've ever known!" Yes indeed!

~Segue~

Interview: Greg Spawton

[Published on *The Daily Vault* 10/4/2012]

For five years now, every time a package has arrived in the mail from Bournemouth, its U.S. Customs stamp cursorily marked "CDs," this writer's pulse has quickened. When the first one arrived in summer 2007, I'd never heard of Big Big Train. Today, three full albums and a remarkable EP later, I count myself as an unabashed fan. Progressive rock music is, by its very nature, difficult to pull off well. It can easily come off as overblown or impersonal or esoteric or even predictable in its attempts to be different. Big Big Train's music is consistently none of these; instead, it is intelligent, diverse, lush, driving, emotional, imaginative, engaging, and at times virtuosic.

The group was founded by Andy Poole and Greg Spawton in 1989 and today consists of Spawton (guitar, bass, keyboards, composition), Poole (bass, guitar, production), David Longdon (vocals, flute, composition and more), Dave Gregory (guitar, ex-XTC) and Nick D'Virgilio (drums, ex-Spock's Beard), often joined by a varied guest cast of modern prog luminaries that on their recent album English Electric Part One *includes Andy Tillison (The Tangent) and Martin Orford (IQ). Over the course of a recent week, co-founder Greg Spawton indulged the Vault with a wide-ranging interview addressing the new album and what's next, the possibility of live dates, Joni Mitchell and James Taylor, and the ongoing search for the transcendent.*

[Editor's Note: The interview was conducted by e-mail, resulting in many English spellings (ploughing, realised, etc.) making their way into the text. These have been preserved for authenticity, and should be read aloud with the proper English inflection for full effect.]

The Daily Vault: English Electric Part One has been out for a couple of weeks at this point. It seems to me this is the group's most anticipated release yet, and it comes at a time when it feels like the progressive rock genre is having another of its periodic resurgences. How has the response to the album been so far?

Greg Spawton: *English Electric* has come out at an interesting time for progressive rock. I can't remember any period where there was such a run of high-quality releases. I did become a little bit concerned about how much time the album would get in the limelight before other releases came along, but I think it's worked out just fine for us. We planned the promotional campaign very carefully and the response has been extremely positive. The album appears to have achieved more "reach" than anything else we've done, including *The Underfall Yard*. Sales have been higher than we hoped for and, in just the first two weeks of release, it's been listened to many more times on Spotify than any of our previous releases.

That's great to hear. So, just to recap a bit, *EEP1* is the group's sixth studio album, and its second full album (plus a very substantial EP) with David Longdon, Nick D'Virgilio and Dave Gregory on board along with you and Andy Poole. Like many groups in the prog genre, Big Big Train has been through quite a few lineup changes over the years. Each has moved the band forward in some way, but this particular lineup feels like it might be the sort of thing you've been reaching for all along, five guys with thoroughly compatible musical sensibilities and a strong commitment to this music.

There was actually another album, called *Bard*, which we have deleted, so *EEP1* is, in fact, album number seven. It is the second full-length release with the new line-up. We have certainly experienced a number of line-up changes over the years and for a while it felt like things would never really settle down. Then, it started to come together. Back in 2007 we began working with Nick and that made us think about whether we could strengthen other areas of the band. As if by magic, David came into our life via a phone call from our sound engineer Rob Aubrey. Rob said he'd recorded this chap called David Longdon who, he felt, would be the perfect singer for BBT. I spoke to David a few times and we tried him out on the title track of *The Underfall Yard*. He turned out to be the frontman we had needed all along. Andy and I are huge XTC fans and we'd wondered about asking Dave Gregory to play for us, but had not plucked up the courage. It turned out that David had worked with Dave previously and so he called him and it went from there. Thing is, I love these guys. We have all become close friends who share a similar outlook. They also happen to be extraordinary musicians who pour creativity into Big Big Train.

I think that sense of common purpose (not to mention talent) really shows through in the music—it's a really rich brew. I love also that it's

dramatic music that's full of emotion even when tackling topics that some might regard as fairly esoteric. BBT has a way of bringing historical narratives and specific times and places to life in your music that's pretty remarkable. It feels like that focus on storytelling has become really central to BBT's music over the last few albums.

It's very important to me that music has an emotional connection. Andy is a big Steely Dan fan, but I can't get on with them as their music, clever as it is, just doesn't move me. I'm glad you have picked up on the storytelling aspect of what we do. I have written a number of personal songs over the years but I didn't want to keep ploughing the "failed relationship" furrow. I discovered that telling good stories with the songs can resonate just as much with listeners as songs built on personal experiences. Of course, finding a good story is one thing, but it's recognising and representing the deeper and more universal themes within the stories that make the songs interesting.

Yes. Just for example, I thought it was remarkable how much emotion the group brought to "Winchester From St. Giles' Hill," which on the surface is about exactly what the title implies: walking up a hill to see the view. But when David sings "A river flowing from the chalkhills / Through the water meadows / And the open fields" with the music surging behind him, I get chills. The emotional subtext is that he is seeing and feeling the entire history of England itself laid out before him, and is deeply moved by it.

Glad to hear it had such an impact. History is too often thought of as a dry subject. I find it intensely dramatic and moving and we tried to capture that within "Winchester From St Giles' Hill." One of David's gifts is to find the emotional core in the material. The connection of the onlooker with the landscape below the hill and the people that helped to forge the land is, for me, a soulful thing and that's what David zeroed in on. Danny Manners' piano arrangement sought to emulate the movement of the river and Dave added drama to the song with the string arrangement and guitar solo.

That's, I think, where the magic happens with Big Big Train—how you guys manage to fit all of these different musical components together. There's the basic rock instrumentation, but then you add flute and violin and on some tracks full string and horn sections, and a lot of complex vocals and harmonies, and even banjo on songs like "Uncle Jack" and "Hedgerow." It must be a bit of a puzzle figuring out how the pieces fit together in the arranging and mixing process, when to add to and when to subtract from individual tracks, and where.

I've always appreciated music where the level of detail is such that you can hear something new even after repeated listens. We spend a lot of time piecing the elements together for songs until we find the right combination of sounds. We're finishing "East Coast Racer," a track for *Part Two*, at the moment, and we're getting down to very fine levels of detail in a song which has a number of movements over 15 minutes. It can sometimes feel overwhelming and, occasionally, strong ideas have to make way for the good of the song as a whole. That can be a shame and can cause protracted discussion within the band. Even at the mixing stage, Rob may express forthright opinions if he feels something isn't working or something more is needed. But we work things through and pan for gold. [N.B.: "Rob" is Rob Aubrey, who mixed, mastered and otherwise fiddled with *EEP1* and most other BBT recordings.]

Count me intrigued by your description of "East Coast Racer." I'd like to ask a few questions about some of the individual tracks on *Part One*, but first there's one other point I wanted to just touch on with you. There was quite a lively discussion on the BBT Facebook page a few weeks ago about how much of a Genesis influence can actually be heard in Big Big Train's music, versus how much is simply projected by fans by virtue of your and Andy's acknowledged admiration for Genesis, and David and Nick's previous associations with the band. Personally, I find the conversation interesting mostly because while I feel like the influence is there, I'm actually not a big fan of early Genesis, whereas I'm very fond of the last few BBT albums. The common touch points that I hear are elaborate arrangements, imaginative storytelling, an interest in history, and a uniquely English flavor to the songs. That, and the occasional guitar or keyboard part with a Hackett/Banks vibe.

I think our music appeals to fans of Genesis but that isn't the same as saying it sounds like Genesis and sometimes those two things get confused. And for reviewers who are inundated with new music it's an easy reference point when they are putting their thoughts into words. Having said that, we're all Genesis fans and if a hint of their sound appears in our songs from time-to-time, as it will do, I'm very relaxed about it. And, certainly, Genesis were great storytellers and that is something we have drawn from in our approach. However, there are many influences on our music which all go into the melting pot and we're certainly not restricted to '70s bands, so our sound will inevitably have moved on from any early progressive template. One of the things that strikes me about the BBT forum is the wide tastes of BBT listeners on there. A thread about Joni Mitchell is as likely to get people talking as something about Porcupine Tree or Marillion.

Very true. Alright then, I promised a few questions about the individual songs on *English Electric Part One*. The album is framed by songs contrasting a claustrophobic life below ground—as explored in "The First Rebreather" and "A Boy in Darkness" in particular—with moments of joy in the wide-open countryside ("Uncle Jack" and "Hedgerow," as well as "Winchester from St. Giles' Hill" and "Upton Heath"). At what point did you realize that was going to be a major theme of *EEP1*? To what degree did that realization shape the arranging and mixing process, and decisions about run order?

We didn't start off with any concept or theme. All we set out to do was to bring together the best collection of songs which would work together as an album. After preparing the early demos we realised that a couple of themes were beginning to emerge by happenstance. David had "A Boy in Darkness" and I had "The First Rebreather," both set underground. David had "Uncle Jack" and I had a tune (with no lyrics at the time) called "Hedgerow." The character Uncle Jack (who is a real person) was a man who had a fascination for hedgerows. Jack was also a coal miner. So, the main theme began to emerge and then that influenced the development of other songs such as "Upton Heath" and "Winchester from St Giles' Hill." That also got us thinking about musical motifs, so we began to look again at some of the arrangements. I worked the keyboard solo theme from "Rebreather" into "Upton Heath" and David worked some of the words from "Uncle Jack" into "Hedgerow." The coda of "Summoned by Bells" is actually based on the ending of "East Coast Racer" on *Part Two*. We ended up with about 105 minutes of material which was too long for one album but too short for a decent double so that gave us an opportunity to write a couple of other songs which seek to bring everything together. In particular, one song on *Part Two* is called "The Permanent Way" which is an attempt to summarise the album in eight minutes while standing on its own as a song. I'm really pleased with it. As to the running order, that was left until very late. We expected "Hedgerow" to be the last track but at one stage "East Coast Racer" was going to be the first track on *Part One*. However, that's quite a challenging piece of music so we decided to swap some of the songs around. We must have had five or six different attempts at getting the track order right. It can make a real difference to an album.

Let me say that I think "Hedgerow" is a stellar closer and have been listening to it probably more than any other track on the album in recent days. So many interesting elements to it. The main opening riff played by Dave feels like it has a strong Byrds influence. Pretty soon Nick comes in with an unusual-for-him straight 4/4 backbeat behind it and it gathers tremendous drive. Then David adds lush vocals and all sorts of quirky textures and sounds begin to mingle in the background, and then the horns arrive, and the strings, and the middle section featuring a violin solo, and the closing march with all the layered vocals and horn section fanfare... I guess what I'm getting at it is, it's quite a musical smorgasbord.

"Hedgerow" is a good example of how we are stronger as a unit than as individuals. I'd had the title and that little 12-string riff for a couple of years and worked it up into a demo. My demos are very humble; David's sound amazing because he has that voice, whereas mine need a lot of imagination. The original demo ended on a fade-out of the violin solo, but Andy insisted that we had to end with a reprise of the main vocal part. That wasn't easy, but I found a way. Dave worked up the guitar parts and then Nick put down this really tight backbeat which gave it a lovely '60s feel. David wrote the words and developed the melody and harmonies and sketched out some of the parts for the brass. Rachel Hall took my sketch of the violin solo and made it her own. Danny Manners re-arranged my basic piano parts into something glorious and Dave Desmond and the brass band came in to do their stuff. The big singalong at the end was Andy's idea and we asked as many people as we could to get involved. Rob mixed the track, but even then we felt there was something missing. Dave then came up with the Mellotron solos to complete the arrangement. It's quite an uplifting tune and a good way to end, although it has its moments of pathos.

Indeed. So, speaking of perhaps unanticipated musical connections, I've been wanting to ask a question about "Upton Heath." Maybe it's just

that the subject matter and choices of instruments go together so naturally, but it sure feels to this James Taylor fan like there must be some sort of musical relationship between "Upton Heath" and "Country Road"—that feeling of uplift walking through quiet countryside as mandolin and violin lead the way.

There is definitely a connection, now you mention it. I don't think it is something we were thinking about during the writing and arranging sessions, but it is there.

So Joni Mitchell isn't such a reach after all... interesting. Anyhow, heading into the home stretch here, back to the big picture. In recent years Big Big Train has been almost exclusively a studio band, and now you have Nick in the band, who is based in the U.S. and has substantial other time commitments. And yet, I have caught tantalizing hints here and there about potential live dates. Anything you can share on that subject at this point?

At the moment the time we have Nick is very limited. We're flying him over in the New Year and we have just a couple of days with him before he has to head back. However, he is hopeful of more time off in the future and we are beginning to plan with that in mind. Even then, it's not easy as our release schedule for the next year or so is busy. *Part Two* is out in March, a single and the special double edition of *English Electric* is out in September and a triple CD called *Station Masters* will be out in early 2014. Whilst we have some admin support, we manage ourselves and I know, from past experience, how much time that release schedule and all the promotional work that goes with it will take. We need to be realistic and not bite off more than we can chew and so the show we're planning will follow on from *Station Masters* in 2014. If it all comes off, it'll be presented as an evening with Big Big Train and we hope to record it for a DVD release. It'll include the brass band and a string section.

Live BBT with brass and strings as well... wow. That could be pretty spectacular, and seems like a great goal to shoot for as the next 18 months unfold. Now, zooming the lens out even farther, I'm wondering perhaps the most basic thing of all: why progressive rock? What do you find special and compelling about the form?

My first experience with progressive rock was hearing "Dancing with the Moonlit Knight" in the late '70s. Up until then I'd probably only listened to my parents' music, some of which was very good, but all of which would fit squarely within the mainstream. But this song, by a band called Genesis, it was different. I found it astounding. Why was the song so lengthy? Why were there so many twists and turns? How could it be so loud and aggressive at one moment and so pastoral and gentle at others? What did the lyrics mean? What instruments were creating the sounds? As I went on to explore PFM and Van Der Graaf Generator and other prog bands I began to understand the genre and the motivation of the musicians behind it, but those initial impressions are, for me, still relevant and explain the attraction. Progressive rock is compelling primarily because it provides the musician with a vehicle to write and perform music which can reach beyond the ordinary. I mentioned in an interview with Brad Birzer a comment that Paul Stump made in his book *The Music's All That Matters*, and it bears repeating. Stump says that progressive musicians are "hankering after the transcendent." That about sums it up.

Does it ever. That feels like the perfect place to wrap this up. Thanks again for your time and best of luck with all of Big Big Train's upcoming ventures.

Very much enjoyed this interview, Jason. Thank you for making it interesting.

7

Discoveries

WRITING ABOUT MUSIC FOR 20 YEARS has produced many moments of joy: finding new angles on classic albums, shining a light on underappreciated music, learning more about the creative process of favorite artists from the artists themselves. Among the greatest joys I've experienced over the course of this journey has been the simple joy of discovery.

As a well-established music review site, *The Daily Vault* typically receives 400 to 500 pitches a week from labels, publicists and, more and more frequently, the artists themselves. Many of said pitches are for singles or videos or tours or share news that is often indistinguishable from what used to be called publicity stunts (and are now called press releases). Since the *Vault* is an album review site, all of the above go straight into the trash. We might review an EP or concert documentary on occasion, but other than that it's albums, albums, albums. (For a brief moment in time I wondered if this made us an anachronism in this age of attention-deficit-challenged, curated-and-playlisted music grazing, but then I realized that, to the contrary, it made us different, and therefore special. Albums are our *thing*.)

Tossing out all of the chaff, we might end up with 80 pitches a week for albums. Of those, I'll eliminate up to a quarter based on us not currently covering the genre (just lately our panel of writers is woefully underrepresented when it comes to interest in reviewing country and/or hip-hop), and another quarter based on a quick listen to a track or two (the good news about the d-i-y era is, anyone can make an album—which is also the bad news). The 40 or so remaining pitches get doled out among the staff for their consideration—except for the one I might pluck for myself.

So: in an average week, I'll select one out of 400 pitches to request a copy of the album. (And I only review physical copies; for me, no liner notes equals no interest in reviewing.) Since I review most, but not all, of what I request, I'd put the odds of sending *The Daily Vault* a pitch and having me end up both listening to your whole album and reviewing it at about one in 500.

That might seem harsh, but it's a system that's all about survival. We are a free site, populated by unpaid writers who review albums in our "spare time," and we are barraged with pitches every single day. There is no practical alternative.

The point of all this backstory being: the albums and artists you're going to read about in this chapter are special. Truly special. Not only did they make the cut to be reviewed, in most cases, I flat-out loved them.

There's Jill Knight, whose elemental voice and deeply personal songs dazzled me on the spot when I first met her busking at Ghirardelli Square in 1999.

There's Casey Frazier, the troubadour whose finely-crafted tunes grabbed my attention from the moment my son brought his 2013 album *Regal* home from a local CD release show.

There's Chris Cubeta, a Renaissance Man producer-arranger-multi-instrumentalist-singer-songwriter whose own work simply reeks of artistry and integrity.

There's Mark Doyon, whose adventurous musical alter ego Arms of Kismet sparked a conversation that grew into a convocation of like-minded creators that persists to this day.

And then there's Last Charge of the Light Horse, the musical vehicle for songwriter-singer-guitarist Jean-Paul Vest of Long Island, New York.

Jean-Paul's musings on the inner life of the suburban Everyman are so piercing, so keenly observant of human nature and brutally honest in their assessments of its consequences that I was thoroughly captured from the first time I heard his work.

What I didn't know, couldn't know, when JP's first disc arrived in my mailbox in 2003 (*If You Only Knew*, by his pre-Last Charge group Blue Sandcastle), was that it was the beginning of a connection that would over time dramatically outgrow its initial boundaries of music writer and artist. Over the course of the next decade, our e-mail conversations developed steadily, even as JP produced two more albums and an EP, and I produced two novels and several hundred album reviews. In the course of our shared musings, we discovered a lot of things we had in common, but none more important than this: each of us is, for the other, that person who is so essential to our drive to create art—the person who gets it. A kindred soul. An audience.

So yes, these past two decades of writing about music have been a voyage of discovery. The opportunity to experience new music from new

192

artists, who show me a new way of interpreting the world, is a tremendous gift, and the day I take it for granted will be my last on this job. But the opportunity to break through all of the crash and clutter of our lives today and really connect—the chance, in short, to make a friend—that is priceless.

*

Last Charge of the Light Horse
Fractures
Curlock & Jalaiso, 2008
[Published on *The Daily Vault* 5/23/2008]

Lyric sheets are a dicey business for a writer-geek like me. I'm often so hung up on the quality of lyrics that I've learned not to look at them before I listen to a disc, because a weak turn of phrase or clichéd idea can color my whole view of the album before I've heard a note of music.

In this case, though, I've been around the block with singer-songwriter-guitarist Jean-Paul Vest twice already—once with his former group Blue Sandcastle and more recently with his newer trio Last Charge of the Light Horse—and both times his songs have completely captured me. Yes, the singing is strong, the playing is excellent, and the production usually strikes a nice balance between raw and sharp, but the words are what's ended up pulling me headlong into Vest's universe each time we've met.

And so, when the new Last Charge disc *Fractures* showed up in my mailbox just a few minutes ago, the first thing I did was pop it in the computer to rip it into iTunes… and what did I do while the CD drive was busy spinning zeroes and ones but sit here and read the lyrics to an entire song.

Big mistake.

Because, you see, the song is the last one on this disc, "100,001," and the lyric is not just brilliant but truly profound in a way that only a person of a certain age and station in life can appreciate. Being one myself, I am now stuck in a purgatory of my own making, waiting forty minutes to hear Vest sing said lyric because I do *not* cheat, I treat an album's run order as sacred, especially the first time through, and especially if I'm going to be reviewing it.

Yes, you read that right. I haven't heard a note of music yet, and I'm already frustrated about waiting half an hour to hear a song whose lyrics

I've just read for the first time. If that suggests to you that this album might just be extraordinary... it should.

It's time to listen now. More after the break.

~

If you think being a teenager is hard, try staring middle age in the face. All those big dreams you had have been reduced to life-sized reality—this is your job, this is your family, this is your life. No do-overs allowed. You're past halfway from cradle to grave and this is *it* and what exactly do you have to show for it? A boatload of responsibilities, a household full of stress, and your friends and siblings all grappling with similar strains and doubts.

Having already established himself as one of my favorite lyricists working today, Jean-Paul Vest is back, and neither he nor father-son rhythm section Artie (drums and background vocals) and A.J. (bass and background vocals) Riegger have lost a step. *Fractures* is a genuine Everyman American gothic, a spare, intense song-cycle that reaches into the mid-life male's closet of anxieties and drags them all out one by one.

"The New Year" quickly establishes the album's themes of restlessness and concern about time passing, the trio's skittering arrangement foreshadowing trouble as Vest sings "Look out ahead / we're coming, coming fast / ready for the good old days to start at last / kick off the party with a laugh and a bang / leave your secrets in the closet / your failures where they hang."

"Face to Face" digs deeper yet as Vest explores the nooks and crannies of a sibling relationship on the rocks ("I can only speculate why you never call here anymore / could be advice I gave came back to bite me / could be you mean to but never write me... the distance between us increases as the years accelerate / we used to share a bedroom, now we live in separate states / with less to laugh about, more to tolerate"). The music is another jumpy rhythm section over which Vest and producer Bob Stander layer urgent, repeating chords, winching up the tension with each powerful verse.

The thing you notice only as the disc progresses is that there truly is an arc to this album's story, but once you see it, no other run order could really work for these songs. "Something Out of Nothing" accelerates the tempo another notch before finally releasing pent-up tension at the chorus of a song about the leap of faith that's required both in creating a family and in keeping it going when times get rough ("All those magicians / they pull the dove from their sleeve / you and I pay down the mortgage / and try to believe").

"One Kind Word" looks farther into the future of a similar relationship, Riegger's drums rumbling gently in the back as Vest decorates his precise lyrics with stark, authoritative guitar strums: "One kind word shouldn't have to last me so long / you leave me sucking on a happy memory until the sweetness is gone / I can't walk away from my faith in a good thing / even if it never comes." Ouch. An extended outro lends an epic, elegiac feel to this quietly devastating tune about losing faith in a relationship that's built on it. Sequel "A New Expression" takes a more playful, sardonic look at what feels like the same relationship, set to a sing-songy electric blues arrangement.

The middle three tracks push the tempo, with "The Switch Is On" sounding initially like the album's first upbeat song, handclaps and sunny acoustic strums setting the mood. And then the last verse comes along and offers what might actually be the album's saddest moment, a vignette about filling the empty spaces in a relationship that's suddenly full of them ("We're grateful now for any little errand / marker in the void / but you forget your wallet / and we're driving back and forth / what's a repetition / in the context of a loop / or a needle in a groove"). Damn.

On the next cut Vest takes on one of his chief tormentors directly, calling out "Time" to a catchy, Byrds-influenced jangle-rock beat: "He's waiting like a bully / at the edge of the beach / kicking down castles / ready to bury me in the sand of history." Next up, the Springsteen influence comes on strong as "Worth in Trade" puts the album into fourth gear, an expansive electric track in which our narrator reaches outside himself to be the sounding board for a friend whose troubled relationship is "going nowhere in a lifetime flat."

Setting up the album's closing volley, "A Song Like Yours" backs things off to just Vest and his acoustic for a pretty tune about seeking your muse. The intense "Spring Ahead" unclenches gradually from there, narrating the last bitter fight in a doomed relationship over Vest's rather eerie piano and the rustling rhythm pattern set by A.J. Riegger and guest drummer Larry Eagle (of Springsteen's Sessions Band).

And then it's here: the closer I've been waiting for. "100,001" does not disappoint; to the contrary, the way Vest speak-sings the lyric frames its poetry perfectly, a kind of hymn to the search for meaning that (hopefully) every sentient being goes through at some point. "The odometer flips to a hundred grand / and it feels like progress / the vague taste of accomplishment helps you feel a little less lost / but it's a random number / you're treading water / it's visually pleasing / but grossly misleading / the accumulation of mundane errands over time."

Fractures displays a more contemplative side of the band that made *Getaway Car*, a carefully contained intensity that contrasts with the previous album's untethered nervous energy. It's indisputably a more difficult disc to inhabit, and I'm honestly not sure what this music might sound like to a 20-year-old—maybe a bit dour and over-analytical. But for this 45-year-old, *Fractures* hit like a target-locked cruise missile.

Fractures can be brutal at times, but that just makes the accomplishment that much greater when Vest succeeds in capturing the restlessness, doubt, yearning and recrimination of mid-life and making it into a beautiful, messy, painful and compassionate piece of art. Albums that challenge you this directly to think and feel and get caught up in another person's perspective are rare today, but *Fractures* is one—a wrenching, magnificent, thoroughly memorable one.

Rating: A

*

Jill Knight
Future Perfect
WobyMusik Records, 1998
[Published on *The Daily Vault* 9/8/1999]

San Luis Obispo, California native Jill Knight might just be the most conspicuously talented singer-songwriter-arranger-producer you haven't heard of—yet.

Gifted with a rich, elemental voice that crests and tumbles like a waterfall, she employs it masterfully on this self-published debut album. The eclectic batch of folk-pop she moves through here ranges from engaging acoustic ballads to smartly conceived rock songs, with small touches of jazz and country thrown in for seasoning.

Equally as impressive as her voice and musical range, though, is Knight's knack for crafting witty, evocative and often passionate lyrics. Take the album's opener, "Jeans" for example. Building off a slumbering, funky backbeat, her voice becomes more and more playful each time she passes by the clever chorus:

Wear me like your favorite pair of jeans
We feel good on each other
Stitch me up mend me
When I'm falling apart at the
Seems like we belong together

From there she dives straight into the richly melodic "She Blows Away." Ironic to its core, the song offsets some of her prettiest vocals and a full band-plus-slide-and-cello sound with lyrics that steadily and matter-of-factly carve out a stark character sketch of a self-destructive woman in a downward spiral of addiction.

The album then threatens to peak prematurely with a truly riveting piece of emotional unburdening. Eric Clapton had his "Layla"; Jill Knight has "Don't Make Me Cry." Framed as a heartfelt entreaty to a conflicted lover, it blossoms into something larger as two things occur: Knight steadily ups the ante with her extraordinarily soulful delivery, and it becomes clear the title's plea is directed as much to society at large as it is to the object of her affection—another woman.

Knight clearly recognized she needed to follow up this powerhouse track with something entirely different, and she does, slipping smoothly into the sultry lounge jazz of "Rain." It's a brilliant move, diffusing the built-up tension with a completely fresh and more measured sound. "Rain" also features some of Knight's more potent poetry: "Hungry and dry to the core / Waiting for the perfect cure / Words swirl above and turn into rain."

Here and throughout *Future Perfect*, Knight's band of supporting players repeatedly shines, particularly the core group of Robin Roth on drums, Jeri Jones on lead guitar and Rob Strom on bass, who offer nuanced, punchy and versatile playing.

Knight rounds out the disc with several steadily rocking numbers (the ringing "Mysterious One," the thoughtful/propulsive title track, the Melissa Etheridge-ish "City" and the beautifully funky "Wonderful Sky") mixed in with three gorgeous ballads (the electric "Roses in Winter" and the acoustic "Eyes Wide Open" and "All in a Day").

The other high point lyrically is doubtless the sharp-tongued "All Good Girls," in which Knight imagines confronting a friend who's gotten so wrapped up in her own pious religious pronouncements ("All good girls go to heaven") that she doesn't realize she's become a judgmental hypocrite. The song again takes on a challenging topic with an airy melody, providing the perfect juxtaposition of sound and subject. The one time Knight lets her deep sense of frustration seep into her vocal delivery comes at just the right moment, too, as she sings: "And if it's true I'm going to hell for my ways / I'll save her a seat by the fire."

As a footnote here, my acquaintance with Knight's music came completely by chance. While wandering through Ghirardelli Square in San Francisco earlier this summer with my family, I came across her in the courtyard with her guitarist and bass player, playing a mix of originals and covers for a small but appreciative crowd of passers-by. After three knockout songs and a plea from my daughter, I became the proud owner of this album.

It's the best impulse buy I've made all year. There's a rare and fearless honesty burning through the core of Knight's often compelling songs. Earnest, playful, frank, vulnerable, smartly arranged and thoroughly confident, *Future Perfect* sounds from here like one of the great singer-songwriter debuts of the '90s.

Rating: A

*

Arms of Kismet
Play for Affection
Wampus, 2010
[Published on *The Daily Vault* 11/26/2010]

Only two tracks in and I'm already thinking hard; that's what Mark Doyon's music does to me.

Doyon, who plies his trade of lush, layered, ultra-literate and idiosyncratic postmodern pop under the nom de musique Arms of Kismet, challenges your senses and expectations at every turn. This is not the stuff that you casually put on in the background to create the low-resonating chatter that makes you forget you're alone. This is music you fall into the same way you fall into a good painting or poem, a total package of concept, sound and execution—except, quirky. Very quirky.

Yes, kickoff cut "The Game" might feel relatively mainstream for a few seconds, with its repeating melody line and rather World Party-esque density. It has a nice bounce to its loose, carnival feel—and then barely a minute in, a banjo rides in out of left field and asserts itself underneath and all around the organ-guitar-drums engine of the track, and you realize Doyon has turned a simple 2:41 pop song into a game of three-dimensional chess. "My Mercurial Nature" similarly begins in a comfortable pop groove, at least until the sitar kicks in, and then halfway through the entire musical balloon expands at once—drums, organ, guitar, sitar and vocals—and it becomes almost an anthem, illustrating the title in concrete musical terms. As for the trademark AoK off-center wisdom: "A ripe Neanderthal / An evolving creature / I grow a little every day / It's my mercurial nature"—what husband has never felt like that?

Single "Emmet Kelly in Love" has so many different things going on in its simultaneously airy and jam-packed three and a half minutes that it's almost hard to take it all in, and really, what that makes you want to do more than anything when you're finished is simply to listen to it again (hear that, radio people?). The frenetic-yet-cerebral "Year of Reckoning" features a late-song breakdown-and-full-stop that puts the exclamation point on an appealing melody. And the cosmic-philosophizing "Waiting for the Bounce" won me over with a single characterization: "Curled up like a hanging slider / Landing in some catcher's mitt." (So I'm a sucker for baseball similes...)

And then, things take a turn for the dark. "The Miserablist" presents a state of sourness toward life as a vocation of its own, an act of will requiring intensity and focus. "He smokes a lot but doesn't speak / He reads a book by Cheever... And where he goes at night / we can only wonder—wonder—wonder—" Strange and sad and surprisingly poignant, "The Miserablist" sets the table nicely for the bizarre curveball that is "Leaving," a track that feels like a waking dream. At first it's a spoken-word bit about getting paid after a gig, but then it takes a turn so gritty and Kafkaesque that Doyon even throws in a direct reference to *Metamorphosis*. "I'm leaving immediately," declares the alarmed narrator. "These are things I do not wish to see."

"Another Song Called Home" brings us back to the plane of reality we're used to with a slightly country-tinged story-song, albeit with a dark O. Henry ending. And then there's the decidedly proggy "Persistence of Mercury," mostly instrumental and full of exotic intrigue as a guitar-sitar duet gradually adds a little of this and a little more of that until you're rotating in a sky-hugging swirl of sound. (Trust me, it's sweet.) The disc closes out in fine style with the suitably elegiac "Beautiful in Plaid," a chiming, wistful number about being true to yourself in a world that will never quite understand.

Play for Affection is as apt as a title could be; this album is both playful and multi-layered, its winks and nudges keeping you open and ready to absorb its sadder, stranger and deeper moments. It's also Arms of Kismet's finest moment on record so far. AoK delivers music that doesn't so much make you want to tap your feet or dance or sing along—although there are chances along the way to do each of those things—as it makes you think. Mostly, things like "Are beauty and sadness really two sides of the same coin?" and "I'd really like to buy Mark Doyon a beer some time."

Rating: A

*

Chris Cubeta
Change (EP)
Galuminum Foil, 2007
[Published on *The Daily Vault* 12/21/2007]

There are hundreds of versions of Bruce Springsteen's "Thunder Road" circulating out there. As I type this I'm listening to the delicate yet undeniably passionate acoustic version from *Live 1975-85*, just Roy Bittan on piano and the Boss on harmonica and dusky, indomitably optimistic vocals.

I don't remember the first time I heard "Thunder Road," the first time I was captivated by its urgent lyricism, the fundamental belief in the power of music that underlies its every note and syllable. It's a moment long since lost in the mists of time.

But I do remember the first time I heard Chris Cubeta's new EP *Change*. It was last night, and it hit me like a freight train.

It was last night, at the end of a long day filled with the demands of my new, involuntary freelance career (my previous employer having shuttered its nearby office three months ago) and dealing with various minor family dramas. I'm a strong believer that things work out how they're supposed to in the end—it's just that my belief is often tested.

Chris Cubeta knows exactly what I'm talking about.

Change is an interesting next step for Cubeta after his previous full-length CDs *Sugar Sky* and *Faithful*. The former was produced solo (Cubeta plays everything—and everything well) and the latter was recorded with his live band the Liars Club, but both feature full-band arrangements pretty much throughout. *Change* has a more stripped-down feel, a seven-track EP that features four new songs, a spoken-word collaboration with Cubeta's songwriting and producing partner Danny Lanzetta, and two re-recorded cuts from *Sugar Sky* and *Faithful*.

The new songs are, as has become customary with Cubeta, all excellent, a quartet of heartfelt vignettes of rootsy, Springsteenesque Americana. These tracks are about the moments of light and darkness that enter everyday lives, about how people struggle with their own natures and how those struggles transform them. The opening title track is a piercing examination of change in all its myriad forms, illustrating how sometimes we seek it and sometimes it seeks us, and how it rarely alters us or our lives in the way we were expecting.

Opening over spare acoustic guitar and harmonica, "Change" does a gradual and deeply satisfying build, accelerating steadily until by the final chorus it's become a full-band piece complete with a driving rhythm section and keening electric guitar over the top. The following "Portrait" and "Hold On" spotlight Cubeta's prowess with the acoustic, a pair of beautifully crafted tunes sung with an intensity befitting the poetry of the words they contain. In between, "Innocence" adds the rhythm section back in and, at the break, a brief burst of striking, impassioned electric soloing.

The Lanzetta-Cubeta collaboration "Examination" is an example of just how potent spoken-word can be, as the deep-voiced Lanzetta spits out his epically pointed poetry over Cubeta's energetic backing track. I'm not sure yet how a full CD of brew this strong would hit me, but employed as an interlude here, it's dynamite.

Ah, but the best is still yet to come—the re-recordings of previously released cuts "Sugar Sky" and "Me and the Radio." In both cases, Cubeta puts the musical focus this time around squarely on the piano. In the case of "Sugar Sky," the choice only amplifies the dreamy surrealism of the wonderful lyric.

And then "Me and the Radio" comes along and delivers the coup de grace. In its previously released full-band iteration on *Faithful*, it's an incongruously bouncy rumination on the power of music to uplift, to interrupt dull or difficult everyday moments with flickers of meaning and hope. The bass line drives the entire song, a loping, companionable rhythm that immediately sets your foot tapping.

In the version found here, Cubeta strips the song down to its emotional core and removes everything but the piano for the opening verse, singing his heart out over its warm phrases and chords. As he hits the first bittersweet chorus—"You know it's hard, keeping up / You know it's hard, baby, to stay in love / Me and the radio song"—he brings in slide guitar and paints the high end with soaring notes that accent and punctuate every potent line.

A little while later it falls back to just piano and voice for the last verse—"Well I'm gettin' older by the minute / Still hear the whistle from the schoolyard / Found a minute with the radio / It's still my favorite way to hear a song"—and when the chorus fades down for the last time at 3:55 you're thinking "Wow, that was AMAZING"—and then he punches right through the fade with "Me and the radio song" and the piano comes back twice as big with cymbals now picking up the beat, and then the bass kicks in underneath, and then the drums, and the piano gathers speed and takes a running, giddy leap and solos into a crescendo once, and again, and again, and then at precisely the right moment the multi-tracked, choired vocals come in singing "Still my favorite way to hear a song" over the top, the drums and now also handclaps loud and strong underneath, and repeats the line one, two, three, four times, pulling a single vocal track out of the last repeat like a thread of sound, drawing the last syllable out into a heartfelt "Oh yeaaaaahhhhh" and bringing the whole song down with it, down and home.

The first time I hear this track I'm sitting at my desk with my mouth open, catching flies. The second time, the next day, I'm walking down the street in my neighborhood on a chilly fall afternoon with the iPod on, oblivious to the whisper and crunch of leaves in my path, with a grin on my face and goosebumps running from my wrists up my arms and shoulders and neck and scalp all the way to my forehead, a solid swath of flesh screaming a kind of inchoate joy. I have felt this before, listening to music, maybe ten, maybe twenty times in my life. It's what keeps me coming back for more, these moments.

This song, in this arrangement, captures everything that ever made me love a song like "Thunder Road." It's that powerful, that genuine, that moving, that essential. It's about nurturing hope when it's most endangered. It's about the persistence of love, and the pure unfiltered joy of making and listening to music. And it's Chris Cubeta's finest moment—so far.

Rating: A

*

Jon Troast
A Person & A Heart
Independent release, 2008
[Published on *The Daily Vault* 7/17/2008]

It's hard to talk about singer-songwriter Jon Troast's new disc *A Person & A Heart* without referencing the blog he's been keeping while performing a series of house concerts around the country. His warm, low-key, yet subtly observant entries help you understand his musical personality and why house concerts would suit him well. His songs are friendly and warm and revealingly wise and he comes across like the charming cousin you'd gladly invite to stay over in your guest room or on your couch, just as long he brings his guitar.

Musically, Troast sounds like the long-lost love child of Lyle Lovett and Jack Johnson, a shaggy acoustic troubadour with a keen wit, a soulful voice and an endearing earnestness about him. *A Person & A Heart* features a full band for the most part—complete with twin saxophones—but the songs never lose their intimacy and immediacy, and Troast's throaty, low-key delivery never loses its inviting vulnerability.

The opening title track is as pop as anything he's ever done, with bells and piano and a supple electric guitar line and a big chorus supplementing his effortless rhymes. The song itself, though, feels like an M.C. Escher painting, circular in its portrayal of the difficulty of expressing three-dimensional emotions and relationships in the form of two-dimensional art. The fact that he chooses drawing rather than songwriting as the art he writes about is what makes the whole metaphor work:

> *'Cause the hardest part*
> *is a person and a heart*
> *That's the only thing*
> *I could never draw*
> *'Cause I don't know where someone starts, where they end*
> *And I can't draw lines that could hold them in*

The next two cuts are sweet-swinging home runs as well, funked-up folk tunes that charm with their silky grooves while widening your smile with their insights. "What We Become" is a smart, observant bit about how we're all mothers and fathers and daughters and sons, living inside a pattern that both repeats and continually evolves; "Heaven's Got the Time" is a loose, giddy, finger-snapping "I'm in love" tune that could melt the heart of the coldest cynic.

From there you get several more flavors of Troast wonderfulness. There's gospel-tinged pop ("Prayer for Better Days'), wry observational folk-funk ("Think I'm in Love," "We'd Be Good for Us"), and a deeply affectionate portrait of his hometown ("Lake Geneva"; "All the local boys / Wait for the girls from Illinois").

Not everything here is light and happy, however. "For the Longest Time" paints in darker tones, with an almost Dave Matthews arrangement of densely layered acoustic/electric interplay. The country blues "A Break-Up Song" has bright instrumentation, but the lyrics are as close as Troast ever gets to brutal:

> *Instead of saying we're just friends*
> *Let's tear it open and call it what i*
> *It's a knife right through my rib cage*
> *It's a hammer to my head.*

Closing things out are a pair of mostly acoustic, mostly melancholy songs that showcase Troast's own very expressive singing and playing. "Loneliest Girl" presents a richly detailed story-song, and then "With A Smile Like That" provides a sunnier finish with a tune about that special someone who becomes "my favorite place to go / You always feel like home."

It's a fitting finish to *A Person & A Heart*, an album that fulfills every promise made by Troast's previous album *Second Story*; it's just as sweet and sincere and finely-crafted, yet more richly textured and musically diverse. Rather than continuing to wax rhapsodic here, though, I'll endeavor to keep this as direct as a Troast punchline: this is a terrific album; you should really buy it.

Rating: A

*

Danielia Cotton
Small White Town
HipShake Music, 2005
[Published on *The Daily Vault* 11/24/2005]

So just where exactly did this come from, anyway? Though the cover photo makes her look all of 19, Danielia (da-neel-ya) Cotton has been on this earth twice that long, which helps explain how she came to sing with the fire, conviction and hard-won knowledge of a Tina Turner or a Bonnie

Raitt, but doesn't come close to explaining where she's been hiding all these years.

The life experience Cotton has under her belt is clear right away on cuts like "Found Another" a world-weary, soaring, gorgeous gospel-blues-rock thumper whose lyric and delivery have the kind of mature emotional clarity that sets a singer of any age apart. The fact that the entire song hangs together on a single crushingly effective line—"What part of 'my baby' do you not understand?"—is also the sign of a master craftswoman at work.

But I'm getting ahead of myself, which is a real temptation when the music is this good.

Growing up in Hopewell, New Jersey (the "Small White Town" of the title), Cotton learned about jazz, blues and gospel music from her mother and aunts, but as one of seven African American students in her entire high school, she ended up gravitating toward her peers' favorite classic rockers, acts like AC/DC, Judas Priest and Todd Rundgren. The combination of these disparate influences, in the hands of an artist with enough raw talent to power a rocket engine, is simply explosive.

The end result is a standout album of soaring, growling, immeasurably potent tunes. Hendrix overtones are apparent on heavy cuts like "Devil in Disguise" and "JC I Try," while the driving "Fast" offers a soulful blues-rock nod to Tracy Chapman, and the introspective, mid-tempo "It's Only Life" achieves lift-off on the strength of its absolutely gorgeous gospel accents.

"4 A Ride" and "Take My Heart" are a pair of superb, slow-grinding gospel-blues numbers where Cotton reaches down in the depths of her soul and wails like a master. The latter also contains the classic couplet "Take the food from the table, take the words from my mouth / Take my man if you're able, I can do without." Another highlight, "Today," is strutting, guitar-heavy, Led Zeppelin-style hard rock with a dash of sax thrown in for spice.

Small White Town is produced and largely co-written by acclaimed songwriter/producer Kevin Salem (Giant Sand Chocolate Genius, and a trio of superb solo albums), who gives the proceedings a warm, intimate feel, like you're in the room with the band. As a measure of how compatible a collaborator he is, he wrote one cut here ("Pride") on his own and you wouldn't know the difference without reading the liner notes. Danielia chose well.

Albums like this from artists like this one don't come along every day. You've been warned—don't miss it.

Rating: A

*

Memphis 59
Ragged but Right
Independent release, 2009
[Published on *The Daily Vault* 2/5/2010]

"Americana" has become such a broad genre descriptor that you almost have to go deeper when describing music that falls within its wide boundaries. Yes, the Arlington, Virginia trio Memphis 59 plays rootsy, verse-chorus-verse alt-country-rock, but what do they sound like? How about Steve Earle and the Jayhawks? Paul Westerberg and the Mavericks? Tom Petty and the Old 97s? Or this: honky-tonk rock n' roll with a twang around the edges that adds depth and character to these songs.

On this strong debut disc, the considerable talents of vocalist-guitarist Scott Kurt, drummer Chris Zogby and bassist Richard G. Lewis are supplemented by a pair of seasoned pros from Mary Chapin Carpenter's band—John Jennings produces and plays guitar and Hammond organ, and Jon Carroll contributes piano and Wurlitzer. The end result is exactly as Jennings described it when he inadvertently gave this album its name— *Ragged but Right.*

Opener "Me, Myself and Eyes" set the tone beautifully, an earnest, clever rocker in which Kurt wraps his dusty yet forceful voice around a lyric that dares to pun successfully in the service of an urgent falling-in-love narrative. From there the album is populated with foot-tapping rockers ("Black and White TV," "Hotel Room," "Killing Time") that churn with dynamic changes, tight solos and satisfying payoffs, alternating with quietly appealing laments ("Way With Words," "Putting Up a Fight").

Fresh colors come to the music by way of choices like the slide guitar that lights up the loping, rather Allman Brothers-ish "Knock Me Out" and the jangle-licious, catchy-as-all-get-out "Gone," with its signature line "Don't be rough on an easy heart / 'Cause baby, I was gone right from the start."

The alt-country influence is apparent in lines like the above and song titles like "Heartbreak Luck," "Girl at the End of the Bar" (better than it sounds) and "Quit Kickin' My Heart Around." The latter is actually only the third-most-obvious Petty reference here, after you get past the group's focus on jangly, propulsive hooks inside arrangements that feel tight and loose all at once, and the "American Girl" homage that opens "Hotel Room."

Jennings is the perfect producer for Memphis 59, adding complementary flourishes to their spare arrangements while respecting and embracing the spacious, beautiful rawness at the core of their sound. The thing about this sort of earnest Americana is that it can come off as contrived unless the songs are both very strong and performed with complete conviction. Here, they are.

Ragged but Right is that and more—a showcase for one of the strongest new alt-country/roots-rock acts to come along in many years. Memphis 59 has got the songs, got the sound and got the conviction and chops to back it all up.

Rating: A-

*

Casey Frazier
Regal
Independent release, 2013
[Published on *The Daily Vault* 5/24/2013]

When my son brought this album home from Casey Frazier's CD release show in Monterey a little while back, he struggled to describe the style of music Frazier plays. After giving *Regal* several listens over the intervening weeks, I can appreciate why. The easy fallback would be Americana, but there's so much more here—a heavy white-soul influence fueled by the driving commitment of classic rockers like Van Morrison and Tom Petty, melded with the narrative instincts of a bluesman.

One thing the sound singer-songwriter Frazier features on *Regal* is for sure, is big. On most of these tunes he deploys a core lineup of guitar, bass, drums and keys, plus a full horn section and backup singers, with a several tracks adding strings as well. Which suggests yet another reference point (for this listener, at least)—the Mavericks—if only in the sense that there's a confluence of styles and sounds happening here that's genuinely different and creates something fresh and new, with Frazier's rough-edged-yet-empathetic Everyman voice at the center.

Most importantly, though, these songs have meat on their bones; I found moment after moment that stuck with me long afterwards.

"Cradle to the Grave" opens things up with a steely intensity, at first just Frazier and his acoustic, though the song builds quickly, adding a rhythm section, piano and strings before blossoming fully at the chorus, horns and Hammond organ and electric guitar providing the final boost of drama and power behind a lyric about a desperate man in a passionate affair. Fellow Monterey habitue Dani Paige provides very complementary female harmony vocals during the opening and closing sections.

"One Day in Kansas City" turns up the gospel/r&b influences as big horns, piano, electric guitar and Hammond back a story-song with genuine swing to it. That swing is amplified in the downright exuberant "Cold Hard Truth," featuring the strongest Van Morrison presence yet in its speed-talking wise-troubadour vibe.

From there, Nashville influences begin to assert themselves in Frazier's tunes, starting with the dusty country-folk of "The Family Tree" and growing with "Rocky Mountain Rambler," a downright country road song. There's an agreeable and appealing earnestness and artistry to these tracks, which turn down the horns and electric guitar to draw greater attention to Frazier's evocative words and stories.

"Evil Man" stays out West with a tale of an unjustly-accused outlaw that features banjo right up to the point where the horns come blasting in as he builds to the punchline: "I never was, and never will be / An evil man." "If We Grow Old" turns the volume back down for a contemplative, mostly acoustic blues about starting over clean: "I never wanted to die / So I found a place to start living / A different kind of born again."

The final four alternate between power and restraint. The muscular "Find a City" offers an interesting mélange of soul, gospel, country and folk, a slightly twangy tale of outlaws from Kansas City set to big dramatic strings, with a steady-thrumming earworm of a chorus. "Nothing's quite as terrifying as your own voice in your head" sings Frazier in a moment of revelation. "I Forgot a Name" is a mandolin-tinged dirge that manages to be languid and exotic in rather Jeff Buckley fashion.

The bluesy, penultimate "Lights at the Bar" returns us to the here and now with this time-honored bit of wisdom: "Things look different under the lights at the bar." (Which is also a much more artful phrase than "beer goggles.") Here Frazier tries his best to channel Ray Charles and does a pretty impressive job of it, especially when the horns and piano lift the song up at the choruses. "Walkin' a Line" closing things out with a wistful country-folk tune that sounds like it might be about moving to Monterey.

Regal is a terrific album that showcases Frazier's facility with and genuine affection for all forms of American music, with the horns and strings amplifying the punch and pathos of these thoughtful tunes. His songs are populated by memorably damaged characters stumbling through scenes both familiar and fanciful, searching for some kind of revelation or redemption, and only sometimes finding it. And isn't that a lot like life?

Rating: A-

*

Amy Lennard
EP
Independent release, 2004
[Published on *The Daily Vault* 8/5/2005]

A lot of music makes it into my CD player... and a lot of music goes right back out. What makes the difference? Sometimes all it takes is one good verse. So it was with Amy Lennard.

This five-song EP—an appetizer for a promised full-length—starts strong and never lets up. Over rhythmic acoustic strums, Lennard eases into the sublimely well-crafted "I Wish It Were Mine": "My best friend got a brand new boyfriend / He brings her flowers, he brings her chocolate / He always picks her up on time / And I wish he were mine." The words are strong and clear and sung without a hint of jealousy or embarrassment—only a deep, unapologetic longing. Soon after, the band kicks in behind her and Lennard sails through several more verses rife with a rich, subtle brew of good intentions and green-eyed undercurrents ("I really want her to be happy," she sings over and over towards the close, until, by dropping a single word, she reveals the underlying, greater truth: "I really want to be happy").

Lennard—who self-produced this disc—describes her sound as "New York City with a twang," and a hint of the latter does show up on "El Paso," where she sings of wide open spaces and adds a touch of steel to the mix toward the end of the track. But really, it's just terrific singer-songwriter material, well-written, well-arranged and full of effective and affecting emotional shadings. In her bio, Lennard also references Lucinda

Williams as an influence, and you can hear it in the delicate rawness of lines like "I love the way when we talked / It felt like I was singing inside... Now my heart's in El Paso / 'Cause that's where you are."

"Holy Night" features a steady-building arrangement that adds instrumental texture with each memorable verse: "Turquiose water, purple sky / I feel the breeze and close my eyes / I can taste the salt that's in the air / In your mouth and everywhere." It's a song about fulfillment — emotional, physical, spiritual — and it's flat-out wonderful. Built around a smoky r & b riff, "Please Don't" is a different kind of sensuous — flirty, conflicted and maybe a little desperate: "Please don't look at me that way / It's driving me crazy... And I want to take you home / But this won't work, it's just not right."

Closing this brief glimpse into Lennard's world is the bittersweet breakup coda "I'm Free," which alternates between verses that are almost spoken — in which Lennard's low, severe tones reminded me of Patti Smith — and soaring choruses with a Sheryl Crow feel to them. "Now I'm free," she sings, "And I don't like the way it feels." In real life, you can get what you want (or thought you wanted) and still not be happy.

And that's the core of this EP's appeal. Lennard nails the essence of everyday emotions — the inner conflicts, the flashes of joy and sorrow and regret and desire, the fundamental uncertainty of anything in life but the moment you're inhabiting. It's real life, set to music and rendered in Lennard's rich, versatile voice. Highly recommended.

Rating: A

*

David Corley
Available Light
Independent release, 2014
[Published on *The Daily Vault* 12/5/2014]

It might take a moment to adapt your sensibilities to David Corley's gravelly, twenty-miles-of-rough-road-and-a-bottle-of-whiskey voice at the start of this album; it occupies a universe all its own, and chances are it's either going to work for you or it isn't. But I listened to the first song here and knew I needed to hear the second, and then the third, and by the fourth song, the dude had flat-out seduced me with his songwriting. Like

Dylan and Waits before him, David Corley is a lyric poet inhabiting the grizzled, remarkably expressive voice of a blue-collar Everyman.

Still, albums like *Available Light* tend hinge on atmosphere. You have to feel like you're in that darkened little dive of a club past midnight and the world has narrowed down to just you and the band and a bottle of something strong. Corley and producer Hugh Christopher Brown absolutely nail that barroom confessional vibe, with production that feels live and organic, but also precise. These songs take their time to develop, with several clocking in around six minutes, and the last over seven, but there's not a wasted note, and every line is crafted with care.

Nowhere is this truer than on the magnificent opening title track, a rumbling, tumbling manifesto about seizing every imperfect moment before it flashes by: "The book / well it's a movie now / 'bout how I was busted up and laid out / tried to grab onto this girl / but she was goin' way too fast around / didn't understand quite how she was wound / but ya know we wound up tight / and I shot it all / with the available light."

Over a rootsy, Band-like bed of acoustic and electric guitar, keys (mostly Hammond organ, courtesy of producer Brown), bass (Tony Scherr) and drums (Gregor Beresford), Corley next leads you out "Beyond the Fences," assisted once again by the background vocals of Kate Fenner and Sarah McDermott, their sweet, uplifting tones offering a smooth counterpoint to Corley's jagged lead vocals.

"The Joke" ups the tempo, adopting a bit of a Van Morrison feel to sketch a gritty street-scene, continuing the thought with the languorous, sighing, equally Morrisonesque "Easy Mistake" ("I'm just tryin' to do the right thing / That's an easy mistake to make"). The pair nicely tees up "Dog Tales," another stunner, a chunky-riffed number that crosses from dream into nightmare and back again. When Corley declares "I am beyond the bounds of all reason / I am standin' alone in the gale, caught in the hurricane / down in the crease under the soft light's veil," it's hard not to envision old King Lear bellowing at the wind.

"Unspoken Thing" and "Lean" both feature Fenner and McDermott again offering terrific support, with the male-female counterpoint vocals developing into a call-and-answer that almost becomes a conversation in places, their suppleness contrasting beautifully with Corley's roughness. "Neptune / Line You're Leavin' On" again ventures into Morrison territory, a gentle, wise train-station goodbye to a restless lover ("I don't believe you're gonna find things getting any easier / on down the line").

"The End of My Run" is a slow and steady lament, a soliloquy of personal calamity that Corley delivers with the sort of deep conviction that only personal experience brings. The album closes with "The Calm Revolution," an anthem of quiet determination highlighted by a silvery electric guitar figure running through it, a single, continuously massaged note that fades in and out like a faraway siren in the depths of night.

At times, Corley's work reminds me of The Hold Steady in the sense that the words stand on their own; the lyrics are complete narratives, so fully realized that the music can feel more decorative than fundamental to the songs. The difference between Corley and The Hold Steady is that Corley actually sings, though at times in a voice so relaxed and comfortable in its craggy skin that it feels more like a conversation.

While Corley has been involved with music in some form for most of his life, this album is, at age 53, his debut as a recording artist. It was worth every year of waiting, every life experience and hard-won insight that led him here to this moment. With a voice like a gravel quarry and the heart of a lion, David Corley constructs a universe of broken souls searching for moments of redemption. *Available Light* is a remarkable achievement, an album aglow with a ragged beauty that's simply magnificent to behold.

Rating: A-

*

Spottiswoode and His Enemies
Wild Goosechase Expedition
Old Soul Records, 2011
[Published on *The Daily Vault* 10/28/2011]

I've always had a soft spot for larger-than-life, over-the-top artistic types—just ask my wife. The only time this had real-world consequences was when I was once impulsive enough to go into business with a trio of rather extreme examples of the species; lesson learned. Leaving that experience aside, though, the appeal remains clear: constant stimulation, endless entertainment, thoroughly unleashed imagination, at-times-riotous fun.

All of which is to say—to paraphrase my dry wit of a son—"Hey there Spottiswoode."

If you mixed the laconic, cheeky British cool of Ian Hunter with the brooding urbanity of Leonard Cohen, added the balls-out Broadway showmanship of *Bat Out of Hell* composer Jim Steinman, and sprinkled it all with the self-deprecating panache of James Bond, you might emerge with Jonathan Spottiswoode's less interesting twin brother, because he's clearly more demented than that.

The latest outing from Spottiswoode and His Enemies, the aptly named *Wild Goosechase Expedition*, veers off in several directions at once, leaving the listener's musical compass spinning in circles. This troupe of seven makes a noise together that is uniquely their own, a sort of twisted urban folk music full of dry, acerbic wit and fat horn arrangements. And yet, each individual track is remarkably distinct, with its own sound, vibe and rhythms.

Kickoff cut "Beautiful Monday" sets the tone right away with a breezy, sing-songy ode to manic self-confidence: "Beautiful morning / Beautiful day / Beautiful people / On a beautiful train / All goin' to work now / So du-ti-fully / Beautiful Monday / Beautiful me... Everybody look at me / Take another look at me / I'm beautiful." Meanwhile, a rather Van Morrison-esque lilting-guitar arrangement executes a steady build to a horn-aided crescendo that feels completely inevitable. Tunes like the character-defining "Monday" and the seductive, uber-urbane "Just a Word I Use" ooze a kind of easy charm and swagger that's rare and thoroughly engaging.

In between that notable pair, you get the playful barroom thumper "Happy or Not," the melodramatic, gospel-tinged "Purple River Yellow Sun," and the alternately smoky and apocalyptic "All in the Past." The common thread throughout this memorable opening sequence is that the arrangements are just exquisite. The sheer versatility of the seven-piece Enemies gives Spottiswoode the ability to match each arrangement to the vibe of the song precisely and spectacularly. Each track is its own little painting, with each brushstroke exactly where it should be.

For track number six, Spottiswoode essays the height of romantic sacrifice: "I'd Even Follow You to Philadelphia." And plays it up like a barroom weeper, sounding like a cross between Joe Cocker and W.C. Fields. "I'd go through any kind of hell for you / I'd even follow you to Philadelphia." It's simply brilliant; how else to describe a song that makes you laugh out loud even as it's grooving up a storm?

"Sometimes" plays out like a down and dirty Chicago soul-ified version of George Thorogood; J. Geils would love it. "Chariot" revels in a gorgeous, languorous melody through its latter sections, nicely setting up the curmudgeonly rant that is "All Gone Wrong."

"Problem Child" arrives as more or less the polar opposite of the AC/DC song by the same name, with tinkly piano, jazzy brushed drums, and Spottiswoode taking the role of the clueless parents attempting to adore their thoroughly entitled offspring into compliance. "Problem child, please forgive us / We know you've been through hell / Remember, we love you..."

From there the album only gets more giddily weird. "Happy Where I Am" is a gospel shouter with a fat horn section, and the title track feels a Dixieland band on acid. The terribly British, terribly fatalistic insouciance of "Wake Me When It's Over" sounds very much like Ian Hunter in one of his sassier moods, declaring with deadpan certainty that "All the great men were just like me / Though most of them were creeps / They made their mark on history / While they were asleep."

The closing pair makes an interesting duo as well. "Wonderful Surprise" is a smoky barroom ballad with a bit of Sinatra to it; Spottiswoode is nothing if not hip, and this tune positively swings. By contrast, "You Won't Forget Your Dream" has a suitably dreamy, elegiac quality; it's perfectly pleasant but does go on a bit as you get into the second half of its 9:07 girth.

By the by, the track listing divides these tunes into four acts, the melodramatic titles of which appear to have little to do with the content of the songs themselves, which carry no detectably consistent narrative. Of course, for an iconoclast like Spottiswoode, this sort of affectation comes off as simply further evidence of attention to detail.

Ultimately, you either get swept up in Spottiswoode's peculiar yet robust creative vision, or you don't. *Wild Goosechase Expedition* is both a big shaggy dog of an album and as sleek as a Maserati. Climb in and take her for a spin, won't you?

Rating: A-

*

The Tom Collins
Daylight Tonight
Terminus Records, 2005
[Published on *The Daily Vault* 10/14/2005]

What's that noise you make as you slam the empty glass back down on the bar after tossing down a spectacularly satisfying cold beverage? Oh yes: *ahhhhhhhhhhhhhh*.

That would be the sound I made after getting a load of the huge, propulsive, grin-inducing guitar hook that opens and anchors this disc's lead-off cut, "Back of Your Mind." Immediate reaction: "I get 11 more of these?!"

Yes indeed. The Tom Collins is an Atlanta power trio that makes a big noise, bold, angular riffs holding court over churning, heavy rhythm patterns. The group features Fran Capitanelli on guitar and pleasantly greasy lead vocals; Craig McQuiston on rumbly intense basslines; and Kyle Spence (late of J. Mascis' touring band The Fog) on thundering drum fills and occasional keyboards.

By three or four cuts in, you can hear every major influence — chiefly a *whole* lotta Zeppelin, but also hints of heavy classic rockers like Aerosmith, not to mention neo-classicists like Jet and singer-songwriter-rockers like Tom Petty. The main ingredient, though, is guitar and more guitar. I had to laugh when the already very Zeppelinesque "Hot and Cold" hit a mid-song breakdown where Capitanelli unleashed an a cappella guitar solo that turned "Heartbeaker" inside out and upside down. You have learned well, grasshopper...

The conjoined pair "Why Don't You Leave" and "That Town You Love" (the titles are two halves of a key line that appears in both songs) may be the most brilliant creation on this entire terrific album, though. The former features Capitanelli on acoustic and vocals and no rhythm section, offering a relatively low-key break in the action until it segues suddenly into the bludgeoning opening riff of the latter. After threatening momentarily to accelerate right into "Immigrant Song" territory, "That Town You Love" then settles back into a fierce groove that never lets up. Sweet, sweet stuff.

I also dug the experimentation with tempo and slide on "Start of the Summer," whose reeling accelerate/decelerate bridge has an almost prog feel to it. Ditto for the shifting textures and tones Capitanelli employs on the sometimes dreamy, sometimes driving "I Can't Sleep." They even throw in a bar-band-singalong electrified country-rock number ("We All Said You Would") for kicks.

Rock has been pronounced dead so many times it's become cliche to even suggest it. Dead, alive or indifferent, rock still has a place in the world; this disc is proof aplenty. *Daylight Tonight* is a tour de force of fiery, sweat-soaked, guitar-hero rock and roll.

Rating: A

Butchers Blind
A Place In America (EP)
Electric Giant Productions, 2015
[Published on *The Daily Vault* 10/16/2015]

As a genre, Americana is fueled by the intangible as much as the tangible. The rootsy, country-tinged indie-rock arrangements, the naturalistic narratives and grounded, often fatalistic wisdom are the foundations. What elevates the genre's finest examples is harder to pin down, but if pressed I'd call it integrity. A willingness to dig deep and put yourself out there emotionally, to not just create but inhabit your songs.

Fresh from their strong 2013 LP *Destination Blues*, Long Island quartet Butchers Blind returns this month with *A Place In America*, a six-song EP that's frustrating only in its brevity. Simply put, this is the most ambitious and accomplished set of tunes yet from Pete Mancini (vocals, guitar, songwriting), Paul Anthony (drums, harmony vocals), Brian Reilly (bass) and Christopher Smith (piano and organ).

The heart and soul of the set resides in three songs, a sort of 21st century American Gothic trilogy. Opener "Dead Horses" starts out running off the piano line before building toward a powerful crescendo. "It's hard to say you're someone when your best is not good enough," sings Mancini, his naturally plaintive voice taking on a hint of Don Henley rasp. (There's a sort of laconic vulnerability to his voice that inevitably reminds of Jeff Tweedy as well.)

Next up is the truly stunning "Black & White Dreams." Against a surging musical backdrop, Mancini sings:

> *Goodbye and good luck*
> *It's all been written before*
> *Just climb this ladder*
> *To keep the wolves from the door*
> *I'm livin' hand to mouth*
> *In this whitewashed town*
> *You spend your whole life*
> *Tryin' to get out*

(Chorus)
I want to feel complete
Leave something behind like the names of these streets
A spark in the eye of those who believed in the great generation
Black and white dreams

Mancini's artful lyric lays out the bankruptcy of a fantasy that's haunted the nation for too long, blind nostalgia for a quote-unquote simpler time whose dark undercurrents and still-reverberating consequences are conveniently ignored in memory.

"Twisting In The Wind" offers a momentary detour, a Hammond-heavy barroom thumper singalong about another hapless romantic chasing dreams that are "going down in flames." And then we get to the heart of the matter, the third act of the aforementioned trilogy, "A Place In America." Starting out slow and stately with just piano and acoustic, Mancini intones:

I see the hearts and minds
Of a simpler time
I feel the cold embrace
Through tangled wires
We paid our dues
We got fenced-in blues
Another broken-glass past
All misconstrued

I'm watchin' it all go down on a screen
They're chasin' their Manhattans and their dreams
Some of us grow old and drown
Bitter rants and screams
Some of us find a place in America

From there, Mancini essays a landscape of "broken homes" and "dead-end jobs" until in the fourth minute, the song finds another gear, moving into a heavier section as Mancini cries out "I wish I had a place in America" with increasing urgency as the music gets bigger and harder and angrier all around him. There's no getting around it; this song locates and taps into the same pooling reservoir of desperation Springsteen sang about on *The River* and *Nebraska*, still haunting us a generation later. It's cinemascope songwriting backed by powerhouse performance.

The final pair of tracks are less fraught but plenty strong. "Ghosts" is an easygoing bit of barroom philosophy ("To be nineteen, to laugh and scream / Like ghosts of who we were") with a sweet lap steel solo. And closer "Only Love" is a rolling, ringing mid-tempo love song, offering the only hopeful note on this disc in its closing moments: "It's taken me so long / I think I've got it right / I see in your eyes / Only love, only love."

This set of songs benefits from a sharp mix by Eric Ambel, guitarist in Steve Earle's band and producer of a couple of terrific albums from Mark McKay. In other words, Ambel knows this strain of earnest, literate Americana inside out, and it shows.

In the end, the only real flaw of this EP is that it's over too soon; you're just learning to fully appreciate what Butchers Blind brings to the table—excellent songwriting, sharp ensemble performances, and a ton of integrity—when the last note fades. *A Place In America* feels like half of a great album; I can't wait to hear the whole thing.

Rating: A-

~Segue~

Interview: Jean-Paul Vest

[Published on *The Daily Vault* 1/16/2006]

Last Charge of the Light Horse is the brainchild of singer / songwriter / guitarist Jean-Paul Vest, and their debut disc Getaway Car was my favorite independent release of 2005. Jean-Paul was kind enough to spend some time over the holidays conducting the following interview. In the course of a series of e-mails we covered ground ranging from the inspiration for the new album, to the transition from JP's previous group Blue Sandcastle, the validity of rock as an art form, and the perils of navigating the New York grid in a car with Last Charge's father-and-son rhythm section, A.J. and Artie Riegger. We even talked about music a little. Enjoy!

The Daily Vault: *Getaway Car* melds purposeful, poetic lyrics with stripped-down rock and roll in a manner that inevitably reminds of artists like Springsteen and Dylan. Who would you say your biggest influences were as you conceived this album?

Jean-Paul Vest: The majority of the songs were written over a period of about two years, and the stack of CDs at my desk almost always includes something by the Replacements, Bob Mould, and Wilco, so I'm sure they figure in prominently. Dylan was definitely an influence on this album, in particular the arrangement of "Cold Irons Bound" that he did for the soundtrack of *Masked and Anonymous*. There's some tremendous writing on Emmylou Harris' album *Red Dirt Girl* ("like falling stars from the universe, we are hurled / down through the long loneliness of the world") that's both intimately personal and grandly poetic. I borrowed a turntable from a friend and got reacquainted with some Miracle Legion discs that I have on vinyl, and spent some time trying to figure out how they communicate so profoundly. Those songs are like old friends—I know them by heart, and they resonate strongly within me, even in some cases where I don't understand the lyrics. In fact, the inspiration for "Miracles" was my long love affair with their music. "Circles" is something that I wrote years ago, when I was on a steady diet of Lloyd Cole and Nick Drake. As Bob Stander and I were mixing the album, we spent some time listening to the second volume of *Le Mystère Des Voix Bulgares*, the Bulgarian women's choirs, to give our ears a break in between songs. Those recordings are very stark and passionate, and listening to that set an interesting tone for some of the sessions, in that it made us seek those same qualities in our own work.

The Replacements, Wilco, Emmylou... yeah, I hear all of them. So, the big question for many independent artists in your shoes is, once the album's done, how do you get the word out? How's it going in terms of promotion so far, and what's the response been like?

Promotion is a long, slow haul. As with the Blue Sandcastle record, we've decided to do the media mailings ourselves, starting with the places that gave us positive reviews last time. You have to be prepared to wait several months before you see the results of your work. This time around we've hired someone to help us with radio promotion, and we're scheduled to begin that in February. The response is definitely encouraging so far. Our parents and friends are all very impressed (laughter). But the fact is that we all have demanding day jobs, and AJ and I are raising families, so we're obliged to work for a slow build, rather than a big bang, and we're only a few steps out of the starting gate at this point.

Promotion can be tough. I'm glad the *Vault* could do our part for such a worthy effort. Now, about that worthy effort. I've gotten into a fair number of arguments over the years about the validity and significance of rock and roll as an art form. Your writing has a genuine literary quality to it, yet the music on *Getaway Car* has all the energy and dynamics you'd expect of a great rock album. Do you think in the era of lip-syncing Simpson sisters it's still possible for people to take rock seriously?

A fastball, huh? Well, how does one measure validity or significance? The wonderful thing about art—or any form of communication—is that the artist (as the artist) never finishes the work. The audience completes it, by combining it with their own emotions and experiences to give it meaning and context. That's where validity is determined, and significance. A friend once described poetry to me as "our attempt to express the inexpressible," a description that I like for any art. There are nuances of emotion, thought and life that elude language, and can only be expressed through granite, or paint, or music.

As for rock and roll in particular, I would argue that there's a broad spectrum of my own thoughts and feelings that are only ever truly expressed by rock music, so it's pretty significant to me. On a cultural scale, I think the answer is fluid—it's going to change every year, as more (or fewer) people listen to rock, and as Dylans and Springsteens come and go. As for seriousness, sure, why not? Artists such as Dylan—whose work is intelligent, moving, and thought-provoking—will always be taken seriously by people who seek those qualities. But let's not confuse seriousness with validity. Joy and silliness need avenues for expression, too. Throw on a *Sesame Street* CD with your kids some time, and play "Mah Na Mah Na." Talk about expressing the inexpressible…

Indeed. At the same time, one of the things I enjoyed about *Getaway Car* is the concrete details you placed in many of these songs. The strand of cool air in "Circles" comes to mind, as does the child's fall that is the central image of "Cartwheeling." In the latter, the narrator loses his job the same day his son falls down the stairs. How much of that song was good storytelling, and how much was personal experience?

Occasionally I recognize an event or thought as a subject for a possible song. More often I pick up the guitar and open my notebook and write whatever stream-of-consciousness gibberish comes out, allowing my subconscious to do the heavy lifting. But once an idea begins to take the form of a song, it becomes storytelling, and I care less about autobiographical accuracy than getting an idea across. In the case of "Cartwheeling," the two events took place a day apart (the layoffs came on Friday, and my four-year-old fell down a flight of stairs on Saturday). The similarities struck me when I began to write about what had happened. Other songs are less literal. The "Second Time Around" sprang from my attempts to verbalize the differences between raising our first child and our second. But the song was drivel, and the more I wrote, the worse it got. After a frustrating few days, I finally quit fighting it and let it write itself, and ten minutes later I had a song about a man driving to see an old lover after a long separation, which expressed what I had intended all along.

To me that's where the real magic in writing comes from—recognizing and sketching out the hidden connections between events and feelings and ideas. You do that a lot, and expertly, on *Getaway Car*. If I had to sum up the ideas and emotions you explore there in a single lyric fragment it would probably be this one, from "Wonderful": "…and at

worst it's more / than you can take / and at best it's more / than wonderful." That right there is life in a nutshell, isn't it?

Well, I don't know about "expertly." I think Emmylou Harris set the bar well out of my reach with "The Pearl." "Wonderful" was meant to be about keeping faith—remembering that life's surprises can be positive as well as negative. I've always been a big fan of C.S. Lewis, and the ideas that he explores in books like *Perelandra*, which is essentially a retelling of the Garden of Eden myth. He felt that most myths have their origin in real events, and the thought of a real Adam and Eve is strangely compelling. What a choice: free will, or eternal health, happiness, and security. I guess the choice between freedom and security is one we have to keep making, over and over... Ironically, I almost decided to leave "Wonderful" off the record, but Bob and the guys talked me into keeping it.

Thank you, Bob and the guys! Speaking of the guys, let's talk about the Rieggers. Your last project was Blue Sandcastle, which was just you plus Erik Schuman on drums for most of the album. What can you tell us about that transition, about the Rieggers' musical background, and about how it changes the dynamics to have a father-and-son rhythm section?

The transition came at a difficult time. Erik and I were both laid off when our respective companies decided to do some downsizing, and Erik made the difficult decision to move back to Texas. He and I have always communicated well, musically, and I'm hopeful we can put another project together some day. But I was pretty crushed to have Blue Sandcastle end so abruptly.

I've known Artie and AJ for quite a while—AJ's sister introduced me to my wife—and they've played together for years, mostly working the island [Long Island] in various cover bands. Artie gave me a call when he heard that Erik had left, and suggested we try to put something together. The change in dynamics has been huge, and very liberating; adapting to their musical styles has afforded me an opportunity to re-imagine myself as a songwriter, for the better. Artie is a much less aggressive drummer than I was used to, and they both play with a great feel for the songs. We're in a fun place right now, and having an album under our belts is a big confidence booster.

As for the father-and-son dynamics, we all get along great. I will say that the back-seat driving is pretty spectacular, especially the discussions about which route to take. I've lived here eight years and still don't know my way around, so I mostly stay out of it...

Heh. Been there, done that... Blue Sandcastle obviously involved a lot of overdubs with you playing both bass and guitar on most of the cuts. To my ears, *Getaway Car* has a more organic, live feel to it. How much (if any) of the album was cut live in the studio, and how long did the recording process take?

We spent five days recording, and four mixing. All of the bass and drums were cut live, with a low-volume guitar track for reference. Bob Stander — our engineer — wanted to mic the room a certain way, to capture the sound of the drums, and we didn't want the guitar to bleed into those tracks. So we overdubbed the guitars, vocals, and organ. We spent some time getting different amp setups for the different guitar tracks. With only a three-piece band, we didn't want the whole record to have the same sound. The key was that Bob was able to capture some really good tones, so that there was very little manipulation in the mixing process, with compressors and whatnot. I don't think we added reverb to anything, just the natural reverb in the room, and some delay on some of the vocals.

Well, I love the way it came out, very immediate and organic. Alright, one more and we're into the speed round. Last Charge Of The Light Horse: what's the significance of that very unusual name?

I always felt that Blue Sandcastle was too static a name, and I wanted something more dynamic. The name came from a few things. I was born in the Chinese year of the horse, and I grew up riding horses. Also I'm a big fan of George Harrison, and his record label was Dark Horse, so Light Horse seemed like a natural counterpoint. And then that got me thinking about *The Charge of the Light Brigade*, and about Peter Weir's movie *Gallipoli*, which is one of my all-time favorites. Finally, I wanted the name to reflect our roots in some older musical traditions, and the attitude that we don't want to hold anything back, because who knows if we'll get another chance to do this.

Now for the speed round: favorite Replacements album & song?

I think I have to go with *Pleased to Meet Me* and "Alex Chilton," but "They're Blind" would be a close second.

Any New Year's resolutions, musical or otherwise?

No resolutions per se. But I'm hoping a few good songs will find their way to me.

Last but not least, where do you see the band and the album six months from now?

Hopefully our audience will continue to grow. But our main goals are always oriented towards personal growth: writing better songs, cultivating new ideas, and not allowing the music to stagnate. I would love it if we could head back into the studio a year from now, with a full slate of new perspectives to explore. I've also toyed with the idea of adding a keyboard player to the band, but it would have to be just the right person.

~Segue~

Interview: Chris Cubeta

[Published on *The Daily Vault* 8/15/2006]

The struggle in finding adjectives to describe Chris Cubeta's talent involves balancing obvious choices like "exceptional" and "brilliant" with the desire not to put too much on the shoulders of a guy who is just beginning to find his audience. Composer of heartfelt, sharp-eyed roots-rock songs that somehow also retain a dreamlike universality, he is the author with his good friend Danny Lanzetta of two CDs' worth of terrific music, 2003's Sugar Sky *and more recently the July 2006 release* Faithful. *An admirer of artists like Pearl Jam, Bruce Springsteen and Lucinda Williams, Cubeta keeps it real in his lyrics, his music and his interviews. Our discussion ranged from the rollercoaster nature of the creative process to how you build a following as an indie artist, from the origins of individual songs to why we bother creating art at all. It's the only interview I've ever done that felt like it was over way too soon. Chris Cubeta is the genuine article in every respect, and a creator whose audience—if there is any justice in the universe—will one day catch up with the size of his abilities as a composer, singer, player, producer and all-around creative talent.*

The Daily Vault: **How's the response been so far to** *Faithful*? **I know you've been working it for about a month now, playing shows in the New York City area...**

Chris Cubeta: The response has been basically fabulous. Everyone that we've gotten the record to has loved it—the small fan base that we have, family and friends, and the people we know in the industry. We've gotten a tremendous response at the last four or five shows we've played—the band is really coming together live. When we get in front of a big audience, by which I mean 100-200 people, we usually end up selling 20 or 30 CDs, which to me is a good sign. I like to think if we were in front of 5,000, we might sell 1,000 in one night. Getting to new fans and new audiences is the bulk of the work right now. We're trying to target the New York City area right now and build a buzz. At some point, hopefully someone will notice, and we'll be able to take it to the next level. Our whole approach is to target a small audience that hopefully gets bigger over time.

I understand *Sugar Sky* wasn't technically your first CD like I thought it was when I reviewed it.

I was a member of a band for years, since I was in high school, and we put out a couple of CDs, and I've produced a lot of records for other people. *Sugar Sky* was really my first foray into the singer-songwriter-slash-frontman realm. I'd always been more of a behind-the-scenes guy, a studio guy and a guitar player, not a mouthpiece for a band. But then my best friend and lyric partner [and co-producer of *Sugar Sky* and *Faithful*] Danny Lanzetta said "You've got all these songs, man, and recording equipment and the ability to make a record. You shouldn't be looking around for a singer, you should just sing your own songs." So even though I never really wanted to be a frontman, that's where we are now.

That's ironic to me, because one of the things I mentioned in my reviews was that I think your vocals are outstanding.

That's a nice thing to hear, because it's still something that I struggle with. I've worked with a lot of singers in the studio and I know how I want to sound. But it's difficult when you hear yourself back on tape, at least for me. You're so exposed and your emotions are so on your sleeve that it can be very unnerving hearing it coming back at you—not because of the way it sounds, but because it's so revealing. For lack of a better example, the only thing I can compare it to is that it's like walking into a crowded room naked. It's very unnerving, but it's also exhilarating when someone tells me that I've connected with them. That makes it worth it.

What I get from your albums is that you're singing like you mean every word, and every word is important. A lot of acts that are looking for commercial success sound like they're focused on that, instead of really investing themselves in the song.

I grew up listening to acts where I connected with what they were singing and what they were playing on an emotional level. I like intellectual music, but for me it was always first—not more, but first—about emotional connection. And that's something that I've always tried to remain true to. I'm hoping to have some sort of success, too—just enough to support myself and my wife and my good friend and my band. Nothing too fancy! But I've always tried to remain true to the art form as much as possible, and also to make sure that it translates to other people. My goal is pretty much to do what music had done for me, for other people. It's really been a savior in my life since I was a young child. And hopefully somewhere along the way, this music will affect someone to that extent.

A worthy goal. About your songs—they tend to pack in details, but still feel impressionistic and dreamy in places. To me, that gives them kind of a timeless, universal feeling. Do you feel like there's a secret to writing like that? Or is that just how it comes out for you?

You know, there's no secret to it. The one thing is, I would love to be able to be more prolific than I am right now, and than I've been over the last couple of years. A lot of that is due to circumstances—I spend a lot of time making records with other artists, so usually time is too short to write as much as I'd like to. As far as theories about songwriting, Stevie Wonder used to say he would write a song every day. And somewhere along the way he came out and said he wrote a lot of shitty songs—but he also wrote a lot of great ones. For me it's always been about just capturing a moment, sitting down with a guitar or a piano and really connecting with a certain moment in time and space. It can be a big moment in my life, or a small moment, or just a random moment in the middle of a day that doesn't really have any meaning. The key is this very small burst where you feel very connected and willing to let something out, and usually those moments come naturally and spontaneously.

I wish I had more control over that, but when they do come it's very important to embrace that—and then the work kicks in. That's the easy part usually, getting the spark or the germ out. The hard part for me, and I think for a lot of artists, is taking that spark and saying, how can I make this into something that other people will understand and connect with? That can be in terms of just finishing off a song, or trying to create a story around a specific moment that people can relate to. I also co-write a lot of my lyrics with Danny, who is a tremendous writer and poet and novelist, and he sometimes is able to help me hone in on some of those moments and tie them into something that maybe can translate to the rest of the world.

As a writer, I'm always interested to hear how other people's creative process works. I know just what you mean about that moment of connection and inspiration. It can feel incredible.

227

I love it. For instance, there's a song called "Clementine" on the record that is probably my favorite song that I've ever written, and it has a story behind it. Danny and I actually took a trip right after the New Year, we left on New Year's Day from New York City and just drove about four hours into Pennsylvania. We didn't know where we were going. The goal was to go out and do some writing because I needed to finish this album. I didn't have all the songs written yet, and we had already started recording it, and set a deadline, and if I didn't get away from my studio and all the people I work with around here I was never going to sit down and do my own stuff. So we drove out there for a couple of days, and it's nerve-wracking, because you go out there and think, you know, you're supposed to sit down and be creative and write a song. And sometimes that can be disastrous, because you're trying to force something to happen. But for me, that weekend was tremendous. I wrote "Clementine" in about an hour sitting in the hotel room one morning, and Danny and I finished "If I'm Okay"—all the lyrics, and the rest of the music. So we got two of the best songs on the album right there in that three-day weekend.

Sometimes it can be frustrating while you're waiting for it to come, but when it does, it's amazing. The hard part is, when it's not there you feel like it's never going to come back. There's times when I tell myself "I'm never getting that back. I wrote my last song, it's never happening again." Knock on wood, so far that hasn't happened in my 10 or 12 years of doing this. I always find one more, you know? It's the reason—besides the people in my life and the support that I have, which is huge—that I get up in the morning.

Talking about composition and where the songs come from, I know you play a lot of instruments. Is there one in particular you're most comfortable writing on?

I write 95 percent of my material with a guitar in my hands. Which is funny because I actually grew up playing piano, which was my first instrument as a kid. When I got to be a teenager, I found guitar and fell in love with rock and roll. I've always found guitar to be a little bit more of an expressive instrument for me. That said, piano and drums are two instruments that I play quite often and there are certain times and certain aspects of composing where they're really helpful.

Back to the new album. I know on *Sugar Sky* you played most of the instruments yourself, and for *Faithful* you had a band working with you. How did having a band in the studio change things in terms of your creative process and the making of the album?

Sugar Sky was quite an amazing experience because, since I have the ability to play all four of the basic instruments well enough to put them down on record, I was in total control of that album, and I made it in a very haphazard way simply because I could. I pretty much did the whole album in my basement when I lived upstate. I would just go downstairs into my basement and decide to do a drum track and if it came out, it came out.

That being said, I don't think of either one as being a better or worse experience, they were both fantastic in different ways. The band on the new album *[Editor's note: John Passineau on bass and background vocals, Jeff Berner on guitars and background vocals and Marc Capaldo on drums and percussion]* has been nothing short of astounding. I've known John for many years and the other two guys, Jeff and Marc, who are the newer guys in the band, have become very good friends of mine and their contributions on the album have been priceless.

As for the future, I'm going to do a small EP in the fall that might be ready for the holiday season. That will probably be four or five songs with just me and a guitar. That's been something I've been wanting to do also—strip it down and try to capture a couple of songs that are as bare bones as possible. I'll record live with no overdubbing and no additional musicians or anything like that. So then I'll have the full range—an album I did playing all the instruments, a band album, and an EP of just me and a guitar or a piano, very sparse.

One of the things I really enjoyed about both albums is that you do pace them to build and fall back. On both *Sugar Sky* and *Faithful* you've got some band songs that have a strong build to them, and then you've got some quiet, sparse ones.

I've always liked records that have that dynamic. I grew up listening to albums, but I know in this day and age with the iPod generation—which I am a part of—it's a little different. People are almost creating their own albums using playlists. In some ways it's very cool—I think it's a neat technology if it's not abused, but by the same token it's a little bit troublesome for me because the art form of the album is not quite as important as it used to be, and I think it's still a very valid art form.

Ironically, my song "Me and the Radio" is about how much I love hearing a new song on the radio. The tagline at the end of the song is, "It's still my favorite way to hear a song." I can remember when I was a little kid driving in the car with my father and a song I knew would come on the radio and you had no control over it and if you caught it at the beginning and you had two and a half verses left and the chorus, you were psyched. Still occasionally in this day and age, I'll turn the radio on and hear a song that I love or something new that's out that I haven't heard before, and it's still something that I cherish. So I have these two sides— obviously I love albums, but I really do love just a great song that happens to hit you at the right moment.

I think the thing about the radio is you feel like there must be a bunch of other people out there who are listening at the same time and feeling the same thing that you are, so it's kind of a group experience.

Absolutely, it's a special feeling, less isolated. That's a really neat aspect of radio which I hope will survive all this technology and b.s. that's going on in the music business.

Do you feel like there's a particular theme or idea that the *Faithful* album is built around? I commented on the title in my review in terms of being faithful to a songwriting tradition.

We actually didn't have a title until a few days before we sent the artwork out to be printed. The title of the record is somewhat ironic. It might not be obvious, but I'm not a huge proponent of organized religion. I was raised Catholic, with Catholic guilt and these ideas of abstract faith that I've spent a lot of my life pushing away because I'm a believer in free thinking and intellectual learning and things like that. We called the record *Faithful* because after all these years, I still have faith in music and art. For some reason, I and the few people who are very close to me have a tremendous amount of faith in it, not only in what we do but in what other people do with music and the arts and moviemaking and literature and poetry. It's very difficult at times in this society to continue doing it, so it does require a tremendous amount of faith.

This is a classic cliché interviewer question, but what the hell: what musical artists, past and present, do you admire the most?

Pearl Jam is number one, without a doubt. They have been the biggest influence in my musical life. They were the band that, when I was 13 or so in junior high school, changed music from something I did into something I was becoming a part of. For the last 14 years I've been a diehard fan. Obviously also Springsteen. Tom Petty is a huge influence. Dashboard Confessional in recent years has actually been a big influence; they're one of the few bands I've heard in a long time that really has no gimmicks, they just go out and play with no pretensions. Wilco is a big influence. Lucinda Williams in the last three or four years has been one of my biggest influences as a songwriter, particularly her albums *Car Wheels on a Gravel Road* and *Essence*.

In the last four or five years, as big an influence on me as anything has been hip-hop, which people generally find pretty surprising. I am a diehard Jay-Z fan, to the point where I have every record and know each of them inside and out, and in my own private moments can rap along with them. Eminem also, in the way that he's been able to express himself honestly, right or wrong. Hip-hop is a different culture for me, in that I was raised in a pretty lily-white suburb in upstate New York. Living in the city now, I've gotten to work with kids and adults who were raised in much different environments. What I've found is that when we step behind the microphone, no matter where we came from, the feeling is identical. An African American kid from the ghetto and I might have nothing in common, but once we get behind a microphone or a keyboard or a computer and start making music together, everything else goes out the window.

What are your goals for the next six months?

The next six months, our goals are to keep playing live around New York and to get the record into as many people's hands as possible—fans, people who come to our shows, and as many people within the industry as we can, artists who are doing something similar who might take a liking to what we do. Over the holidays we're going to playing a big benefit show for an AIDS charity. We've been doing this for years for a good friend of ours upstate, a man living with AIDS who runs a very small organization that constantly gets its funding cut by the government, and we've been able to occasionally raise $500 or $1,000. This year we're hoping, since we're based in New York City now, that we can put together a really big show. I wish I could give you some names, but we don't have any confirmations yet. However, if a few things come through, we'll be able to book a big room. We hope that will be a centerpiece for the end of 2006. And then we'll continue working, maybe pushing out to play in Boston and places around there, and then in early spring if we don't have a deal or don't have something bigger happening, we're going to do our own tour. We're trying to save for that right now so we can buy a van and try to do half the country in a month or so on the road. After that, we'll come back to New York and keep working it.

Let's take that one step further. Imagine it's next spring, the album's started heating up and you get offered an opening slot on somebody's summer tour. In your dreams, who's the headliner?

Pearl Jam, without a doubt. I love Springsteen and I love Dylan and all these guys, and obviously we wouldn't be here without them, but if I ever got to set foot on a stage and play some music with any of those guys, particularly Eddie Vedder, I could probably drop dead happy right then and there. As big as they are and as unreasonable as the idea is, they're one of the bands who I feel like, if they ever actually either got to see us perform or got to really hear the record in a good situation where they could spend time with it, they would really get what we do. Because they come from a very similar place of just trying to be honest, and I think that they've done that their whole career.

8

Zebras

EVERY MUSIC WRITER WORTH HIS or her salt enjoys being contrary from time to time. The opportunity to tread familiar ground and express safe, widely held opinions presents itself every day. Half the point of bothering to write about music at all is to try to add something fresh to the mix if you can, to maybe steer a few members of the herd away from the direction they're all busy stampeding.

This chapter is about breaking free from the herd. And while we all know what happens to the zebra who turns the wrong way, don't expect any blood to be spilled on these pages. A majority of the albums found here are ones I liked, that others didn't. A few are the flip-side of that equation—widely-praised albums that I either struggled with or didn't care for—but the ranting is mostly done. The point here is to, as Mr. Jobs might say, hear differently and speak differently.

And indeed, at least one of these reviews—you'll know it when you stumble across it—is as much about the writing process as the album it describes. It was a radically different approach, and in this one instance, it worked. It's another zebra that got away; long may they run.

*

Bruce Springsteen
Lucky Town
Columbia Records, 1992
[Published on *The Daily Vault* 5/29/1998]

Bruce Springsteen is first, a great lyricist, and second, everything else.

Each of Springsteen's studio albums tells a story. Sometimes the story is a virtual mirror-image of his own life, as on *Tunnel of Love*; more often he constructs characters to explore the dilemmas churning in his mind, an approach that reached its zenith on the desolate folk albums *Nebraska* and *The Ghost of Tom Joad*. But each album is itself just one chapter in the larger story he's been telling with almost every song he's issued since 1972: his own.

Springsteen's albums, taken as a whole, trace the middle arc of a life from youth into manhood, and then adulthood, and then fatherhood, and lately, creeping middle age. The tones and styles and relative degrees of separation between author and narrator have fluctuated over time. But the life at the center of the story has always been Springsteen's, and in this, one of his most important—and sorely overlooked—albums, a man who's spent eighteen years struggling to get a grip on the sense of purpose so desperately sought by the narrator of "Born To Run" finally grasps it.

The surprise, at least for those among his longtime fans who once worshipped him for his road-wise, hard-living, freedom-craving image, is that he found the keys to his happiness in his own hand, in his own home, with his own wife and children.

He begins with a statement that captures both where he's been and where he's just arrived, in "Better Days." He's grown tired of "sittin' around waitin' for my life to begin / While it was all just slippin' away," and, with a gospel-tinged organ and background chorus urging him on, resolves to live more in the moment and savor the good place he has come to in his life.

This change in attitude is just the thing, he sings in "Lucky Town," to help him "lose these blues I've found" since winning "some victory that was just failure in deceit," a seeming reference to the undesirable side of fame he experienced after *Born In The USA* made his name a household word. The more his success drove his existence away from his blue-collar roots, it seems, the more it drove his core values back to them.

He takes a few more shots at his own rarefied image in the rollicking story-song "Local Hero," in which he comes across a portrait of himself screened onto black velvet and the checkout girl informs him it's "a local hero, he used to live here for a while." In the end, he comes to appreciate that bittersweet station in life, though, and to almost long for the good old days when his aspirations could only reach that high.

The gorgeous country ballad "If You Should Fall Behind" brings things back close to home with a look at how lovers must pace one another to stay on the same path, and leads nicely into the hard-rocking "Leap of Faith," a rousing tribute to the almost-religious powers of sexual healing ("And in your love, I'm born again").

Next "The Big Muddy" takes things down to the swamps for a brief, eerie wade into the kind of moral ambiguity that troubles any man with a conscience. But this evocative piece (a character study in more ways than one) is really just the set-up for the album's knockout punch.

"Living Proof" is one of the most heartfelt songs Springsteen has ever recorded (which is in itself a statement). He's taken stock of his entire life and still been left searching for something that's missing, and now, to a slowly building backbeat, over a stream of jangly guitar chords, he's struggling to find the core of certainty and meaning that's eluded him for so long. Then, like a gift from above, it appears:

> *Well now on a summer night, in a dusky room*
> *Come a little piece of the Lord's undying light*
> *Crying like he swallowed the fiery moon*
> *In his mother's arms, it was all the beauty I could take*
> *Like the missing words to some prayer that I could never make*
> *In a world so hard and dirty, so fouled and confused*
> *Searching for a little bit of God's mercy*
> *I found living proof*

It's a song of redemption, of the spiritual rebirth of a new father whose struggles with his own father are nearly legendary, delivered with the ragged voice of an ancient wolf howling triumphantly at the full moon. Perhaps especially if you have a child of your own, it is a thing of breathtaking beauty to behold.

There is more: an achingly pretty wedding song ("Book of Dreams"); a thundering elegy to those who die too young ("Souls of the Departed"); and a surreal country-folk coda—"My Beautiful Reward"—that suggests even now, Springsteen's search for meaning continues. It's just taken on a different scope, searching for answers beyond the reaches of the essential contentment he's achieved within his own life. It points, inexorably, toward the larger issues addressed by the subsequent *The Ghost of Tom Joad* album.

Lucky Town is a masterful, moving, essential piece of work. What it isn't, is *Born To Run II*, or *Born In The USA II*. But it isn't meant to be. Instead, it's just one more fascinating chapter in the autobiography of one of the great American storytellers of the 20th century.

Rating: A

*

John Hiatt
Walk On
Capitol, 1995
[Published on *The Daily Vault* 10/13/2007]
[Adapted from a review originally published in *On the Town* 4/16/1996]

It's been three decades now since John Hiatt launched a career defined by his sure-handed mixing of styles—rock, folk, pop, R&B, country and gospel influences are all apparent—and his skewed vision of human relationships. A songwriters' songwriter, Hiatt has built a career composing wryly observant tunes that have often met their biggest commercial successes via voices more radio-friendly than his reedy, attractively road-worn instrument. His work has been covered by The Neville Brothers, Dave Edmunds and Bob Dylan, and his "Thing Called Love," a typically off-center romp, played a major role in resurrecting Bonnie Raitt's career in the late '80s.

Critics tend to view Hiatt's 1987 outing *Bring The Family* as his career high point—but for this listener at least, that honor goes to *Walk On*, Hiatt's equally understated and underappreciated 1995 disc. Song for song, arrangement for arrangement, it's a picture of consistency with a ton of heart and a notable team of players behind it.

The core group is made up of frequent Hiatt collaborator Davey Faragher on bass, the excellent Michael Urbano on drums, and the stupendous David Immerg   lück (Camper Van Beethoven, Counting Crows) on guitar, slide, mandolin, pedal steel and just about any other stringed object within reach. And then there are the guest stars...

Thematically, *Walk On* finds Hiatt continuing to build his encyclopedia of relationships that don't quite work. Opener "Cry Love" is a propulsive, mandolin-driven anthem to love's greatest paradox—no matter how many times it hurts us, we always want more. "Cry" segues beautifully into "You Must Go," a thoroughly lovable mid-tempo bust-up-and-hit-the-road tune whose choruses invite you to sing along with background vocalists Gary Louris and Mark Olson of the Jayhawks.

As the rather somber title track fades in, we find the shell-shocked protagonist wandering the streets of New Orleans, terrified to return to the arms of the woman with whom he thinks he may be falling in love. The tune has an aura of combustibility that lurks just beneath the surface, stoked by Hiatt's heavy acoustic strums.

From there, you get Hiatt's usual complement of bouncy, whip-smart rockers ("Good As She Could Be," "Ethylene"), beautifully executed contemplations ("The River Knows Your Name, "Friend of Mine") and even a chilling, Stephen King-like tale of obsessive love gone wrong ("She Wrote It Down and Burned It"). The best track for showing off the man's biting wit, though, is clearly "Shredding the Document," a brilliant five-minute bludgeoning of talk show exhibitionism which Hiatt closes with a kicker that left me laughing out loud.

Another highlight is the knockout r&b number "I Can't Wait," on which Bonnie Raitt returns the favor with absolutely gorgeous harmony vocals. It's the perfect straight-faced intermission between the sassy "Ethylene" and the biting "Document."

Walk On finds Hiatt covering a wide range of tonal ground on a set of songs that nonetheless offer a unifying theme—the distance we put between ourselves and our loved ones, physical or otherwise. Everyone in these songs is leaving or returning, yearning or frustrated or sad. They're all searching for connection, and there is no one on earth who hasn't felt that way before.

Marry such a universal theme to some of Hiatt's best lyrics and an all-star cast of players, and you have an album that deserves to be ranked among Hiatt's very best. Walk on, John.

Rating: A

*

Coldplay
A Rush of Blood to the Head
Capitol Records, 2002
[Published on *The Daily Vault* 8/27/2003]

Ah, Coldplay.

Dramatically-flourishing, melodically-sparkling, dourly-British Coldplay.

Brooding, plaintive, are-we-really-as-good-as-they-say-well-all-right-then-I-suppose-if-you-insist Coldplay.

Weighty, philosophical, desperately serious—except when dating Gwyneth Paltrow, though maybe even still then*—Coldplay. (*Of course she isn't dating the whole band. It's a figure of frigging speech.)

I was prepared—no, anxious—to be impressed by this album. Many worshipful fan reviews of it and its 2000 predecessor *Parachutes* had come to my attention. Many an expectation had been raised by the hoopla, as well as by the rippling melodicism and enticing urgency of the hit single "Clocks" (a simply fabulous tune, no qualifiers necessary). And no wonder; I loved U2 back when the goal of their music was to change the world instead of just their chart position, and I still pretty predictably go apesh*t when ol' Bruce-from-New-Joisey wrinkles his brow, brandishes his guitar and belts out a lyric as if—wow—he really means it. That's what Coldplay sounded like to me, heard only through the voices of their fans— the kind of band that makes music that's both real, and entertaining.

I strained to hear that magic over several weeks of listening sessions. A number of them were quite enjoyable as the songs on this disc gradually revealed themselves before my ears, uncovering a nice little turn of phrase here, a bewitching melody there. Special compliments are due to "God Put a Smile Upon Your Face," where the band actually sounds a bit rock and roll for a few minutes, building up a healthy sweat behind an enigmatic lyric that made itself comfortable inside my imagination.

But.

Normally, this would be the part where I rattle off quick observations on a number of other tracks. Problem is, I can't. Don't remember any of 'em. Well, no, I do remember the bombastic-to-the-point-of-utter-silliness "Politik," which quickly earned an appearance from my wife's favorite blunt instrument, the scorn-drenched "What *is* this?" But as for the rest, after a good twenty listens this album has left me with as much substance to sift through as bottled water poured through a strainer.

The one impression that does stick with me is a truly remarkable amount of repetition. The Coldplay modus operandi seems to be to select a chord progression of modest merit, match it to an inscrutable lyric and repeat it obsessively until it either assumes an air of false profundity or drives the listener loony (or both). Song after song teases, building and layering and building some more without ever shifting gears or reaching any kind of coherent musical conclusion. It's as if they came up with seven or eight decent ideas and then just quit and said "Eh. Those'll do."

With this album, Coldplay aspires to grandeur, but too often achieves only tedium. Real is good—real boring, isn't.

Rating: C-

*

Shawn Mullins
Beneath the Velvet Sun
Columbia Records, 2000
[Published on *The Daily Vault* 1/6/2003]

Sometimes I just don't get you people. Maybe it was the whole millennium thing distracting everybody or something. Maybe it was criminally poor promotion by the labels involved. But the year 2000 probably set a modern record for "Most Really Good Albums That Hardly Anybody Bought." In a just universe, bestsellers that year would have included The Jayhawks' *Smile*, Fastball's *The Harsh Light of Day*, and this, Shawn Mullins' sophomore try as a major-label bonus baby.

The Mullins backstory is the stuff of legend. Ten years of coffeehouse gigs and self-published acoustic CDs led up to Mullins' 1998 indie album *Soul's Core*. Then one day some bright fellow at a big Atlanta station took a chance on the local guy and threw "Lullaby" on the playlist. Boom: regional hit single, major label signing, national hit, platinum album, etc., etc.

The inevitable big-budget follow-up album, however, may have been doomed from the start by short-sighted label execs. Seamless as *Beneath the Velvet Sun* might appear on first listen, it's actually a two-part affair. The nine-song core of the album was recorded in Atlanta and co-produced by Mullins and Anthony J. Resta. It's a restless set of songs, veering from the edgy, literate folk that had been Mullins' trademark as an undiscovered regional artist ("Yellow Dog Song") to airy, atmospheric rock ("North On 95," "Santa Fe") to a soaring piano-and-strings ballad co-written with his wife ("We Run"). The highlight of this set is a funked-up, temperature-heightening duet between Mullins and very special guest Shelby Lynne on the grinding, memorable "I Know."

The first four tracks, however, were apparently recorded after Columbia decided they didn't hear a single (read: a "Lullaby" clone) among Mullins' initial set. So, they dragged him out to LA to record a few follow-up tracks with Julian Raymond, hit-making producer for, ironically enough, Fastball. The results were strong, including a pair of highly melodic pop-rock tunes (the clever "Amy's Eyes" and the unremarkable yet pretty "Everywhere I Go") and—hey, folks, there it is—a name-dropping, spoken-verse-over-a-hip-hop-beat, "Lullaby"-like piece of Mullins magic called "Up All Night." It was the perfect follow-up to "Lullaby"—so, naturally, the label chose "Everywhere I Go" as the first single. (As Casey Stengel famously said of the hapless 1962 New York Mets: "Doesn't anybody know how to play this here game?")

The fourth song of the Raymond set, and quite possibly the best on the album, is a stirring, largely acoustic anthem to personal integrity called "Something to Believe In." The fact that it was recorded under pressure from the label to conform to their creative tastes is about as close to perfect irony as you're likely to encounter, and doubtless lost on those whom you suspect it was aimed at.

But I've dwelled too long already on the circumstances surrounding this ill-fated album. The essential information here is this: Shawn Mullins has a remarkable voice equally capable of rumbly, rough-edged lows and billowing high notes; a terrific ear for melody; and a fiction writer's touch with character details. This is a superb set of songs that is compromised only by Mullins' apparent desire to please the people who took his gentle, idiosyncratic music and tried to make a quick buck off it. Don't hold against him the fact that the label chose for the first single the only somewhat weightless, predictable song on the entire album. There's a ton of good music on here that's worthwhile either for the long-time Mullins fan or the casual listener intrigued by artfully conceived, highly melodic singer-songwriter material.

Like the Jayhawks, like Fastball, Mullins found himself in 2002 once again without major-label backing. In the case of Fastball, the result has been a premature breakup. The Jayhawks have soldiered on at half-strength, working as a largely acoustic trio. The answer has been simpler for Mullins, the once-and-again troubadour. He simply shrugged off the disappointing sales of this album, continued performing solo and producing others' albums, and is now hard at work on a fascinating collaboration with fellow outside-the-mainstream songsmiths Matthew Sweet and Pete Droge. Hint: buy their album. The majors probably won't touch it, which will be your first clue that it's really good.

Rating: A-

*

Hanson
Middle Of Nowhere
Mercury Records, 1997
[Published on *The Daily Vault* 10/2/1998]

A cynic couldn't help but hate this album.

Consider: three gorgeously-scrubbed white kids, ages 12 to 17, all blond, all brothers, with a sound that's frequently so Jackson Five you half expect to find "A-B-C, 1-2-3" on the track list. A long list of managers, legal consultants and executive producers, help from some seasoned pro songwriters (Barry Mann, Cynthia Weil, Mark Hudson), big-time promotional backing from a major label, media saturation, frothing-at-the-mouth teenage fanclubs...

I mean, this album just about HAS TO suck, right?

Wrong. Not only does *Middle of Nowhere* sincerely NOT suck, it's a pretty impressive accomplishment. One of the big reasons is the smart, lively Phil-Spector-meets-Will-Smith production by Stephen Lironi (Moby Grape), and on two tracks, The Dust Brothers (Beck's acclaimed *Odelay* album). They add layers of depth and complexity to the music while simultaneously making sure the Hansons are allowed to be themselves, rather than a whitewashed corporate product.

And—surprise—what the Hansons turn out to be is three young, vulnerable, intensely energetic and precociously talented musicians. Fourteen-year-old Taylor Hanson's vocal delivery is full of the kind of hyper-kinetic enthusiasm that made Michael Jackson into a superstar before puberty. The joy coming from behind the mike on this album is palpable and—unless you're hopelessly jaded—fairly awesome to behold. This is music made by people utterly unashamed of enjoying what they're doing.

This is truest on the way-beyond-infectious pop gem "MMMbop," whose hip-hop edge (courtesy of the aforementioned Dust Brothers) cements the Hansons' musical connection to that predecessor quintet of singing brothers. Still, maybe the most impressive aspect of the song is the lyric, written solo by the three brothers. It's a simple yet surprisingly sophisticated take on mortality and learning what's really important in life ("Hold on to the ones who really care / In the end they'll be the only ones there"). A lot of full-grown adult songwriters couldn't pull off the combination of knockout power-pop music and subtly thoughtful lyrics; coming from the Hansons it sounds perfectly natural.

The Hansons rock out to similarly pleasing effect on "Thinking of You" and "Where's the Love," both full of punchy grooves and soaring harmonies that are pure ear candy. The fact that Taylor and older brother Isaac alternate (and sometimes share) lead vocals helps widen the band's musical range, with 17-year-old Isaac's more mature voice showing a strong resemblance to veteran rock-and-balladeer Bryan Adams on tunes like "A Minute Without You," and especially "I Will Come to You."

The boys also dip into some funk on "Speechless," pulling it off better than you might think, and offer predictably sweet but well-crafted ballads in "Weird" and "With You in Your Dreams," the latter dedicated to their deceased grandmother.

It's not exactly Springsteen, but for a trio of wholesome, suburban teenagers, it's a pretty auspicious debut, much more sophisticated musically and lyrically than any of the pre-fab, disposable teen idols that went before. If you can put aside your cynicism—and c'mon, be honest, maybe a little envy, too—for a few minutes, you ought to be pleasantly surprised by this album. And if, like me, at some point you suddenly catch yourself singing along with your ten-year-old at the top of your lungs, you've basically got two choices: cut yourself off and return to your former life as a cynical, repressed, fatalistic grown-up, or let it rip.

I know what your therapist would say.

Rating: B+

*

Train
Save Me, San Francisco
Columbia, 2009
[Published on *The Daily Vault* 10/31/2010]

I waited a long time to buy this album, and a longer time to review it. When you're talking about a band you've followed for more than a decade, that's rarely a good sign.

Of course, Train today is only 60 percent of the Train that started out in 1998 with their self-titled debut and hit single "Meet Virginia." In the process of cutting 2003's *My Private Nation*, the band shed first bassist Charlie Colin and then rhythm guitarist Rob Hotchkiss, replacing both with studio musicians and sidemen, leaving lead voice Pat Monahan, guitarist Jimmy Stafford and drummer Scott Underwood as the sole official members of the band for subsequent albums.

Save Me, San Francisco kicks off with the title track, an ode to the boys' hometown that is by turns rousing and embarrassing. The hook is a monster… but so is the lyric. "I been high / I been low / I been yes / And I been oh hell no / I been rock and roll and disco / Won't you save me San

Francisco" goes the sing-songy, cringe-worthy chorus. The entire carefully modulated construction—even the sloppy moments appear precisely calibrated to charm—feels like nothing so much as a commercial jingle (more on that thought soon), in the sense that the catchiness of the hook demands that you sing along even as the lyric makes you feel like a moron for doing it.

Follow-up track "Hey, Soul Sister" does nothing to dispel this first impression. As calculated as a television ad's background music—which is how most people now know the "hey—hey-AY—hey-ay-AY-ay" chorus thanks to Samsung's ubiquitous campaign—"Hey, Soul Sister" is in fact about as soulful as a slice of Wonder bread. The idea that it's become the biggest hit of the band's career is a compliment to every act that refuses to cater to the lowest common denominator; this is what you get when you do that, and it isn't a pretty sight. Never has a string of superficial, self-indulgent lyrics ("Your lipstick stains / On the front lobe of my left-side brains / I knew I wouldn't forget you / And so I let you go and blow my mind") meant so fleetingly much to so barely-paying-attention many.

And the rest of the album gets worse.

I would go into greater detail, but you really only need one song description: spare intro builds quickly to swelling chorus with Monahan's voice way out front, melodramatic vocals delivering pseudo-hip, often-ridiculous lyrics, repeat, crescendo and you're done. Times nine. The roaming, diverse musical landscape of the Brendan O'Brien-produced discs *Drops of Jupiter*, *My Private Nation* and *For Me, It's You* is gone, washed away by a sea of lame white-boy-soul posturing. Even borrowing half a song from the Doobie Brothers ("Black Water" interpolates with "I Got You") doesn't accomplish more than pointing out how creatively bankrupt the rest of this disc is.

This album in fact sounds after the first two tracks like a Pat Monahan solo release; with rare exceptions (the lively but annoyingly repetitive "You Already Know" and the overcooked second half of "Breakfast in Bed") Stafford and Underwood come off as faceless as any of the studio musicians Monahan employed for his 2007 solo disc *Last of Seven*. It's a wonder he bothered to come back, but he seems to recognize that a brand name is a brand name, and Train have surely pumped new life into theirs with this smartly marketed effort.

Plenty of critics have slagged Train over the years as mainstream sell-outs, a group that seemed all too eager to sacrifice their musical imagination on the altar of commercial success. I've defended them in the past because until now they've always managed to be more than that, dipping their toes in a variety of genres and offering a sort of quirky, earnest charm with flashes of genuine grit and imagination. *Save Me San Francisco* arrives 100 percent grit-free; it's 50 percent commercial calculation and 50 percent pure narcissism, a pair of mindlessly catchy pop tunes grafted onto an album otherwise littered with weak hipster posturing and assembly-line power ballads. This album will surely make Train Inc. a handsome buck, but there's little here that any fan of music that matters will care about beyond next Tuesday.

Rating: D

*

Fastball
The Harsh Light Of Day
Hollywood Records, 2000
[Published on *The Daily Vault* 11/15/2000]

Once upon a time there was a band with not one, but two talented singer/songwriters, who alternated on lead vocals. One played guitar; the other, bass. The guitar player had a throaty, bluesy voice, and his songs ranged from moody ballads to furiously energetic rock songs. The bass player had a buoyant sense of melody and a penchant for romantic pop songs, yet would also rock out when the mood struck him.

Different as they were, their styles complemented one another perfectly, like two sides of the same coin. These divergent approaches kept the group's sound constantly evolving, peopling their exhilarating range of song-styles with quirky characters and creative sonic embellishments. The lead pair were aided and abetted throughout by the group's mop-topped drummer, an unassuming but remarkably steady and versatile backstop.

Well, actually... once upon the time there were two bands. One came from Liverpool and changed the musical world forever with albums like *Revolver, Sgt. Pepper's* and "The White Album." They were called the Beatles.

The other came from Austin, Texas, and just delivered the best album of their career. They're called Fastball. (And right about now, they probably hate me. Just give it a chance, guys...)

Let's be clear right up front—Miles Zuniga (guitar/vocals) is not John Lennon, Tony Scalzo (bass/vocals) is not Paul McCartney, and Joey Shuffield (drums) only resembles Ringo when his face is in the shadows.

What Fastball is—much like the Jayhawks—is a band that fearlessly mixes the old with the new, creating music that's both obviously influenced and determinedly original. On *The Harsh Light of Day*, Fastball pays frequent homage to middle-period Beatles without ever sacrificing their musical identity.

The album kicks off with a fantastic one-two punch. Zuniga's "This Is Not My Life" harnesses the rage of the rejected to a heavy-duty electric guitar riff that's half muscle and half melody. He hammers his point home over and over, alternating his approaches between full-out electric barrages, midrange rhythm, and a pair of tinny, mono, volume-on-two interludes that would make George Martin chuckle. The closing sing-along rant is eventually drowned out by feedback that cuts right into the next track, veering 180 degrees into the hyperactive dueling-acoustic-and-electric-piano melodies of "You're an Ocean." The first single from the album, "Ocean" is powered by its unabashedly silly, yet deliriously well-rhymed chorus.

Scalzo and Zuniga trade tracks the rest of the way to similarly entertaining effect. Scalzo's exotic yet philosophical "Love is Expensive and Free," featuring a full orchestra plus mariachi horns and percussion, cuts directly into Zuniga's silky, creepy "Vampires," which could pass for a sequel to the Blue Oyster Cult classic "(Don't Fear) The Reaper." Later on, Scalzo's languorous, acerbic "Funny How It Fades Away" contrasts string-accented verses with hammering choruses, then cuts straight into Zuniga's "Don't Give Up on Me," a parade of sturdy electric licks and urgent vocals.

In the middle, Zuniga and Scalzo each take two in a row. Scalzo's "Wind Me Up" is an insistently catchy power-pop track heavily spiced with symphonic flourishes. The bizarre little coda that follows it features trains rolling by as a sultry-voiced woman speaks incomprehensible French. Before Billy Shears or Mr. Kite can arrive to translate for us, though, we cut to "Morning Star," a guitar-driven blast of sarcasm that proves Scalzo isn't all sweetness and light.

Zuniga follows with one of my favorite cuts of Y2K. "Time" is a rip-it-up piece of rock n' roll that grafts all manner of edgy sonic twists and turns onto a killer electric hook that's topped off by Zuniga's best belting "Twist And Shout" vocals. From those thundering heights, Zuniga slides smoothly down into the ironically light "Dark Street," all layered harmonies and upbeat chords.

Finishing strong, album closer "Whatever Gets You On" opens contemporary with acoustic guitar over electronic percussion, before the chorus throws the song into an affectionate pastiche of "White Album" Hammond organ, descending "aahhh-uuhhh" harmony vocals, and "weeping," Harrison-esque guitar licks. It's about now that you remember the cinematic, run-the-songs-together-into-a-single-diverse-and-dynamic-soundscape strategy is descended directly from *Sgt. Pepper's*.

Even with all the intriguing parallels, I might still have exercised compassion for Fastball and left the Beatles thing alone, if not for one little nugget hidden away in this disc's liner notes. The album features terrific keyboard work throughout by sidemen Bennett Salvay and Kim Bullard. Still, for one track at least, our boys went right to the source. Thus, we find that "You're an Ocean" features piano by none other than... Billy Preston.

I'll bet he felt right at home.

Rating: A-

*

Steve Winwood
Roll With It
Virgin Records, 1988
[Published on *The Daily Vault* 6/16/1999]

The first thing you have to do when reviewing a Steve Winwood album is to acknowledge the legend, before setting to work separating it from the man.

Joined the Spencer Davis Group at the age of 15 in 1963... scored (and co-wrote) a huge (immortal, even) hit in "Gimme Some Lovin'" in 1966... was admired early on by the likes of Eric Clapton, whom he later partnered with as the twin towers of supergroup Blind Faith... joined with drummer Jim Capaldi as one of the principal creative forces behind late '60s-early '70s progressive stalwarts Traffic... and as a solo artist, scored big with six Top Ten hits and three Grammys for his 1986 smash hit album *Back in the High Life*.

That is the good news—and plenty of it—about Steve Winwood.

The bad news is that for every high point in his catalog there seems to be an equal and opposite low. Part of this is directly traceable to Winwood's unfortunate fascination with synthesizers. He was a dynamo tearing into rhythm and blues tunes on the old Hammond B-3 organ, but during the '80s wrung much of the life out of his music by overusing electronic keyboards and percussion.

Roll With It is more or less a classic in the category of "missed opportunities." In 1988 Winwood had just scored the biggest hit of his career in the brilliant, highly melodic *Back in the High Life* album, and was poised to consolidate the status as a solo superstar that had largely escaped him since Traffic disbanded in 1974.

You can tell that's what's on his mind by the artwork—a Herb Ritts glam-rock portrait in leather jacket with WINWOOD superimposed on it—and the songs, a slick, formulaic set of largely mid-tempo blue-eyed soul numbers co-written by top industry lyric doctor Will Jennings. Winwood wanted to grab the brass ring, and how.

He missed.

The music that makes up the bulk of *Roll With It* is so pallid it barely manages to go in one ear and out the other. Too slick for rock, too pop for fusion, too heavy for r&b, too progressive for pop, and too bland for progressive, for the most part it ends up nowhere... and nowhere is not a happy place to be.

Not that it isn't without some charm; the album actually starts off strong with the title track (a #1 hit), a tight, horn-heavy r&b number. This is Winwood at his most appealing—focused, singing soulfully, and relying principally on piano and Hammond organ from his keyboard rig. "Holding On" is solid, as well, with a beefy rhythm section and nicely arranged horns and synths. Both incorporate the Memphis Horns to good effect.

Too bad it's largely downhill from there. "The Morning Side" desperately seeks to create a glimmering, twilight feel with its brittle electric piano trills, looming synth washes and chirpy electronic percussion, but in the end it's all atmosphere and no substance. The mood is there, but the song lacks any emotional payoff.

Worse yet, next comes the low point of the album, the improbably plodding "Put on Your Dancing Shoes," whose cheesy synths and sterile drum machine are capped by a truly embarrassing lyric. Winwood seemed to have realized at some point that the song was barking at him like the dog it is, because he ends up throwing in every trick he can think of to salvage it. There's a bridge that shifts in odd but uninteresting ways, a weak faux-blues guitar solo, and the tried-and-true but here totally unsuccessful call-and-answer vocals at the end. It's a groaner.

Winwood kicks off the second half of the album using the same tools, albeit executed with a little more flair, on "Don't You Know What the Night Can Do." Still, even a stronger melody, more interesting synth flourishes, and nicely arranged background vocals only bring the song up to the level of a memorable advertising jingle—a fact quickly grasped by the musical geniuses in Michelob's marketing department.

Nothing kills a guy's musical credibility quite like making a beer commercial instead of a song.

Bouncing back yet again (inconsistency, thy name is Winwood), the track that follows creates the most excitement on this entire disc—"Hearts on Fire," a driving dance track co-written with Winwood's ex-Traffic mate Jim Capaldi. They clearly had a good time putting this one together, as evidenced by its irrepressible bass line and the sly self-reference Winwood throws in: "She said no, but while you see a chance / You better take it" (harking back to his 1981 solo breakthrough single "While You See a Chance").

Closing out the album, "One More Morning" offers a sweet lyric (I'm a sucker for songs written "For Mom") well-sung, but otherwise barely registers musically. "Shining Song" likewise bounces along harmlessly without ever leaving a lasting impression. There's nothing intrinsically bad about these songs; they're just so bland and full of sheen that they fail to connect with me as a listener.

Unfortunately, Winwood never really recovered from this album. He has managed only two solo albums since (with a short-lived Traffic reunion sandwiched between), and both have sounded like yet another try at the *Roll With It* formula.

The basic problems with the formula seem obvious in hindsight: Winwood is hindered throughout by lyricist Jennings' pedestrian approaches and cliché renderings, and doesn't help matters with his own propensity for slicking up r&b music whose very nature shouts for a looser, grittier approach. After all, what's left of a soul album—blue-eyed or otherwise—if you take out the soul?

Rating: C+

*

Ben Folds Five
The Unauthorized Biography of Reinhold Messner
550 Music, 1999
[Published on *The Daily Vault* 5/4/1999]

Writing reviews is one weird gig. With me at least, they're sometimes longer being born than the McCaughey septuplets. And then sometimes lightning strikes...

While shopping for my nephew's birthday, I spot Ben Folds Five's new disc *The Unauthorized Biography of Reinhold Messner*. This isn't hard to do given that the cover is a bizarro black, white and red movie-poster image, a multiple exposure of an oddly sinister man in a double-breasted white suit. The band's 1997 album *Whatever and Ever Amen* remains a favorite of mine, with its alternately sad, sardonic, angry and blissed-out attitude coupled with wildly creative piano-bass-drums musical backing. Still, I'm shopping for my nephew, not me...

Two for him, one for me, I think.

I've got six minutes between Borders and home in the car, long enough for maybe one song after I'm done wrestling the shrinkwrap into submission at the first stoplight. Four bars into "Narcolepsy" I know I made the right choice. It opens in classic Ben Folds Five style—all of them. Folds begins solo on the piano massaging a soft, bluesy melody—that suddenly jolts into a rippling, baroque arpeggio—that just as suddenly explodes as Robert Sledge's fuzzed-out banshee bass and Darren Jessee's crashing drums and a goddamned *string quartet* all plow into you at once, rumbling and careening around like a psychedelic orchestral thunderstorm.

And then it's back to Folds solo on the piano again beneath his plaintive voice as he spins the tale of a guy who literally shuts down every time anyone outside himself challenges him to feel a real emotion. Calling this song "different" is like calling Slobodan Milosevic "testy."

The amazing part is how the band throws everything—kitchen sink and all the cabinets, too—into this song and it all holds together in one exhilarating burst of sonic surprise. The ever-evolving Folds style is so original—so melodic and yet aggressive, so urgent and bouncy and yet often sadly matter-of-fact, that the comparisons really get lost. A little Joe Jackson in the punk attitude and the fondness for big band music, to be sure, a dash of McCartney in some of the nakedly romantic pop tunes, yes. Maybe even a pinch of Freddie Mercury in the showmanship and the occasional layered vocal chorus. But the truth is Ben Folds Five sounds like nothing you've ever heard before—*nothing*.

The song fades with "I'm not tired / I'm not tired / I'm not tired / I just sleep." I check the booklet and note that the string quartet—frequently supplemented by a flugelhorn—is utilized on about 2/3 of the songs. A flugelhorn. With that I come to my senses sitting in my garage with the engine off muttering "effing genius" under my breath.

The next morning on the way to work the treats emerging from my car's CD player include the exquisitely melancholy—yet somehow also indescribably loopy—"Don't Change Your Plans," with its Chicago bridge (flugelhorn, anyone?), and the Jessee-penned, simply stunning "Magic." A classic BFF ballad in the "Brick" neighborhood, it's all gorgeous piano lines, deadpan vocal delivery and a devastatingly raw and beautiful lyric ("You're the magic that holds the sky up from the ground... Trading places with an angel now").

"Genius," I mutter again, pulling into a parking space at work.

Lunchtime. I'm parked in a dead-end a block from my office eating in my car and listening to "Army" for the first time. This qualifies me for *Daily Vault* writer's combat pay, since the lyric keeps making me cackle out loud with my mouth full and there's no one in sight I could possibly lip-sync "Heimlich maneuver" to.

"Well I thought about the Army / Dad said, 'Son, you're fucking high' / And I thought, 'Yeah there's a first for everything' / So I took my old man's advice / Three sad semesters / It was only 15 grand spent in bed / I thought about the army / I dropped out and joined a band instead..."

Beyond his talent for painting cool shades of sad confusion, there is probably no one sharper and funnier out there today than Ben Folds at matter-of-factly skewering the lives of the self-absorbed and semi-delusional. The narrator of "Army" is the kind of endlessly scheming, absurdly romantic and shamelessly pathetic character Woody Allen used to write for himself before he turned into a bitter, self-worshipping old bastard. You can tell Folds identifies with the fellow in "Army," and yet he never flinches in his description of the ludicrous fantasies that propel him blindly through life.

On the way home I'm entertained by the clever "Your Most Valuable Possession" (whose chief lesson seems to be never to erase the really interesting phone messages friends and family leave on your machine when they're half-asleep). But then Folds turns back to nailing hard emotional truths... to a lounge piano beat. The music to "Regrets" bounces along deceptively underneath a brutally honest lyric: "I thought about... all the great ideas I had / And how we just made fun / Of those who had the guts to try and fail."

Just about every song on this disc offers a piercing lyric or killer keyboard tone or exotic percussion run or thundering bass line or whacked-out time signature that flat-out startles you with its inventiveness and brilliant incorporation into the rest of the tune. It's such blindingly original music that you almost lose track of the bare fact that, despite its complexity, it is completely guitarless and almost completely acoustic. Even Folds' own tongue-in-cheek label for the band's genre—"punk for sissies"—is deceptively limiting. No category can hold these guys, or would dare try.

Our story ends with your scribe scribbling the above paragraph furiously on the bag that had earlier contained his lunch as he inches down the rush-hour-clogged freeway toward home, navigating by peripheral vision, using the steering wheel as his desktop, stopping between words to shift gears, energized by the realization that he's crafted the guts of a full-blown 1,000-word review in a handful of stolen moments over the first 24 hours he's owned the disc... only to realize all at once what the drivers around him must be seeing: a dangerously obsessive-compulsive writer-geek incapable of turning off the voices in his head long enough to get himself home in one piece.

I may just have to change my name to Reinhold Messner.

Rating: A-

*

Rush
Clockwork Angels
Anthem, 2012
[Published on *The Daily Vault* 7/24/2012]

Rush: the band critics (other than this one) love to hate. I've always thought one reason for this is that Canada's #1 power trio have never—not for five minutes in a career now spanning five decades—tried to be cool. To the contrary, besides being world-class musicians, Geddy Lee (bass/keys/vocals), Alex Lifeson (guitar) and Neil Peart (drums) very early on embraced their destiny as the high priests of uncoolness. They are the geeks in the corner who played for the other geeks, who all told a friend, and so on and so on until, in today's geek-ascendant world, Rush has evolved into a money-making machine the likes of which the rock world has rarely seen.

That said, latter-day Rush has tended to feel a bit tepid. For this listener—this fan—the appeal of the band has always been the drive and hookiness behind their best songs and best albums. The common theme of the core of Rush's catalog—the *Hemispheres*-through-*Moving Pictures* trilogy, with maybe *A Farewell to Kings* and *Signals* tacked on either end—is an extraordinarily potent combination of power and melody. In that era the trio achieved a sort of creative balance point between the longer, proggier songs they had favored earlier and the synth-driven group they would become in the 80s. They were also building songs around hooks and riffs and choruses, songs that held focus musically even when the lyrics drifted into philosophy and fantasy.

With *Clockwork Angels*, Rush returns in some sense to the epic scale of earlier works. This is a 66-minute concept album featuring a single, continuous, semi-coherent narrative, rather trendily set in a steampunk universe. It's a story that the band—one supposes simply because they can—has also made into a full-length book. (It *would* be nice to be an artist AND have money, right?)

On to the music. Rush has a history of strong album openers, and "Caravan" is another one. The chorus is a bit of a soft spot—consisting principally of the line "I can't stop thinkin' big" repeated over and over—but the song itself is a muscular, emphatic overture to the story ahead. With "BU2B," however, they veer immediately into the philosophical debate that has occupied lyricist/drummer Neil Peart for decades: faith vs. reason. Unfortunately, "BU2B" also brings to the fore a key flaw in the production by Nick Raskulinecz and the band: despite a welcome emphasis on the trio's terrific musicianship, the mix is surprisingly muddy in places, obscuring the vocals and reducing the impact of individual riffs.

The title track isn't an especially memorable tune, but does feature a snazzy Lifeson solo around the midpoint of its overlong 7:31 girth. It's essentially an exploration of the tension between belief and unbelief, predestination (in the form of this particular imaginary universe's overseer, the Watchmaker) and free will, with an appropriately grand chorus.

That grandness, however, begins to wear by the time you get into the fourth straight track in this vein, "The Anarchist." The boys simply throw themselves headlong into every song, running at full-tilt more often than not, burning pavement without stopping to savor individual riffs and moments along the way. The instrumental prowess of these three is rightfully legendary but when you're not halfway through and the songs are already blurring together, it's not a good sign. "Halo Effect" feints at a change of pace, opening acoustic before almost immediately diving back into the fray. The opening section of "Seven Cities of Gold" features Lee's fantastic, frenetic "lead bass" and Lifeson atmospherics before moving into yet another heavy, hammering number free of the sort of hooks that lit up an album like *Moving Pictures*.

The heart of the album lies in the next three tracks. In "The Wreckers," a rather open-minded look at skepticism ("All I know is that sometimes you have to be wary / Of a miracle too good to be true") Lifeson delivers a riff that actually sticks in your head and there's an actual chorus that is somewhat memorable. "Headlong Flight" starts with some fabulous Lee riffing that builds into a dynamic Lifeson-led jam; there might not be that sticky riff, but there's genuine drive happening. And then the brief (1:28) reprise "BU2B2" sends an arrow to the heart of Peart's concerns, reflecting his own personal tragedies of the '90s, the grief that he went through and his decision to keep on living, despite the fact that "No philosophy consoles me."

Interestingly, the penultimate "Wish Them Well," after charging in with abundant heaviness, eases off the pedal to deliver a message full of Christian heritage: essentially, turn the other cheek and love thine enemy. Closer "The Garden" is a kind of elegy / summing-up bit that attempts to draw the threads and themes together into some sort of conclusion: "The measure of a life is a measure of love and respect / So hard to earn, so easily burned."

The core problem seems to be that Lee, Lifeson and Peart appear to have shaped these songs around their narrative concept rather than around riffs and melodies. My lasting impression is of a continuous torrent of music, some of which was pretty cool, but whose individual tracks don't really have structure—beginnings, middles, ends, choruses—they just kind of go and keep going until it's time to move on to the next chapter of the story.

If you simply rated this album for musicianship and/or artistic ambition, it would rate an A of some sort. In the end, though, *Clockwork Angels* falls victim to its own hubris and scale, focusing on the forest while losing track of (groan-worthy Rush pun 100% intended) the trees. Highbrow concepts and instrumental virtuosity abound here; what's missing are memorable songs.

Rating: C+

*

Ben Kweller
Sha Sha
ATO Records, 2002
[Published on *The Daily Vault* 6/14/2004]

You just never know, y'know?

Here I was, thinking I'd give Ben Kweller a try and then sit down and write a fresh entry for the pantheon of Glowing Reviews by Star-Struck Critics of the Young Prodigy Himself. Raised in a musical family, Kweller was solid on piano and guitar at an early age, in a band at 12 (Radish) and had logged musical appearances on *Conan O'Brien* and *Letterman* before his 17th birthday. The critics all but drooled on the guy.

But when I stuck his 2002 solo debut *Sha Sha* in the player and sat back, a funny thing happened—a really funny thing for someone who's lauded the innocent genius of any number of young-and-sincere singer-songwriter-savant types. I hated it. Really, viscerally "yousucksucksuck" despised it.

Notes from my first listen: "calculated sloppiness... not even trying to hit the notes with his tone-deaf singing... self-conscious composing geared for shock value... Zappaesque in places but not half as funny..." Then I reached "In Other Words" and noted "Ahh, here's the good stuff, a quality, thoughtful, melodic ballad free of affectations... before he fucks it up with that ridiculous, accelerated close. Why??" Next-to-final thoughts: "if the jarring transitions were more organic, they might be interesting— instead they feel pretentious and manipulative." And then, regarding closer "Falling": "the best track on the disc, a pretty piano tune with no sonic graffiti added to screw it up. It's about damn time."

Yeah, those expectations can be murder. Need proof? Notes from my second listen to that overrated, pretentious spaz Ben Kweller, a full two weeks later:

"A brilliant pop alchemist. Charming, vulnerable, fearless, a great sense of melody, totally uninhibited. 'Sex reminds her of eating spaghetti'... ha! 'Wasted and Ready' matches French horn and power chords like an exotic cocktail served in a storefront dive. The closing jam on 'In Other Words' is a jarring, cathartic emotional release of surprising power."

Yeah, it's starting to feel like that whole "I feel strongly both ways" thing again.

Kweller is as adept at rocking out on cuts like the rollicking "Commerce, TX" and "Harriet's Got a Song" as he is at tugging on your heartstrings with earnest ballads. The place he sometimes stumbles is in his insistence on keeping things raw at all times. The lack of polish is part of what makes uptempo cuts like "Walk on Me" and "Make It Up" fun — they sound like the giddy, sloppy early takes from a teenager's basement studio. But the lyrics veer between clever and dopey, and the off-pitch singing on tracks like "No Reason" crosses the line between endearing and annoying.

Just as young Ben's act is starting to wear thin, though, there's the big finish, that lost Ben Folds number "Falling." Gorgeous, brilliant, wonderful, insert your own favorite exclamation of musical joy here. Yeah, dammit, he is good, even if it's sometimes in spite of himself. Bottom line, I didn't make the Star-Struck Critics' Hall of Fame, but I did get to know Ben Kweller a little — and that's a worthwhile endeavor.

Rating: B-

*

Garth Brooks
No Fences
Liberty Records, 1990
[Published on *The Daily Vault* 9/26/2003]

File under "Things That Probably Shouldn't Be Admitted in Public": am I the only person in the Western world whose first exposure to Garth Brooks was watching him serenade the Olsen twins on a long-forgotten episode of *Full House*? Maybe so.

I don't recall the year, or the song (Was it "Unanswered Prayers"? Help me out here, fans...), but I do remember the impression he left. Country, yeah, that was a little off-putting for a rock n' roll guy like me, but it wasn't the kind of country I knew, or thought I did. The guy was a gifted balladeer, blessed with a huge voice and abundant charm, and he came across as unflinchingly sincere.

I won't try to re-tell the entire GB legend here; suffice it to say that *No Fences* was a milestone in his career, the sophomore album that catapulted him from promising newcomer with a couple of strong singles to national crossover star. Given this career trajectory, it seems likely Garth first showed up on my small screen within a year after this album came out.

The reasons why this album performed like the booster-rocket it was designed to be are pretty self-evident. It isn't a stretch to say *No Fences* has something for just about everyone who isn't terrified to listen to an album with steel guitar and twangy vocals (don't worry, all you rawk-boys, your ears won't fall off). There's clever rhymes, sentimental ballads, raucous party anthems, soaring guitar solos and several more-than-passable pop songs dressed up with just enough country trappings to make it through the door in Nashville.

The disc kicks off with the sounds of a storm and powers right into "The Thunder Rolls," a rocking, melodramatic but ultimately compelling tale of infidelity and consequences. The video for this song went even further, extrapolating the song's lyrics into a controversial tale of spousal abuse and revenge, which made for good drama *and* smart marketing, the perfect trail-blazer to ensure crossover success on the pop charts.

From that notable beginning, the album flip-flops between somewhat generic, mid-tempo country-pop ("New Way to Fly," "Victim of the Game," "Wild Horses") and three of the best songs this guy has ever recorded. "Two of a Kind, Workin' on a Full House" flat-out swings, an upbeat rock song with a country arrangement and a lyric so clever and genuinely joyous that it won over even my hopelessly jaded teenage daughter. And "Friends in Low Places"... fight it if you want, but this song is rock and roll all the way in terms of attitude, people—the hilarious tale of a jilted good ol' boy crashing his ex's wedding. If you haven't hit "skip" by the second verse, you'll be singing along for sure.

Perhaps the best song here, though, is "Unanswered Prayers." Most of the time I find songs in which the singer addresses his/her God directly pretty tiresome; if I want a sermon, I know where to go. It's hard not to make an exception for this tune, however, because it's so sincere and so well-crafted. A deceptively simple ballad about overcoming regret and being grateful for not getting the things you once felt certain you wanted, it's not just a song, it's a life lesson.

It's impossible to review a Garth Brooks album without taking a hard look at the persona he projects here. He is, after all, a master at the game of image, and he fosters one here, to be sure, of the lovable rebel, edgy yet charismatic, and ultimately tender-hearted. The weakness of this stance is in the way many of his lyrics employ clichés and platitudes to get his ideas across—he wants to push the envelope musically and lyrically, but he's all too anxious to bring everyone along with him. Are rebels who play it safe really rebels?

That's the album's flaw for me—that, and the way it peters out after "Unanswered Prayers" with a chunk of mostly forgettable filler. Still, there's no denying the power and stylistic reach of the hits on *No Fences*, and the significance of the crossover musical career they helped propel into the stratosphere. This is a key album in a major country figure's catalog, even if it isn't necessarily a great one.

Rating: B

~Segue~

Interview: Danny Federici

[Published on *The Daily Vault* 2/17/1998]

Danny Federici is a happy man.

After spending much of the last twenty-five years as an integral part of one of the great concert units in rock and roll history—Bruce Springsteen's E Street Band—Federici is on the brink of a new career, with a posse of old friends still lined up at his side. Almost a decade after Springsteen walked away from the band, this E Streeter is busier than ever, building his own record label and promoting his very first solo album.

The album, Flemington, *is named after the New Jersey town he grew up in, but that's about as close as it gets to the Jersey shore sound popularized by his old Boss. The album is essentially contemporary jazz, a smooth blend of Latin, soul and jazz fusion influences, shot through with Federici's trademark keyboard and accordion playing. He throws in a few familiar touches for good measure—a little organ-glockenspiel interplay on the title tune, and brief guest appearances by E Street Band bassist Garry Tallent and guitarist Nils Lofgren—but the sound is distinctly Federici's, a fact he is justifiably proud of.*

In the course of a long conversation over the phone one recent evening, we talked about Federici's new perspective as a bandleader and record label owner, his plans for promoting and touring behind Flemington, *and the ever-constant speculation about the possibilities for an E Street Band reunion.*

The Daily Vault: You've been a member of the E Street Band and a session player your whole career up until now. After thirty years in the music business, what led you down the road to want to do a solo album?

Danny Federici: It was something I never really thought about; that's why it came out so late in my career. I had written a lot of music for film and TV for many years, I'd studied classical accordion. I actually used to write my own music and stuff all the time, before I hooked up with Bruce. It's something that's always been with me. It just didn't all come together until recently. Part of what finally led to doing an album was that I'd listen to the kind of music I like to listen to, which is mostly contemporary jazz, on stations like The Wave in LA and 101.9 in New York, and think to myself,

"How'd that get on the radio? I could do better than that." So eventually I had to try and actually do it. I think this music I'm involved in crosses all barriers. I had some stuff to start with that I really liked. And then I'd give out tapes to my friends and kind of say "Hey, what do you think about this?" And Bruce and the band and my partners at Deadeye Records, all my friends heard it, and pretty much all of them said "Hey, let's do this, you need to get this out there." And that was a great feeling, having that kind of validation from my peers, my buddies, the guys whose opinions mean the most to me. Bruce was very surprised by the music. I think he didn't know what to expect. But his reaction made me feel really good.

What was it like in the studio, going from being one of the guys in the band to being the guy in charge—the songwriter, the producer and the bandleader?

Actually, the thing I liked the most about it was being in a position to make sure I got all the proper credit. In the early days, a lot of things went on in the studio where I did things and nobody really paid attention, so I ended up not getting credited for accordion, or background vocals, or whatever on songs. People just forgot to put it all down for the credits. And so it's neat to be able to put myself down for everything I did on the record—you know, I played all the keyboards, the accordion, produced the album and co-engineered it. And I wrote all the songs and all the parts. I didn't just come up with a melody and then bring it to the players and say, "Here's my song, what do you want to do with it?" I wrote all the bass parts and everything else and then had people come in and play them. The whole process helped me see I can trust myself. I was never sure until people came in if I'd done it right, and then I realized it would only sound right if they played the way I'd written it. Toward the end I was editing my ass off. I'd change something and have my partners at Deadeye listen, and they'd say "It's fine, it's fine," and I'd have my wife listen and she'd say "I can't hear anything different," but I always heard a way to improve it—until we reached a certain point where I just had to say, okay, that's it. We're done.

How did you end up starting your own label, getting into that side of things?

I have a music publishing company, Shark River Music. And I advertise in a couple of papers and get a lot of people sending me music. Eventually I got to the point where I felt like I didn't have time to develop the talent, but if people had their product already ready, with good songs and artwork and a sample pressing of CDs and everything ready to go, but they couldn't get a record deal, then I would consider taking a listen to it, because I know how hard it is and how much belief you have to have in yourself to get your music out there. There a lot of people out there with a thousand CDs they paid to have made themselves sitting in their closet because they can't get any backing. My original idea was to have a record company with a website, so that I could just get it out there.

Is the website one of your main distribution outlets?

No. At first I thought it might be, but we ended up signing a deal with a company called Music Masters back in New Jersey to get distribution through BMG. And that got me into Tower and Blockbuster and Virgin. We're not talking huge numbers of CDs, but we're in all those stores, all over the country, and that's great.

Back to the album a little bit—it's got a real smooth, confident feel. You've got a couple of old friends on there, Garry Tallent and Nils Lofgren. Did that help your comfort level, having some familiar faces there in the studio?

I actually sent the tape to Garry and he did his parts in Nashville and then sent the tape back.

Well, there goes my image of you guys in the studio! (Laughter)

Yeah. But Nils, he was in town directing the music on the ACE awards. He's done that for something like three years in a row. And in his case, guitar is only instrument I'm really not familiar with. So we talked about it a little off and on, and then he came by the studio and said hello, and then he's like "Hey, let's try something out." And in the end it took him about 20 minutes, and I couldn't be more pleased with it. The stuff he played just fit in perfectly.

Yeah, those were very nice little touches he added. Listening to the album, I heard a lot of different sources and styles in the music—a little

bit of Latin here, a little bit of contemporary jazz—how would you describe it yourself?

Just the way you put it. With more time and more money I would like to have put more of the Latin feel in it. I just love that Latin sound. Some of the music you hear in the background on the album is Latin samples. I kept it in back so it wouldn't sound fake. My intention is to use a percussionist on the next album; I'm actually going crazy right now trying to find a percussionist. I can't get the sound I want with just a drummer; I need both a drummer and a percussionist. The accordion did bring some other influences in, too. Like on "Mr. Continental," the accordion gives it a very European feel, kind of a romantic touch.

That was actually a perfect segue—you must have known what my next question was, because I was going to ask you about the stories on the Deadeye Records website about the accordion lessons your mom used to take you to.

It was just like the image you probably have. I was an unpopular, overweight kid going off to accordion lessons with my mother pulling me by the ear. At the time it was pretty miserable; I was this red haired freckle-faced accordion-playing kid. As I got older, I got more serious about not wanting to do it. But Mom was a stage mom. She stayed on me, worked me hard, made me practice all the time. I wasn't that great in school, but she didn't care—she had other ideas for me. I was going to be a classical accordion player. If things had continued the way they were heading, I think today I'd be really good friends with Wayne Newton. (Laughter) She had me dressed up in these really schlocky clothes, playing classical music on the accordion. If nothing had changed, I'd be playing Vegas right now with Don Rickles and Frank Sinatra. Thank God the Beatles came along. Like everybody else, I got all excited about them, and right after that one day my accordion professor got sick and we had a substitute who played some jazz for us. Once I'd heard jazz played on the accordion, there was no going back. The music moved me so much I quit altogether about a year later. And to her credit, my mother was hip enough to respect my wishes.

Did you ever see yourself playing accordion in a rock and roll band? I was actually listening today to the BoDeans' "Heart of a Miracle," and

the accordion you played on that song is just great, and it's a great rock and roll song.

Yeah. Accordion's a really unique instrument. When I play it today I still think of my mom all the time. It's changed a lot since I was a kid, though—(laughs) here's a good story. I play part time out here with a zydeco band, and I was playing a couple of weeks ago in Santa Monica. I was standing there playing and these pretty girls walked by and sort of smiled at me, and I just naturally smiled back at them, and then I'm thinking to myself "Yeah, right, you're playing the accordion"—but things have changed since I was a kid. Girls like the accordion now. When I was a kid—well, that's why I picked up the organ! (Laughter) The girls were not going for the guy playing the squeeze box!

As long as we're on instruments, I'm curious—who got the idea back in 1972 or '73 to put glockenspiel on a rock and roll record?

It was Bruce's idea to do it. He was heavily influenced by Phil Spector, you know. It's sort of ironic, because that influence ended up creating this whole Asbury Park sound with the organ and glockenspiel playing off each other.

You mentioned a couple of stations you like—how has radio responded to the album? Are the contemporary jazz stations picking it up?

We're getting played—(stops and laughs) you know, I'm really having a hard time getting used to not being in a band where it's "We this" and "We that." I'm getting played on about 70 radio stations nationally. There are only a couple of hundred stations in the contemporary jazz market, so that's not too bad. When I put this record out I didn't think too hard about what songs would fit the kind of radio that plays the style that I was writing in. I didn't have any real commercial intentions. I just really needed to put this record out. Once I put it out my job is basically over; what happens from there, happens.

I've got a good story for you, though. A little while back I called Max Weinberg and said "Hey, Max, can you do an old pal a favor? Can you get me on the show," —you know, *Late Night*, with Conan—"and play a couple of my songs with me?" So Max lines it all up so it can happen while I'm in New York doing a video shoot with Bruce. And I get out there on stage and Max's horn section in the Seven [the Max Weinberg Seven, the *Late Night* house band] is a bunch of the old gang that used to back up Bruce on the E Street albums [see *Live 1975-85* and *Chimes Of Freedom*]. It's La Bamba [Richie "La Bamba" Rosenberg, one of the original members of Jersey shore legends the Asbury Jukes] and Mark Pender and those guys. It was such a great feeling, having these guys I've known for years and years behind me playing my songs. I mean, on the show I had that five-piece horn section right in my ear for three songs. And so afterwards I get to the video shoot and start telling Bruce about it. And I'm saying "Bruce, I gotta tell you it was soooo great having the horn section behind me playing my songs," and he was laughing with me, because he got it, you know? He got that it was something really special for me, having that band up there playing *my* songs.

You were saying you're putting together a band to do some live dates. How's that coming together? Who's going to be in the band?

Michael Cates is this great sax player I know from New Jersey. We met a long time ago back there and then sort of lost touch, and then ended up crossing paths again. He actually found my website address and then sent me an e-mail. Then I went to see him at the Long Beach Jazz Festival, and now he's in the band. Ben Arrington, my partner at Deadeye Records, is my bass player. And I've been playing with a couple of drummers and guitar players, doing a few local dates to try things out, but I'm not firm on who I want to keep yet. We've got some dates set toward the end of May in France, and something in Switzerland. We'll probably come back to the U.S. and do some stuff on east coast in May or June.

Who are some of your favorite musicians in the business, both folks you've had a chance to work with, and maybe folks who you haven't had the chance to work with yet, but you'd like to?

I like David Sanborn a lot; he's a great sax player, just terrific. I've always loved Jimmie Smith. And I've always wanted to play with Bruce Hornsby—his style of piano playing is very rhythmic. This might surprise some people, but I'd love to play accordion with Garth Brooks. I've called his people before and said, "Hey, give me a call sometime." I haven't heard anything back, though.

You think Garry Tallent out there in Nashville has any Garth connections he could put to work for you on that?

I don't know. He probably does! I just haven't really pushed it.

That gets me to the question that all the Springsteen fans out there would crucify me if I failed to ask...

...is there going to be an E Street Band reunion? Is there going to be a tour? (Laughter)

Well, there you go.

You know, we talk about it all the time... but that's all we've been doing. A couple of years ago, I thought maybe it would happen, but it just didn't come about. I still play with Bruce all the time. I played on *Ghost Of Tom Joad*, "Dead Man Walkin'," the *Jerry Maguire* soundtrack. I just shot a video with Bruce in New York for *Rolling Stone*'s "30 Years of Rock and Roll" special, playing accordion and organ. Bruce and I are better friends now then we've ever been, and that's great. I've got my own album out and I'm great friends with Bruce. I really couldn't ask for anything better.

One last sort of oddball question someone suggested to me that seemed interesting— has anyone ever floated the idea of doing an E Street Band album WITHOUT Bruce on it?

We've thought about it through the years. We played as the E Street Band at one of the inaugural balls in 1992, with Johnny Rivers and Southside Johnny. It was really a blast. But our problem with trying to do that is, who are you going to get to sing lead? Whoever it is, is going to get crucified. It's a very tricky thing to put somebody in that spot. I think the only thing you could even try would be to put a girl in that spot. But you know, the biggest problem is that we wouldn't have a boss. I wouldn't listen to Clarence, and Clarence wouldn't listen to Max, and Max wouldn't listen to me... none of us would listen to each other... but we would all listen to Bruce. He's always been great at that—"You, play this. You, play that." "No, that's too much," or too little. With Bruce, we all know what our piece of the puzzle is. I don't think we could really work together without Bruce. That's what that whole band is about; he's our leader.

9

Miscellany: Concert, Book & Film Reviews

A GREAT ALBUM, LISTENED TO uninterrupted in an otherwise quiet space, is one of life's sublime pleasures. That said, it only captures one aspect—one channel, if you will—of the communication that is possible between musical artist and audience. This chapter is about exploring some of those other channels: concerts, books and films.

Seeing and hearing an artist live in concert is a fundamentally different experience from listening to an album. The music is rarely as cleanly played or carefully arranged as on the original recording; it's apt to be both livelier and sloppier, an adrenalized rendition with abundant freedom for the artist to reinterpret their own work in new and unexpected ways. Whatever gap exists between audience expectations and what comes out of the speakers can usually be made up for by the vital human connection forged between performer and witness, as the sterility of a studio recording is replaced by the intimacy of watching a performance unfold in real time before your eyes.

Plus, y'know, it's kind of fun.

Watching a musician you've long admired from afar play a song you love right in front of you can in fact be genuinely transcendent. You're both inside your memory of the song and keenly present as it's unfolding in front of you. You're watching the expressions and body language of the song's creator as he/she brings their creation to life, the performance and the audience's real-time reaction to it creating a feedback loop of sizzling, primal energy. A great concert by a great artist is like an endless dream of flying, or the best sex you've ever had. It transports, it transforms, it sanctifies and rebirths you.

So, yeah: it's fun.

Of the four concert reviews reprinted here, three are of artists I've long admired; the fourth was a night where I went along rather than leading the way, and was pleasantly surprised by what I experienced.

Ironically enough, I've never reviewed what I still regard as my favorite concert experience ever: seeing U2 live in November 2001, with the heart-shaped runway allowing Bono and the Edge to race out into the midst of the audience and play to every corner of the arena, singing anthems of hope and affirmation to a crowd desperate to hear them, less than two months after the devastation of 9/11. It was a singular, indelible experience that I could never do justice to with mere words.

*

Regarding rock books: first, there have been a lot of them, and second, a lot of them never manage to rise above retelling clichéd me-against-the-world / overcoming-tremendous-odds narratives in predictable ways. To surpass that standard requires a gifted storyteller with a firsthand account of a genuinely memorable sequence of events. Most rock books fail one of these three tests: the writing isn't that good, or the writer is one step removed, telling someone else's story for them, or the story itself doesn't feel all that special.

The three book reviews in this volume include my two favorite rock books published to date. Both were written by the principals themselves, without outside assistance, and both authors are extremely perceptive and witty observer/participants in a narrative that's both compelling and meaningful in a broader sense. Their understanding of their own value and foibles as musicians and human beings, and their thoughtful, incisive renderings of life inside the bubble of fame each has inhabited, make for a pair of books that rival the best novels in terms of insight offered and impact achieved.

An interesting footnote is that each is penned by one of the less well-known players in a successful trio, offering a view of the action that is simultaneously inside of it and off to one side. It seems that not being the frontman/spokesperson whom everyone wants to interview may allow—for the right person with the right skills and temperament—a certain detachment that allows for greater perspective and insight.

Or maybe Jacob Slichter and Andy Summers are just both really good writers. I'll leave that for you to decide.

As for Mike Doughty's book—well, you'll see.

*

Film is a tricky medium when the subject is popular music. Most concert films feel dull and predictable; the directors all watched the same concert movies growing up and ape the same shots over and over. Meanwhile, the audience gets all of the drawbacks of live music—reduced sound quality and multiple visual distractions—and none of the benefits of direct communication and interaction between artist and audience.

The end result is that I haven't reviewed many concert films at all; most of the reviews would be along the lines of "You're better off buying the album and catching a show." The main value of a concert film in my mind is historical—the opportunity to see someone play a live show who isn't playing them anymore.

More interesting to me are the kinds of rock-centric films represented in the two reviews found here. Stewart Copeland's aptly named documentary *Everyone Stares: The Police Inside Out* tells the same "life-inside-the-bubble" story as Andy Summers' book, but from a slightly different angle, with candid photos and scruffy super 8 film supplying the visuals to go with Copeland's wise, acerbic narration.

Baillie Walsh and Ridley Scott's film *Springsteen & I* is another beast entirely, an enveloping, charmingly naturalistic examination of Bruce Springsteen—the man and his music—through the eyes and ears of his biggest fans. It's once again a fresh and unique perspective on a familiar subject that both promises and delivers new insights on a story most viewers will already know.

I'd like to think these concert, book and film reviews offer more than just a Jeopardy-style Potpourri category—they extend the conversation about these artists and their music in interesting ways, like the special features on a DVD release, or the liner notes on an album. At least, that's what they did for me.

*

Concert Reviews

Montrose
Mystic Theatre / Petaluma, CA, USA / November 16, 2002
[Published on *The Daily Vault* 11/21/2002]

Hearing the name of a legendary '70s hard rock band like Montrose mentioned in the present tense is bound to generate two emotions among its audience: hope, and fear. Hope, that it means what fans have been waiting for all these years—the chance to hear all those early classics, the ones that basically ignited the heavy metal flame in America, played again for the first time in a quarter century. Fear, that it may be what we've seen far too much of in the past few years from other '70s bands—a quickie milk-the-audience reunion that draws a half-hearted effort from a group of guys who don't really care anymore.

After seeing the new Montrose band recently at Petaluma's Mystic Theatre, I'm here to say: put away your fears and let hope rise again. For this is no half-hearted retread; it's a new band for a new era, and this time, that's a good thing.

The original Montrose—Ronnie Montrose on guitar, Sammy Hagar on vocals, Bill Church on bass and Denny Carmassi on drums—was in its day the ultimate stateside power trio with vocals, the American answer to Led Zeppelin. Their single effort as a unit, 1973's self-titled *Montrose*, formed the template for nearly every American hard rock band to follow, beginning with that virtual Montrose tribute band, Van Halen. Its 1973-74 golden era was over all too soon, sundered by tensions within the young, headstrong and indisputably passionate band.

So how do you recapture that passion, almost 30 years later? Most bands wouldn't even try. But for a Jedi master like Ronnie Montrose, there is no "try"; there is only "do." And what he's done this time is to reconstitute the band with an entirely new cast of players with no history or baggage in the Montrose saga, only a passion for playing the band's music that's absolutely palpable.

That much is obvious from the first note as Montrose himself strides to center stage, acknowledging the surging tide of cheers from the crowd as he rips into the opening chords of "Rock the Nation," the immortal air-guitar anthem that opened that monumental *Montrose* album in 1973. The sold-out audience of 600 partisans seems to sense already what's coming—the real thing, baby, right here in your face after all these years.

And they are not disappointed. If you took the average Montrose fan and asked them what their ideal set-list would be, this would be exactly how it starts. "RTN" segues straight into "Good Rockin' Tonight," the band's rave-up heavy-guitar version of the Elvis hip-shaker, which segues straight into a double-shot of the chord-crunching classics "Make It Last" and "I Got the Fire."

By now the crowd is in ecstasy, realizing exactly what they're in for. Pat Torpey on drums and Chuck Wright on bass are a pair of hard rock pros who probably played the opening to "Rock Candy" a hundred times at sound checks for their previous bands (Mr. Big and Quiet Riot, respectively). They know and love these songs instinctively, and it shows in every move they make on stage.

More surprising is the new vocalist, Keith St. John, who looks like a 22-year-old cross between Jim Morrison and Robert Plant, his long dark curls, peekaboo eyes and open shirt eliciting repeated hoots and hollers from the ladies in the crowd. You see how young he is and wonder if he's up to the task—and then discover that not only is he an obvious fan who's got Hagar's distinctive phrasing nailed, he's leagues beyond the average hard-rock shouter in terms of vocal talent. The kid has serious pipes, strong and sure and ready to rip.

And rip they do as Montrose himself leads the band through the wailing sci-fi blues number "Spaceage Sacrifice" before dropping straight into the party-time boogie of "One Thing On My Mind" (subtle, these guys weren't...). Next up is "Paper Money," a cut Mr. Montrose has long said may not have gotten enough attention from the original band. Here, it flat-out rocks, Torpey outdoing himself on the rumbling, extended intro, the crowd stomping right along with him until Wright and Montrose kick in with the melody. Bass and drum solos follow somewhat predictably, proving not so much that these are rock-solid players—we knew that already—as that Montrose is determined to be a generous host to his new bandmates.

Next up is the debut of a new song, a ringing, somewhat nostalgic tune called "'69" that fits in so well with the rest of the set that your mind begins to boggle at the potential for this band to generate a fresh new set of Montrose classics. The crowd welcomes the newcomer right alongside another taste of the old, the somewhat neglected anthem to attitude "I Don't Want It."

Saving a pair of nuggets for the big finish, the reborn Montrose closes out the main set with rip-roaring renditions of "Rock Candy" and "Space Station #5." The band runs right into a goosebump moment in the midst of the former, as after the first chorus, St. John gives up, grinning like a lottery winner, throws his mike down on the drum riser and lets the crowd sing the entire second verse note for note with no competition from him. The blistering "#5" arrives unadorned, no spacey intro, just Montrose himself slamming home those incendiary opening chords as every head in the crowd bangs to the beat.

By the time the band re-emerges for a two-song encore, the crowd has already guessed what must be next; there's only one song left from the original *Montrose* album to play. Their cries dissolve into delirious cheering as St. John moves center stage, assumes a wide stance, sticks his hands out in front and leans back as if astride an invisible Harley. You got it—it's time to get on your "Bad Motor Scooter" and ride.

The night's closing words go to the man himself, as Ronnie Montrose explains that when he went about putting together the original Montrose, "There were three bands that I had in mind, three power-trio, guitar-bass-drums-type bands that did it for me—Free, Led Zeppelin, and this band." With that, they launch like a rocket into the opening bars of The Who's immortal "My Generation." The whole band does background vocals on the choruses, straining to make themselves heard over the crowd.

As the band departs leaving the audience begging for more, it's hard for the long-time Montrose fan not to feel a little euphoric. Because it's clear this is more than a nostalgia act; this group is entering the game with fresh legs and fresh commitment, bringing with them a catalog of classic tunes that are the answer to 25 years of pent-up audience demand. It's hard to say what the upper limit might be for a band whose reconstitution inspires this kind of fervor... and that's a great place to be.

*

Bruce Springsteen and the E Street Band Live
Arco Arena / Sacramento, CA, USA / April 9, 2003
[Published on *The Daily Vault* 4/13/2003]

They tried to draft Bruce Springsteen last year. A group of New Jerseyites got it in their head that what their state really needed to turn things around was for Springsteen to represent them in the U.S. Senate. That idea only seems preposterous if you have never seen the man live in concert. For there may be no one in the history of rock and roll—hell, the history of popular music—with this man's capacity to inspire.

As he has throughout the 2002-2003 tour supporting his Grammy-winning album *The Rising*, he arrived in Sacramento, California last Wednesday night with the entire reconstituted E Street Band on board to deliver a performance that achieved the man's own vision of what a rock concert should be: "part political rally, part dance party, part religious revival."

It was the first date back in the states for the band after a month-long swing down under to Australia and New Zealand. When Springsteen left, the U.S. was engaged in a tense standoff at the U.N.; while he was gone we attacked Iraq and he began opening shows with "War"—as in "War / What is it good for? / Absolutely nothin' / Say it again," the ferocious Edwin Starr standard he first played live back during 1984's *Born In The USA* tour. At home, popular opinion about the war remained divided despite the steady success of the military campaign. How would Springsteen bridge that gap in front of a home crowd, while remaining true to his principles?

His approach was, typically, both passionate and ultimately unifying. With the initial offensive nearing its close, he opened with an acoustic rendering of "Born in the USA" that has become familiar to Springsteen-ites but was likely foreign to most casual fans. With the anthemic electric guitars and keyboards removed, the song was stripped down to its bare bones and revealed once and for all as the bitter lament of a war veteran battered by the ravages of combat both abroad and at home. With the often-misinterpreted chorus excised, the song emerges as a gripping plea for the salvation of the narrator's soul. Bringing the full band into play, Springsteen followed with a ringing, memorable rendition of the CCR classic "Who'll Stop the Rain," an anti-violence hymn you can sing along to.

The remainder of Springsteen's two-and-a-quarter-hour main set was a challenging mixture of familiar classics and a substantial cohort of songs from *The Rising*, an album that interweaves desolate laments with a steely backbone of hope. The title song in particular translated beautifully to the stage, the crowd singing along like it had already taken its rightful place among the band's most powerful numbers. Springsteen and the E Streeters also offered strong readings of *Rising* tracks "Lonesome Day" (a reflective rocker) and "You're Missing" (one of his most affecting ballads). The album's lone upbeat party number "Mary's Place" offered time later in the set for band intros and a hilarious little mating dance Springsteen presented to wife/background vocalist Patti Scialfa ("She's being cool about it, but this always works at home!").

The clear highlights of the show, though, remained the old chestnuts. The leadoff track to 1978's seminal *Darkness on the Edge of Town*, the ringing "Badlands" retains every ounce of its desperate determination 25 years later, the crowd singalong toward the end swelling like a gospel chorus. Moments later as they pulled out old nugget "She's the One," a secondary track from 1975's breakout hit *Born to Run*, drummer Max Weinberg's hammering fills brought the crowd energy to an early peak. (If there was ever a vote for Most Improved Over the Years among E Streeters, Weinberg would win hands down. He started out in 1975 solid but unspectacular. Today he is simply the best there is in rock n' roll when it

271

comes to plastering a 4/4 backbeat across the back of the audience's brainpan.)

Stunning is the only way to describe Springsteen and company's rendition of the operatic "Jungleland," also from *Born To Run*. From the gorgeous opening piano melody played by Roy Bittan, to the stylized Leonard Bernstein street-fighting verses, to Clarence Clemons' magnificent sax solo, right down to Springsteen's soul-baring moans over the closing notes, it's a song designed to enthrall that still succeeds in doing so a quarter-century later.

The first set of encores quickly moved into the heart of Springsteen's catalog, an energetic full-band reading of "Thunder Road" dropping right into an all-out house party on the rave-up roadhouse rocker "Ramrod," featuring that hammering backbeat, great turns by Roy Bittan and Danny Federici on piano and organ, another tasty sax solo from Clemons, and a seven-bandmember conga line circling the stage. By the time they finished the crowd was—despite an average age hovering in the late 40s—ready to tear the roof off the place. There was never any question what had to come next.

"Born to Run" was, well, "Born to Run." Springsteen wrote it in 1974 as "my shot at the title, a 24-year-old kid aimin' at 'the greatest rock n' roll record ever.'" Whether he succeeded is still the subject of debate, but the song remains decades later one of the most succinct and complete renderings of the poetry, majesty and sheer power to thrill that rock and roll can be.

During the second set of encores Springsteen made his only overt reference of the night to world events. Introducing "Land of Hopes and Dreams," a soaring, gospel-tinged anthem of salvation, he said "Tonight our prayers are for peace and for the safety of our sons and daughters and the Iraqi people." And there it was—the bridge across that gap. He spoke his mind, no one walked out, and the party went on.

Surprisingly, the soundtrack for the last ten minutes of the show was taken entirely from *Born in the USA*. First came a brilliant reworking of "Dancing in the Dark," that dated '80s synthesizer sound banished for good and replaced by dominating guitars and organ over a jacked-up backbeat. With just a few adjustments the song went from swaying melancholy to a flat-out rocker. For all-out goofy fun, though, it's tough to beat closing with "Darlington County," complete with all the "sha-la-las" the audience could possibly take. Hoarse, spent and all smiles, the crowd headed home with a bounce in its step. Some of us even felt a little inspired. And in a cynical world, that may be the highest office an artist could ever aspire to.

*

Green Day / Jimmy Eat World
Arco Arena / Sacramento, CA, USA / September 30, 2005
[Published on *The Daily Vault* 10/7/2005]

A funny thing happened to me last Friday night; I went to a Jimmy Eat World concert and came home a Green Day fan.

Y'see, I've listened to Billie Joe Armstrong and company quite a bit over the past two years by default thanks to my teenaged kids, but I was always more of an admiring bystander than an actual fan. It was the presence on the bill of Green Day's current opening act, Jimmy Eat World, that motivated me to buy tickets to the recent show at Arco Arena and make it an evening with the kids.

It's a good thing I wasn't totally focused on Jimmy as the be-all end-all of the evening, because their set was abominably short. They sounded great, big guitar hooks ringing out over rich vocal harmonies, playing all the hits off of their last two terrific albums ("Pain," "Work," "Sweetness" and of course "The Middle"). But their set was a bare seven songs and 35 minutes. Opening for a band as huge as Green Day is right now is a thankless task; you just have to hope you make a good first impression on all those potential fans out in the audience—and then get the hell off the stage before they turn on you.

Of course, in true bitter-early-fan style, one snarky Jimmy "fan" couldn't resist texting onto the cellular-provider-sponsored video screen at the front of the hall between sets something about how he guesses—based on the setlist—that the band's first two albums *Clarity* and *Static Prevails* "don't exist." Actually, they do exist—they're just not very good, not to mention several years old. Which means, if you're playing a half-hour opening slot for one of the biggest acts on Earth today, and have a half a brain, you don't play anything from them.

And then there was Green Day.

There was only one logical opener for this show, and the East Bay trio did not disappoint. The furious opening riff to "American Idiot" had the entire arena on their feet in a split second, jamming, pogoing and/or moshing to one of the great guitar hooks of the new millennium.

It was maybe 15 minutes into the breakneck opening sequence ("American Idiot" right into the nine-minute "Jesus of Suburbia," right into "Holiday") when it struck me that this was like seeing one of the classic '70s bands at their peak. It's true that I was probably influenced by the band's choice of preshow music, a batch of memorable AOR hits spanning 1977 to 1982, concluding with "We Will Rock You." But I also saw a combination of unleashed musical ferocity and untethered artistic ambition that made me think of those original guitar-smashing, epic-writing mods The Who.

Later in the set, Green Day confirmed their admiration for the once-upon-a-time "world's greatest live act." Billie Joe used a wireless mike for most of the night, but for one song late in the main set he went with a wired one, whereupon halfway through the song he started twirling the mike by the cord in big vertical loop-the-loops. It wasn't five minutes later I caught him and Mike Dirnt both windmilling their guitars. You think these guys didn't watch *The Kids Are Alright* about a thousand times when they were younger?

No, they're making modern music, but that doesn't mean they didn't study the masters. The stage show — which saw Green Day simultaneously mock and embrace any number of rock-star excesses — featured multiple backdrops, LED screens, a mirrorball, flashpots galore and enough two-story columns of fire to make Gene Simmons drool. The essence of the show, though, was a total sweaty commitment to leaving nothing on the stage that would've made Bruce Springsteen proud. Forty bucks to see these guys, when tired acts like the Eagles are getting $150 a ticket, has got to be one of the best deals on earth.

Beyond the nods to their forebears, though, Green Day offered up a sustained blast of riff-rocking music that defied you to sit (no one did). Bassist Mike Dirnt, looking somewhere between a refugee from the Stray Cats and a tattooed, leather-clad Ichabod Crane, bounced around the fringes of the stage like a teenager with springs for legs, busting one rock star move after another while never missing a note. Drummer Tre Cool is a round-faced, deadpan goofball whose looks belie his skills, one minute still and calm, the next throwing huge fills all over his kit like Keith Moon reincarnate, tossing drumsticks aside after every verse. The touring band also features a talented group of sidemen to help flesh out the arrangements, especially on the newer material.

In terms of what was played, Green Day focused on *American Idiot*, for reasons both obvious (it's all over the radio) and artistic (the concept album approach more or less demands playing big chunks of it on the ensuing tour). The ringing riffs of "Holiday" had the crowd fist-pumping by the thousands, but perhaps even better were the soft-hard dynamics of "Are We the Waiting" and the simply gorgeous "Wake Me When September Ends" (kind of a given to be on the setlist considering the date of the concert...). Here is where the whole categorization thing throws me off, though. On one hand, calling this trio's music punk-pop makes good sense; it's punk attitude and anger melded with pop hooks and melodies. But at its core, *American Idiot* is simply high-energy, politically-aware rock and roll, music that burns with both energy and purpose.

The boys managed to touch on past glories as well with tracks like "Longview," "Basket Case," "King for a Day" and main-set closer "Minority," which hit new highs in both volume and energy. They nailed the encore down with the old nugget "Maria," followed by a straight-off-of-radio take on the disillusioned-youth anthem "Boulevard of Broken Dreams," followed by a deliriously swaggering sing-along cover of Queen's "We Are the Champions." The coup de grace came when, after announcing "Champions" as their last song, Billie Joe turned to leave at the end and just stood there... until every other band member had walked off stage... until the stage lights had come down... until the crowd had yelled itself hoarse... until he finally turned back around to deliver a solo guitar-and-vocals rendition of "Good Riddance (Time of Your Life)."

Was the song itself punk? Only in the way it gave the finger to the expectations of the band's core following when it first came out in 1997. Was it punk for Billie Joe to stand alone in the middle of a sea of adoring fans crooning to them "I hope you had the time of your life" at the end of a rib-cage-rattling, high-production-value arena rock show? No. But Green Day isn't a trio of sweaty little wiseasses from the neighborhood anymore. They're global superstars and, as Billie Joe himself might put it, they're having a fucking good time with it. You got a problem with that?

*

Lindsey Buckingham
Sunset Center / Carmel, CA, USA / May 10, 2012
[Published on *The Daily Vault* 5/12/2012]

Alone on a bare stage decorated only with an area rug and a sizable amp rig, two songs into a taut 90-minute set that epitomized words like "intensity" and "masterful," Lindsey Buckingham paused to contemplate the long, twisting trail that has led the Palo Alto native to the top of the rock world, around the globe and back to Carmel's 800-seat Sunset Center as a still-vital solo act.

The "big machine" — the musical juggernaut Fleetwood Mac, of which Buckingham has been a part for 27 of the last 37 years — and the small machine, solo recording and touring — nourish and feed off of one another. After a long struggle to achieve balance between the two, Buckingham has concluded that both are necessary and each has a vital role to play in fueling his growth as an artist.

This sort of semi-obsessive self-examination lies at the heart of Buckingham's work both inside and outside of the Mac. His songs, both solo and with the band, almost always navigate those critical moments in which life-altering choices are made, sometimes at great cost.

All of which was in ample evidence Thursday night at the Sunset Center, but so was this simple fact: dude can play guitar like nobody's business. I wouldn't exactly call being named one of *Rolling Stone*'s Top 100 Guitarists of All Time a badge of honor — like most things *RS* does these days, the list was driven more by sales than merit — but Buckingham has surely earned a place on any such list imaginable.

Snapping off notes like little firecrackers, executing and repeating complex strummed figures on a small army of acoustics — he changed guitars after every single song, thrashing each within an inch of its life and killing one dead onstage in a moment of frustration — Buckingham put his virtuosity on full display from the opening notes of "Cast Away Dreams," a pretty, somewhat contemplative number from 2006's *Under the Skin*.

Buckingham's well-paced show alternated between solo and Mac tunes, deftly drawing the audience into his less familiar solo catalog while sprinkling the set with old friends and FM radio classics. "Cast Away Dreams" was followed by "Bleed to Love Her" from FM's 2003 comeback album *Say You Will*, both full of Buckingham's trademark drive.

After another pair of solo tunes — the gorgeously rendered "Not Too Late" and a very pretty instrumental that might have been "This Was Nearly Mine" — Buckingham paused again to introduce "Big Love." In one of several revealing monologues, Buckingham described how this particular Mac tune was intended quite differently from the way it's generally been interpreted by audiences, the phrase "looking out for love" having been intended as a defensive hunkering down against love's onslaught. Hearing the backstory definitely changed the way this listener heard the song — the sort of insight and interaction you can only get from an intimate evening like this.

The gorgeous "Never Going Back Again" from *Rumours* followed to huge response, though Buckingham chose to make numerous changes to its arrangement, altering tempo, build and vocal phrasing throughout. The crowd, to its credit, rolled with the changes and rewarded Buckingham with a standing ovation.

Returning to solo tunes (including the suitably manic "Go Insane") Buckingham showed a tendency to execute the same sort of vocal/instrumental build on every song, soft to medium to furious to soft again, in an almost-verse-verse-chorus-verse arrangement. His delivery at times felt a bit overcooked and repetitive in that respect, but you can't fault his intensity; the guy brings it 110 percent every time he steps up to the mike. Amazingly enough, the 62-year-old Buckingham's voice sounds, if anything, better than it did ten years ago—richer, stronger, and under his complete control.

On a couple of tunes mid-show Buckingham accompanied himself with prerecorded, rather subdued rhythm tracks. At the close of the main set, he brought out a pair of electric guitars and used full prerecorded backing tracks (bass, drums and acoustic rhythm guitar) to pull off powerful, extended versions of Mac classics "I'm So Afraid" and "Go Your Own Way," bringing the crowd to its feet once again. As one of our party put it afterwards: "That man loves to play guitar."

Encores of solo cuts "Trouble" and "Seeds We Sow" were well met and the evening ended with a sense of wonder and satisfaction at seeing an artist of unique intensity and focus bare his soul on a naked stage. The little machine and the big machine roll on, both filled still with life and power and a remarkable, timeless catalog of music. Long may they run.

*

Book Reviews

So You Wanna Be a Rock N' Roll Star
By Jacob Slichter
[Published on *The Daily Vault* 6/30/2004]

What is it about rock and roll drummers? Keith Moon was a genius behind the kit and a self-destructive madman everywhere else. Charlie Watts looks like your kindly uncle and plays jazz like a born master when he's not busy banging out "Satisfaction" for the 79,000th time. In the past ten years Counting Crows has had four hit albums and three drummers.

And then there's Jacob Slichter, a mild-mannered, occasionally panic-attack-stricken average Joe who went in a matter of five years from being friends with musicians to drumming behind them in small clubs, to riding an exhilarating wave of mainstream success, to getting spit back out by the music industry monster, thereby granting him the opportunity to write one of the wittiest and most entertaining books ever published about life inside the rock and roll bubble.

So You Wanna Be a Rock N' Roll Star is the book you or I might write if we were to trade places for five years with someone who had just scored a major-label record deal (and hopefully had some actual musical talent as well). It's a remarkably clear-eyed and self-aware chronicle of a trip through the looking glass of fame and back again. Slichter, drummer for Semisonic (remember "Closing Time"?), chronicles his wild ride with an Everyman mixture of bewilderment and lust (for affirmation, mostly).

Along the way he experiences awe, shame, revulsion and giddiness, wonders if he's actually famous yet and waits for the money and respect that mostly eludes this talented but criminally misjudged and underpromoted trio from Minneapolis. Slichter never loses sight of the fickleness of fame and fortune or of his own status as a tiny cog inside a vast and indifferent machine. Having been enlisted into Semisonic by his much more experienced musician friends Dan Wilson and John Munson, he describes their initial weeks as a side project to Wilson and Munson's band, the regionally renowned Trip Shakespeare, like so: "A pair of jumper cables had thus been fastened to my lifeless career."

Four years and 115 pages later, Slichter sits in his apartment, rereading the rave review a senior editor at *Rolling Stone* has given the band's debut disc *Great Divide*, mentally tallying the 30,000 copies the disc has actually sold against the million dollars of debt the band owes their label for its shoddy promotion of three different singles—none of which included the two most radio-friendly songs on the album—and ponders returning to his day job.

Eventually, of course, the band breaks through with "Closing Time" and goes on to earn some measure of fame and respect, even if they're forever being mistaken for, bumped for, or slighted by someone with more "juice" in the industry. This section of the book is entertaining mostly for Slichter's narration of life on the road and under the glare of the music video-making lights, neither of which endeavor is one thousandth as glamorous as any rock and roll movie ever made would have us believe.

The latter part of the book charts the band's return to earth as it makes a follow-up album that dares to be different and falls victim once again to the fickle tastes and short attention spans of industry insiders.

Some of the most potent passages consist of Slichter's acute observations of the perversity of a system where the people with actual talent—the artists—can only earn a living off their art by first agreeing to become "rock and roll sharecroppers," deeply in debt to a cadre of know-nothing music industry executives whose function is basically that of giant leeches, albeit leeches with a global promotion and distribution network.

The numerous anecdotes and asides Slichter shares like a chatty, yet introspective old friend are the book's highlights, from his panic attacks and fears that a professional record producer would replace all his drum parts, to his rampant and faintly ridiculous rock-star fantasies during the band's first photo shoot, to the ins and outs of choosing which plastic wastebasket to use for percussion during on-air radio studio performances.

You are also reminded of some of the reasons why Semisonic's peculiar brand of cerebral rock and roll never really fit into any genre the industry tried to stick them in. It all starts to make sense when you read that Slichter and bandleader Wilson became friends while both were attending Harvard. I don't think you'll find Keith Moon on the books at Oxford, nor any of the industry execs or radio station program directors whose super-sized egos and fickle antics doomed Semisonic to the vastly undeserved status of one-hit wonders. (For the record, "Closing Time" is just one of many superb tracks to be found on the trio's truly terrific 1998 disc *Feeling Strangely Fine*, reviewed on p. 105.)

If you've ever been curious whether budding stars practice their autograph inscriptions, wondered how to tactfully negotiate a better final mix for your instrument with your bandmates, or fantasized about playfully pretending to machine-gun a roomful of music executives who hold your professional future in their hands, this book will entertain. Jake Slichter tells his tale with the same qualities of intelligence, wit and winking self-knowledge that he and his bandmates put into their music. Enjoy the ride.

*

One Train Later
By Andy Summers
[Published on *The Daily Vault* 10/28/2006]

There's a familiar feeling I get when reaching the end of a book I've really enjoyed. It's a bittersweet, slightly disorienting sensation of departing—against your will—a world that's thoroughly captivated you, even if some part of you knew all along that your time there was destined to be limited.

In this insightful musical autobiography, guitarist Andy Summers shares in intimate detail how he came to experience that same sensation, arriving—after great tribulation—at the peak of a legend-making career with the Police, only to face the inevitable yet all-too-soon breakup of the band that transformed him from a rock and roll footnote into a global superstar.

One Train Later—so named out of karmic respect for the chance meeting on a train with Police drummer Stewart Copeland that would change the course of Summers' life forever—is hardly an "insider's expose," though. Rather, it's a knowing rumination on the joys and trials of a life devoted to making music, told with self-effacing and thoroughly endearing wit. Every person who picks up this book knows where it is headed—to the collision of Summers, Copeland and bassist/vocalist Sting and their 1979-1983 ascendance into the ranks of rock demigods—but the journey turns out to be at least as interesting as that glittering destination.

Summers speaks frankly but unsentimentally of a difficult family life as a child, dwelling only long enough to establish the roots of a passion for making music that blossomed from the first time he held a battered old Spanish guitar: "It is an immediate bond and possibly at that moment there is a shift in the universe because this is the moment, the point from which my life unfolds. I strike the remaining strings, which make a sound like slack elastic. It's horribly out of tune and I don't know even the simplest chord, but to me it is the sound of love."

From that pivotal moment, Summers tracks forward into his adolescent initiation into the secret brotherhood of chord-sharing among poor teenaged Brits who learn by ear off the radio and a handful of LPs; no lessons, no music books. His adventures as a young adult, after moving to London to try to make it in the music business, are the stuff of a serio-comic Dickens novel, full of great expectations and dashed hopes, daft bandmates and ridiculous gigs. As Summers' skills and reputation grow he links up with Zoot Money and the Big Roll Band, which evolves into Dantalion's Chariot, which lands him a gig with Soft Machine, which leads to touring and recording with the 1968-69 lineup of Eric Burdon's Animals.

Through this period Summers relays anecdote upon wonderful anecdote—told with a rich mixture of classically British deadpan humor and entirely appropriate amazement—of life in the mid-'60s London music scene. From scamming beers and gigs to jamming with Jimi Hendrix, Summers lives through a remarkably fertile musical era that sees him cross paths with the likes of Jimmy Page, James Brown and Eric Clapton, to whom Summers sells the Les Paul guitar that Clapton makes famous while playing in Cream.

The path to the top is hardly a straight one, though. The vicissitudes of the rock life eventually land Summers in Los Angeles, jobless, in 1969. Almost five years, hundreds of guitar lessons taught and one ill-advised marriage later, he returns to London with a new bride for one more shot at making it as a professional musician. It takes another three-year slog through various groups of varying merit—highlighted financially by a stint as the hired-gun guitarist for (this is not a misprint) Neil Sedaka—before Summers runs into Copeland on the tube, and his life begins to change once again. This is the halfway point of the book.

From there, things take off like a rocket. The acceleration of the narrative parallels the acceleration of the life being lived within it. Things spin faster and faster and faster until it becomes dizzying. Gigs, tours, recordings, singles, more gigs, press, fans, more recording, and the rocket leaves the launch pad and heads off into its well-chronicled orbit. It feels like a matter of weeks—though in fact it was three years—before Summers the struggling, near has-been guitarist with wife and child finds himself a single, rootless millionaire rock star, drowning his celebrity sorrows on a shroomed-out madman's safari across the island of Bali with John Belushi. Three more years, many lines of cocaine and a great deal of in-studio tension later, the Police quietly call it quits at the very height of their popularity.

The beauty of this book is that Summers, having been to the mountaintop and returned to tell the tale, appreciates in equal measures the glorious affirmation and the absolute insanity of life in the rock and roll circus. He renders in vivid detail the rapid disconnect from the everyday, the protective bubble in which one must exist or be rent limb from limb by one's ravenous, hysterical "fans," and the seductive, destructive nature of the machine which works 24/7 to feed both itself and the egos of the trio at the top. Managers are carted off to jail, marriages disintegrate, and wild times and assorted odd injuries ensue (note: it's always handy to have an ENT on your small Caribbean island when you absent-mindedly stuff a candy wrapper all the way into your ear canal).

For all that, Summers the author never loses sight of what propelled him—his passion for the guitar and for the power of music as tool of self-expression, spiritual exploration and connection with an audience. Fittingly, the book proper—embellished with a brief afterword— ends not with the band's breakup, but with the band launching itself onstage at Shea Stadium in August 1983 to play the first concert there since the Beatles. "We walk into the center, the luminescence, the incandescent blaze of electric power, and there is a deep roar like the end of the world. Eighty thousand lighters go on in the stadium, an incendiary salutation. Like a prayer, it is now, it is forever. I strike the first chord."

For the curious, Summers is frank but generally kind when speaking of his former bandmates, and contrite about his failings as a husband and father. Sting does come off as aloof, controlling, and taken with his own celebrity, but that hardly qualifies as news. Summers still speaks of him (and Copeland, for that matter) with the affection of a long-time mate who stood shoulder to shoulder with him more times than toe to toe.

Writing entirely in the present tense—a device which lends immediacy to every moment—Summers renders one scene after another with a rich mixture of clarity and bemusement, conveying both the intimate details and, with the benefit of twenty years' perspective, the greater significance and/or absurdity of any given situation along his twisting path. *One Train Later* is a captivating ride through both a musical era and a life made in music, narrated by a gifted storyteller—a treat for any music lover, and essential for any Police fan.

*

The Book of Drugs
By Mike Doughty
[Published on *The Daily Vault* 5/12/2012]

I made it.

That was my first reaction upon finishing *The Book of Drugs*, the memoir by singer-songwriter and former Soul Coughing frontman Mike Doughty. It was no sure thing for a while there; after the first 120 or so pages I was pretty sure this was the most infuriating book I'd ever read.

The form alone irritated me—a faux-epistolary style where there's no attempt at building any sort of narrative; one anecdote simply blurs into another for page after page after page. But what really drove me to distraction around page 100 was my strong desire to grab Doughty by the shoulders, slap him hard across the face and tell him to either (a) get a grip and do something about it, or (b) shut the hell up with his endless litany of victimhood and self-pity.

My perspective may or may not have been affected by the fact that I am not a fan of—in fact, before picking up this book, I'd never heard a single song by—the band that Doughty spends most of these pages writing about, Soul Coughing. His 1994-2000 role as singer-songwriter-guitarist for the group offered a launching pad for his current, successful solo career, a point which at times seems lost on Doughty himself.

Instead—once he's sped past what sounds like a genuinely tortured childhood that inspires genuine sympathy—he occupies the next hundred or so pages cataloging in excruciating detail the horrors associated with achieving his dream of being in a band with a record deal, radio play and a steady following. Managers: horrible. Producers: horrible. Engineers: horrible. Fans: horrible. Life on the road: horrible. Doughty himself—a hot mess of expensive drugs, cheap sex and bottomless self-loathing—horrible.

But the most corrosive acid in the table of elements lurking inside Doughty's pen is reserved for his former bandmates. Doughty from the start refers to them only as "the sampler player," "the bass player" and "the drummer." Perhaps his publisher's attorneys demanded this before printing a book that paints such an unrelentingly bitter portrait of each— the drummer who willfully refuses to follow the arrangements of songs, then denies it; the bass player whose blood-sugar issues and prima donna outbursts constantly create chaos; the sampler player whose petty rants are all pre-chewed for him by his shrewish, paranoid wife. Whatever the case, this no-names affectation, besides being annoying, has the opposite effect from what Doughty seems to have intended. By painting such an obsessively one-dimensional picture of these individuals—who are, after all, real flesh-and-blood human beings with names and friends and moms and dads and most likely a kid or two by now—Doughty throws the reliability of his entire narrative into question, i.e. what else are you exaggerating?

It's said that all great art comes from great suffering, but in the early going at least, Doughty doesn't come off as a tortured artist so much as a whiny, immature kid with a victim complex and an insatiable appetite for drugs and impersonal sex. His frankness in describing events feels brave and bracing the first time, but soon grows tiresome. ("You really needed to share that little detail? To what end, sir? What conceivable artistic purpose is served by your assertion that you outperformed the other guy in the threesome when giving oral sex to this particular groupie?") (And, by the way: when exactly did exhibitionism come to be equated with artistic integrity? Why is the sharing of unsavory personal details generally viewed today as courageous rather than self-indulgent, entertaining rather than off-putting, important rather than trivial? Sorry, folks, I don't get it.)

About two-thirds of the way through this 252-page memoir, things finally take a turn as, in no particular order, Doughty bottoms out as a shaky, constantly out-of-breath junkie, gets into therapy, kicks heroin, and quits Soul Coughing. Soon he's attending 12-step meetings daily (in "the rooms," his favored shorthand for addiction recovery groups) and beginning to build a life and career outside of the band and the drugs that nearly consumed him.

This is also where the big reveal occurs: Doughty is diagnosed with bipolar disorder. This was, given my own experiences with several people I've been close to in my life, a "whack the forehead" moment. *Of course he is.* The black-and-white thinking, the episodes of lethargic hopelessness intercut with bursts of creativity, the headlong pursuit of self-medication. A textbook scenario. On *The Daily Show* recently, author Jonah Lehrer (*Imagine: How Creativity Works*) asserted that creative people (writers, artists, musicians, etc.) are somewhere between eight and 40 times more likely to manifest bipolar disorder than the general population. I can't vouch for the reliability of those numbers, but anecdotally speaking, they seem in the ballpark.

The last third of *The Book of Drugs* does a decent job of redeeming what came before. In the late going, Doughty's struggle to build a healthy life becomes genuinely poignant and affirming, without a hint of sentimentality. Doughty's discussion of his bipolar diagnosis and treatment is brave and candid, and its coda reflects what I've heard from others in similar circumstances: "The cocktail of meds has wrought amazing relief. There aren't any notable side effects, sexual, soporific or otherwise. Though I sometimes feel naggingly inauthentic. As if it were cowardly to need medical help." It's never easy to admit you need help, let alone that you need it every day; that admission is the single most courageous thing Doughty does in the entire book.

Doughty also writes movingly of the rewards offered by staying in "the rooms" long after he's achieved and maintained sobriety: "Once you get your shit together, you stay in to help other people. It astonishes me that I get one of the best feelings in my life when I encounter a stranger, suffering from the same thing I suffer, who needs help." Beats the hell out of dying young in a Paris bathtub, right?

I imagine writing this memoir was cathartic for Doughty—a purging of negative memories that might help in the continuing process of moving on from the person he used to be and becoming the person he wants to be. *The Book of Drugs* was by no means an easy read, but in the end, I made it, and I hope Doughty makes it, too. He seems like a decent enough sort now that he's gotten off the bad drugs and onto the good ones, not to mention grown up a bit. And if I wish I could un-read a few of the things I read, well, at least I didn't have to live them.

*

Film Reviews

Everyone Stares: The Police Inside Out
[Published on *The Daily Vault* 6/29/2007]

One of my first luxury item purchases as a young adult was a video camera. And that about covers the parallels between my life and that of Police drummer Stewart Copeland, who spent some of the first actual cash he earned off of the Police's debut album *Outlandos D'Amour* purchasing a Super 8 video camera.

Copeland then proceeded over the course of the next five eventful years to take over 50 hours of film of the band, crew, management, fans, airplanes, busses, street scenes and who knows what else. Twenty years later Copeland had the footage digitized and began assembling and editing what would become a 74-minute peek behind the curtain of a rock band in the process of conquering the world, full of moments and vignettes that alternately entertain, amuse and enlighten.

Copeland's first challenge was that his footage covers only about 70 percent of the band's lifespan; as a result his direction employs all manner of creative tricks to cover the ground necessary to fill out the band's story. The first two years of the group's existence is reconstructed via a series of stills and clever crossfades as Copeland's narration leads you up to the point where the camera was purchased, just after the release of *Outlandos*.

Over the course of the film, Copeland's narration in fact turns out to be as much a highlight as any of the sometimes grainy footage. With the benefit of two decades' hindsight he views with deep clarity the surreal experience of going in less than three years from a struggling London club band to instantly-recognizable global superstars. A segment titled "1981: Life becomes a Duran Duran video" is especially piquant and on point:

"We're getting kind of disconnected from the world. Inside our bubble, the suitcase life feels normal. Stepping out into the streets among regular folks feels alien. When people come rushing at you, even with love in their hearts, the instinct is to recoil; a wall goes up. Pretty soon the real world that most people live in just seems like wind rushing past the car window. If you grab hold of anything, you'll lose an arm."

The ensuing footage, full of agitated, sometimes screaming Japanese fans encircling Copeland and bandmates Andy Summers and Sting as they wander the streets of Tokyo, plays to one of Copeland's whimsical "derangements" (remixes) of the band's then-hit single "Don't Stand So Close to Me," its meaning transformed from "stop flirting with me" to a more visceral "get out of my face, now."

There is also a wonderful, superbly constructed sequence where Copeland lays the band's brilliantly evocative instrumental "Reggatta de Blanc" over a ridiculous bit of footage involving sheep hired for a video shoot running wild all over the set, culminating with a documented example of Sting's notable sheepherding skills. As he approaches the camera with a babe in arms, the caption reads: "Can't Stand Losing Ewe." (Cue rimshot.)

From there we cut to Montserrat, where the band is recording its troubled fourth album *Ghost in the Machine* amidst increasing internal tensions as Sting begins to dominate the musical proceedings. The segment is a short overview of what was by most accounts an unhappy time for the band as egos collided and the trio's divergent views of the future became more and more evident.

The end comes mercifully quickly after that, as Copeland intones "This is it—the target moment—this is what we came for." "Synchronicity 1" plays in the background with perfect, well, synchronicity.

Copeland's closing narration, over faintly hilarious footage of the band's management sorting a mountain of bills into stacks after getting paid in cash for what one presumes must have been an earlier gig, is appropriately elegiac: "Bands don't get any higher than this. The screaming fans are gone, or at least if they're still screaming we're too far up in our ivory tower to hear them anymore. Looking at all this money makes me think it's time to jump off this pirate ship and abscond with the loot... You know what? We're done. When you get to where you're going, the ride is over."

Indeed it was, but with *Everyone Stares*, Copeland has given Police fans a chance to relive the ride from the inside out, and it's a worthwhile trip led by a witty guide who knows intimately whereof he speaks.

*

Springsteen & I: The Story of Rock's Biggest Fan, and His Fans
[Published on *The Daily Vault* 11/19/2013]

They used to call Eric Clapton "God," but the highest anyone's ever placed Bruce Springsteen in the pecking order is "The Boss." This is ironic only insofar as anyone who has ever observed the fervor and absolute devotion of Springsteen's most loyal fans can attest to the fact that the man has been essentially deified.

As more than a casual fan myself, I have witnessed this firsthand, and the results aren't always pretty. I remember one particular run-in I had in the early days of the Internet with a fan on the old USENET group rec.music.artists.springsteen who was basically furious with Springsteen for ever making another album after 1978's *Darkness on the Edge of Town*. After those first four albums, the guy had this perfect image in his mind of who Bruce Springsteen was supposed to be, and in this fan's mind he was supposed to stay that person forever, to never grow or change as an artist and a person. Speaking angrily of Bruce's more exploratory work in the '80s and '90s, he said words to the effect of "Bruce left me," sounding for all the world like a bitter, jilted divorcee.

Fortunately he doesn't show up in *Springsteen & I*, Baillie Walsh and Ridley Scott's love letter to the man, a crowd-sourced documentary splicing together snippets from thousands of video-selfies in which various longtime fans (and the occasional long-suffering family members) attempt to explain with varying degrees of eloquence what Bruce Springsteen and his music mean to them. Their thoughts and stories are interspersed with concert footage of Springsteen and the E Street Band, sometimes simply illustrating the raw passion of Springsteen's embrace of his own audience, the preacher before his congregation, and at other times revisiting actual incidents from concerts past, now narrated by his fans.

The latter is done with particular pathos in a sequence involving a fan who dressed up as Vegas Elvis and held up a sign at a recent Philadelphia show begging for the chance to sing "All Shook Up" with the Boss. You can guess what happens next, and in its own way this vignette sums up the entire experience of this film, and the person it's about; it's insightful, goofy, poetic, overblown, a little odd, deeply empathetic, and in its best moments, knee-weakeningly spectacular.

Another funny sequence features a devoted female fan and her long-suffering British husband, who has been force-fed Springsteen music without ever developing a taste for it, and is visibly resigned to being dragged to one three-hour show after another. His voice is both genuine and in its own way quite sweet; whatever his misgivings, he's long since accepted that loving his wife requires that he put up with this Bruce guy, too.

Some of the best moments are the quietest; the young Asian female truck driver sitting in the cab of her rig who talks about how Bruce's songs of hope for the working class have inspired her, the suburban dad talking while driving about how Bruce's songs make him feel ("...like I was going through someone's family photo album and looking at their life, and feeling what they felt... feeling their sadness, and their triumph...") before being overcome and breaking down weeping as he drives.

The concert clips selected from 40 years of footage are fantastic as well, ranging from a very early clip of Bruce singing "Growin' Up" solo and acoustic, to recent shows with the now-stadium-sized E Street Band. Footage of "Candy's Room" from the 1978-9 *Darkness* tour is especially electric, showing the ferocious energy young Bruce delivered every moment of every night, and that older Bruce still manages to reach back and grasp a few times during every show.

The DVD bonuses are nice as well—some awkward but happy footage of Bruce meeting several of the fans featured in the film after a show, and six songs from a 2012 Hyde Park concert. The latter segment, including a two-song guest appearance by Paul McCartney, is wonderful not so much for the music itself as for expressions and body language. Sir Paul is happy to be there, gives due respect to his host, and has a good time. Standing next to him, Springsteen is visibly thrilled, the still-neurotic superfan standing next to one of his musical idols, singing together, sharing a mike, living out a younger man's dream.

Which brings me back around to a famous Springsteen quote, from around the time *Born in the USA* made him a global superstar: "I believe that the life of a rock & roll band will last as long as you look down into the audience and can see yourself, and your audience looks up at you and can see themselves—and as long as those reflections are human, realistic ones." Standing next to Paul McCartney, Bruce is revealed for what he is and always has been at his core: one of the world's biggest fans of rock and roll itself.

The fans want Bruce to live his dream, because it's their dream, too, and they know that he knows that they know it. If that sounds complicated, it really isn't. *Springsteen & I* is the perfect title for this film because every passionate Springsteen fan has found a reflection of themselves somewhere in Springsteen's songs and onstage persona. His words speak to their dreams, and his very human voice feels like it could be their own.

~Segue~

Remembering Ronnie Montrose: An Unexpected Friendship

[Published on *The Daily Vault* 3/4/2012]

Like a math problem I could never quite solve, my teenage years were filled with more variables than constants. Through the changes—and occasional outright chaos—one of the constants was my passion for music. And one of the constants I measured that passion by was Ronnie Montrose.

Five years after it came out, that first eponymous album (1973's *Montrose*) was a staple of my high school years, one of those rare albums that every single member of our group of compadres—Geoff, Tor, Neil, Jason C., Mike, Khal and Andy (RIP)—would always say yes to giving another spin. Songs like "Rock the Nation" and "Bad Motor Scooter" and "Rock Candy" and "Make It Last" were the soundtrack to our 16- and 17-year-old lives. When Ronnie's first solo album *Open Fire* came out in 1978, we embraced it completely, different as it was from anything he'd done before. The same held true when he formed the futuristic Gamma in 1979; he was an adventurer after our own hearts.

Three of the highlights from my teenage concert-going days featured Ronnie. First was original Montrose vocalist Sammy Hagar's New Year's Eve show at San Francisco's Cow Palace in 1978, at which Ronnie joined the rest of the original Montrose lineup on stage for the third encore, closing out the night with a thundering run at "Rock Candy." And then there was the literal last waltz of my high school days, a pair of Gamma shows in San Francisco in September 1980, at the Old Waldorf and then again the next day on Justin Herman Plaza. I was right up front for both, with Tor at one and Mike at the other. Two weeks later I was off to college.

All this stuff about the music, though, is really just the preamble. (If it's album reviews you want, stop by *The Daily Vault*; they're all there.) Today, the day I learned of Ronnie Montrose's passing, I want to talk about the man I came to know not as a legendary guitarist who practically invented American hard rock, but as my friend Ronnie.

After high school, as the years passed, I would occasionally revisit *Montrose, Open Fire,* and the rest, but my life revolved more around family and work and less around music during those years (and after all, it was the '80s... talk about a musical desert). I still loved the classics, but Montrose seemed like part of my past, not my future.

Then in 1998, a few months after I started writing reviews for *The Daily Vault*, I wrote my first Ronnie review, of *Open Fire* [see Chapter 4]. I waxed pretty rhapsodic about it (opening line: "The worst thing I can say about guitarist Ronnie Montrose's moody, inventive 1978 solo debut is that it's too damn short"), and when I was done, I did an Internet search that turned up an e-mail address for the man himself. On a whim, I e-mailed him a link to the review, with a brief cover note. I figured there was about a one percent chance I'd ever hear back. I mean, it was RONNIE MONTROSE, rock guitar god, idol of my youth. No way he's going to write back to some random punk like me (even if I was 35 by then).

Within two or three days he e-mailed me back, friendly and appreciative. It was the beginning of a conversation that continued for 14 years.

The e-mail correspondence went on, and I interviewed the man a couple of months later [see Segue 2]. That's when we really got to know each other. I understood quickly why Ronnie's musical situation never seemed stable. He was an adventurer at heart, a restless soul who was constantly driven to follow his muse wherever it might take him. He was also unbending, never one to compromise, and always confident in his decisions. Anyone who couldn't follow his lead — and then follow it again, when he inevitably changed course — wasn't going to last long. It wasn't personal; it was just how he was built.

One of my favorite anecdotes from that interview was Ronnie talking about how he related to fans, how sometimes when he would meet them, they'd be drunk or flustered and just kind of say "You rock, dude!" and then back away. And he was cool with that, but he also liked it when the conversations went deeper. He liked connecting with people, and the guitar was his bridge to get the conversation started.

I got to witness this phenomenon firsthand soon afterwards when Ronnie, who was set to play a show at The Boardwalk in Sacramento, invited me to come to sound check. I brought along a friend who played guitar himself (I can't play a lick), and we watched the man get everything just right for a good half hour before he ambled off stage and down the steps to greet us. We spent ten minutes or so chatting. After he departed I looked over at my friend, a guy I would describe as not easily impressed. He just stared at me like he couldn't believe what had just happened, until three words finally tumbled out: "Ronnie Montrose. Fuck." Couldn't have said it better myself.

The following summer I somehow convinced my ever-tolerant spouse Karen that we should time our southwest vacation with the kids around a show Ronnie was playing at the Texas Station casino in Las Vegas. We caught the end of sound check and hung out with Ronnie afterwards taking pictures. While we hung out, Ronnie invited us to watch the night's show from backstage. My older son Josh and I sat on a low riser directly behind the front-of-stage speakers, ten feet from Ronnie while he played his heart out, smiling and waving at us—an incredible thrill.

A couple of years later, Ronnie decided to hire a vocalist and start playing the old Montrose tunes again for the first time in years. I wrote an equally rhapsodic review of a show I went to in Petaluma on that first time back out playing the Montrose classics [see Chapter 9]. It remains one of my favorite shows I've ever been to, for two reasons that have nothing to do with the music he played. That was the night I reconnected with a friend from high school whom I hadn't seen in twenty years (hey, Tor), and after the show, when I went up to say hi, Ronnie immediately broke through the crowd clustered around him and wrapped me in a bear hug.

In 2004 or so, Ronnie invited me to come to his house for a Super Bowl party. "Bring the kids!" he said in his usual declarative way, halfway between invitation and command. My daughter Sarah and younger son Eric spent halftime in his home studio, noodling around on his guitars while we talked. They loved it and both took guitar lessons for a couple of years afterwards. The guy they took lessons from had previously taken lessons himself from Jerry Jennings, whose album *Shortcut to the Center* was produced by Ronnie. All that joy and passion for the guitar, all connected back to Ronnie.

In the ensuing years we'd e-mail and chat on the phone a couple of times a year without fail. Sometimes the talk would grow deeply personal. Like a lot of passionate artists, there were things in Ronnie's past that troubled him and drove him. He was a private person in a lot of ways, sometimes seeming almost unknowable, but then he'd come right out and share these incredibly revealing, sometimes painful moments from his life—which inspired me to do the same. Whatever you got from Ronnie— whatever he chose to share of himself with you—it was real. It was genuine. You could always count on that.

A few years ago Ronnie dropped out of sight for a long stretch, stopped playing out, stopped answering e-mails. Through this period I sent him a brief note every few months, asking how he was doing, sharing a little about what I was up to, keeping the lines open for whenever he was ready to talk. Finally, as he was wont to do, he called me up out of the blue. Explained that he'd been sick and out of touch, but he was doing better now. We ended up talking for almost an hour. Ronnie was the fourth person I've been close to who's battled prostate cancer, so we had a lot to talk about—life, death, love, family, art. We covered it all, and then some.

We had to. I only saw him once more, catching a show live when he played Santa Cruz last year. I was up in front again and when our eyes met he gave his usual smile and nod and kept right on ripping it up. When the show ended it was late and I skipped the after-show, much to my regret. But that's okay. We'd already said everything we needed to say to one another.

When you read the obituaries and tributes this week, most likely you'll read some of my words. I wrote Ronnie's last three or four professional bios for him, gratis, including the one up on his site right now. It was an honor.

Rest in peace, my friend. It still boggles my mind sometimes that I got to call you that. But I did, and I'll never forget you, the talks we had, the brotherhood that you made it easy to feel. You rock, dude.

Conclusion

THANK YOU FOR THE DANCE.

That's where this closing conversation has to start, because art—whether in the form of music, or writing, or dance, or even architecture—is about building human connections, and that requires attention and care, and therefore gratitude.

Beyond that simple acknowledgment, here's a closing thought: learning about what you respond to in art is learning about yourself. What I've come to understand over the years is that the music I respond to most readily has two elements: integrity and emotion.

Integrity, because I am so turned off by artifice. If you can't be yourself, how can I respect you? Be real. Don't worry about whether I'm going to like you or not, just be authentic, and have confidence that that act of courage alone will earn my respect.

Emotion, because for my entire life I've been the shy kid, the reserved one, the one who usually only speaks when he has something to say. One of the side effects of this is that I reflexively admire anyone who invests their art—their outward expression—with genuine, unself-conscious emotion. It's more than just admiration, though—it's a craving. As an adult, those moments of emotional release have become my drug of choice; they set every neuron in my brain to firing and, to borrow a phrase from Peter Gabriel, make my heart go boom-boom-boom.

That's why my breathing deepens and my scalp tingles when The Who explode with righteous fury in "Won't Get Fooled Again," or when James Taylor plumbs the deepest caverns of his grief in "Fire and Rain," or even when those young bucks Sammy Hagar and Ronnie Montrose proclaim that "Whether I'm twelve or whether I'm sixty-four / I spend my time like there ain't gonna be no more."

When these moments arrive, the world disappears, because the emotional experience these artists are conveying to me in their songs is real, and has the power, still, to transport and transform me in a way that no other art form can.

The artists praised in these pages, both the well-known and the unknown, invite you with every song they sing to share a moment of pure human connection with them, a moment that can be repeated, but never replicated. The song will end, and new songs will come along. But that moment—that moment is immortal.

Index of Reviews

Chronological

1959

Miles Davis – *Kind of Blue*

1967

The Beatles – *Sgt. Pepper's Lonely Hearts Club Band*
The Doors – *The Doors*

1969

Quincy Jones – *Walking in Space*
Led Zeppelin – *II*
Les McCann & Eddie Harris – *Swiss Movement*

1971

The Who – *Who's Next*

1972

Carly Simon – *No Secrets*
Yes – *Close to the Edge*

1973

Montrose – *Montrose*
Pink Floyd – *Dark Side of the Moon*
Stevie Wonder – *Innervisions*

1975

Pink Floyd – *Wish You Were Here*
Queen – *A Night at the Opera*
Bruce Springsteen – *Born to Run*

1976

Boston – *Boston*
Peter Frampton – *Frampton Comes Alive*
James Taylor – *Greatest Hits*

1977

Fleetwood Mac – *Rumours*
Foreigner – *Foreigner*

1978

The Kinks – *Misfits*
Ronnie Montrose – *Open Fire*
Bob Seger & the Silver Bullet Band – *Stranger in Town*
Van Halen – *Van Halen*

1979

Tom Petty & the Heartbreakers – *Damn the Torpedoes*

1980

AC/DC – *Highway to Hell*
The Pretenders – *The Pretenders*
REO Speedwagon – *Hi Infidelity*

1982

Asia – *Asia*

1986

Peter Gabriel – *So*

1987

Bruce Springsteen – *Tunnel of Love*
U2 – *The Joshua Tree*
Yes – *Big Generator*

1988

Steve Winwood – *Roll With It*

1990

Garth Brooks – *No Fences*

1991

Starship – *Greatest Hits (Ten Years and Change 1979-1991)*
U2 – *Achtung Baby*

1992

Eric Clapton – *Unplugged*
Gin Blossoms – *New Miserable Experience*
Bruce Springsteen – *Lucky Town*

1993

Counting Crows – *August and Everything After*
Bruce Hornsby – *Harbor Lights*

1994

Mary Chapin Carpenter – *Stones in the Road*
Dream Theater – *Awake*
Dave Matthews Band – *Under the Table and Dreaming*

1995

John Hiatt – *Walk On*
Stevie Ray Vaughan – *Greatest Hits*

1997

Pat Boone – *In a Metal Mood: No More Mr. Nice Guy*
Hanson – *Middle of Nowhere*

1998

Jimi Hendrix – *Experience Hendrix*
Jill Knight – *Future Perfect*
Semisonic – *Feeling Strangely Fine*

1999

Ben Folds Five – *The Unauthorized Biography of Reinhold Messner*

2000

Angie Aparo – *The American*
Fastball – *The Harsh Light of Day*
The Jayhawks – *Smile*
Shawn Mullins – *Beneath the Velvet Sun*

2001

Ben Folds – *Rockin' the Suburbs*

2002

Coldplay – *A Rush of Blood to the Head*
Sheryl Crow – *C'mon C'mon*
Josh Joplin Group – *The Future That Was*
Ben Kweller – *Sha Sha*

2003

Death Cab for Cutie – *Transatlanticism*
Fountains of Wayne – *Welcome Interstate Managers*
Jet – *Get Born*

2004

Jimmy Eat World – *Futures*
Amy Lennard – *EP*

2005

Danelia Cotton – *Small White Town*
The Redwalls – *De Nova*
Switchfoot – *Nothing Is Sound*
The Tom Collins – *Daylight Tonight*

2006

John Mayer – *Continuum*

2007

Chris Cubeta – *Change* (EP)
Ian Hunter – *Shrunken Heads*

2008

Last Charge of the Light Horse – *Fractures*
Jon Troast – *A Person & A Heart*

2009

Big Big Train – *The Underfall Yard*
John Mayer – *Battlefield Studies*
Memphis 59 – *Ragged but Right*
Train – *Save Me San Francisco*

2010

Arms of Kismet – *Play for Affection*

2011

Black Keys – *El Camino*
Spottiswoode and His Enemies – *Wild Goosechase Expedition*
Styx – *Regeneration Volume I & II*

2012

Gary Clark Jr. – *Blak and Blu*
Maroon 5 – *Overexposed*
Rush – *Clockwork Angels*

2013

Casey Frazier – *Regal*

2014

David Corley – *Available Light*
Elbow – *The Take Off and Landing of Everything*

2015

Butchers Blind – *A Place in America* (EP)

Acknowledgments

THE LIST OF PEOPLE WITHOUT Whom We Wouldn't Be Having This Conversation is lengthy, and begins where it must: with the musicians. Your talent, creativity, persistence, and willingness to open up about your process is the reason this book exists. Sincere thanks to each of you whom I've been fortunate enough to interact with, but especially the late Ronnie Montrose, whose freely offered friendship helped me to understand, among other things, the possibilities. Peace.

We definitely would not be having this conversation if not for two editors who said yes, both genuine originals. First Christopher MacDonald, and then Christopher Thelen, gave me the chance to write about music for an audience. Thank you, thank you.

The cast and crew that keeps *The Daily Vault* humming day after day over at www.dailyvault.com are legion, but special thanks are due to Assistant Editor Melanie Love, Publisher Emeritus Duke Egbert, social media managers Vish Iyer and Tom Haugen, and my friend and former assistant editor Benjamin Ray. Big thanks also to Rick Watkins, *The Daily Vault*'s technical guru since 2006 (and a man of his word), and Angela Tannehill, graphic designer extraordinaire.

A round of applause for the publicists and label representatives who helped to arrange the interviews found herein—Billy James, Anne Leighton, Rob Evanoff, Jamie Sisley, Danny Lanzetta, Ben Arrington—as well as the many others who have provided review material over the years. Good eggs, every one.

Over the past decade or so, on and off the 'net, I've been fortunate enough to connect with a number of musically-minded brethren of a certain age who share my enthusiasm for writing about and/or making music. Big thanks to Mark Doyon, Roger Trott, Richard Fulco and Spencer Critchley for inspiration, encouragement and friendship.

Another member of that fraternity is Jean-Paul Vest, a gifted creator, a kindred soul, and a good friend. His terrific cover design for this book is just the latest volley in a conversation that's been going on for more than a decade now. Thank you, sir.

To my extended family of Warburgs, Stoddards, McKibbens, Hoecks and Dittmars, thanks for always being in my corner and keeping me honest. Special thanks and love to Mom for always believing.

It should be clear to anyone who's read this far that hanging out with my older brothers Andy, Pete, and Gerry while growing up was, among other things, a critical part of my musical education. Thanks for letting me in.

You know love is real when your spouse is willing to listen to any music you put on (once). Everlasting thanks to Karen, whose love and support make all things possible.

This book is dedicated to our children, Josh, Sarah, and Eric, not just because I love and believe in each of them profoundly, but because whatever else was going on at the time, music has been a language we've always shared. As a result, references to each of them show up in these pages. These mentions were never gratuitous, "thrust-my-kid-in-front-of-the-camera" stunts; each one grew out of a genuine moment of connection, set to music. Remember the autobahn.

As for the rest of you, until next time: take care, and be good to each other.

Seaside, California
January, 2016

www.ingramcontent.com/pod-product-compliance
Lightning Source LLC
LaVergne TN
LVHW051038080426
835508LV00019B/1584